Psychoanalysing Horror Cinema

Inspired by her *Wild About Horror* segments on the Evolution of Horror Podcast, *Psychoanalysing Horror Cinema* sees Mary Wild investigate 50 films across six core subgenres—Mind, Body, Nature, Aliens, Vampires, and Home Invasion—through close readings of key titles including *Mulholland Drive*, *Black Swan*, *Jaws*, *Predator*, *Twilight*, and *Misery*.

Informed by Freudian, Lacanian, and Jungian theory, Wild deconstructs each film with her signature blend of insight and playfulness. Writing with startling emotional clarity, she invites readers to engage with popular media through a psychoanalytic lens, treating films as projective tests to uncover meaningful subjective associations. Spanning an eclectic range of titles, from arthouse to blockbuster, these case studies reveal how genre cinema expresses universal psychological truths. Referencing both classic and contemporary horror, this stylish compendium renders complex theory accessible without sacrificing depth.

Featuring a foreword by Mike Muncer, *Psychoanalysing Horror Cinema* speaks to students, cinephiles, and curious general readers alike. Practising and trainee analysts seeking fresh ways to engage with clients will find inspiration in its pages. Addressing both seasoned theorists and those new to psychoanalysis, Mary Wild champions horror as a vital site of introspection, catharsis, and erotic awakening.

Mary Wild is a writer, lecturer, and podcaster based in London, England. She is the creator of the *Projections* lecture series at the Freud Museum, where she applies psychoanalytic theory to film interpretation.

"Even though an intrinsic connection exists between psychoanalysis and the horror film, the number of books addressing this intersection has been scant, and none has gotten to the foundation of the connection. This all changes with the publication of Mary Wild's *Psychoanalysing Horror Cinema*. Wild has long engaged with both psychoanalytic thinking and the horror film. *Psychoanalysing Horror Cinema* is the result of this lengthy study, and it promises to influence how we look at the horror film both as a genre and as a cultural phenomenon. It's a groundbreaking work not to be missed."

Todd McGowan, *philosopher*

"Mary Wild makes a unique and timely contribution with her book *Psychoanalysing Horror Cinema*. Using both psychoanalysis and related critical paradigms to explore a series of classic and new examples of the horror genre, Wild offers concise and insightful explorations of each film in a welcoming tone. The reader senses the genuine pleasure Wild takes in the interpretive act that each film elicits her to undertake. Readers ranging from the casual fan to the dedicated viewer of horror cinema—whether their bookshelf exists in physical or digital space—will find Wild's book merits a place."

Richard C. Ledes, *filmmaker*

Psychoanalysing Horror Cinema

MARY WILD

LONDON AND NEW YORK

Designed cover image: Susana Vilchez (www.suspirialand.com)

First published 2026
by Routledge
4 Park Square, Milton Park, Abingdon, Oxon OX14 4RN

and by Routledge
605 Third Avenue, New York, NY 10158

Routledge is an imprint of the Taylor & Francis Group, an informa business

© 2026 Mary Wild

The right of Mary Wild to be identified as author of this work has been asserted in accordance with sections 77 and 78 of the Copyright, Designs and Patents Act 1988.

All rights reserved. No part of this book may be reprinted or reproduced or utilised in any form or by any electronic, mechanical, or other means, now known or hereafter invented, including photocopying and recording, or in any information storage or retrieval system, without permission in writing from the publishers.

For Product Safety Concerns and Information please contact our EU representative GPSR@taylorandfrancis.com. Taylor & Francis Verlag GmbH, Kaufingerstraße 24, 80331 München, Germany.

Trademark notice: Product or corporate names may be trademarks or registered trademarks, and are used only for identification and explanation without intent to infringe.

British Library Cataloguing-in-Publication Data
A catalogue record for this book is available from the British Library

ISBN: 978-1-032-54511-0 (hbk)
ISBN: 978-1-032-54509-7 (pbk)
ISBN: 978-1-003-42523-6 (ebk)

DOI: 10.4324/9781003425236

Typeset in Dante and Avenir
by KnowledgeWorks Global Ltd.

This book is dedicated to artists.

Contents

Acknowledgements   ix

Foreword   xi

Introduction   xiv

1 Mind   1
Identity, memory, delusion, and psychic fragmentation

Mulholland Drive, Donnie Darko, Antichrist, Oldboy, Climax, The Silence of the Lambs, Possessor, Possession, Paranormal Activity, Kiss of the Damned

2 Body   31
Abjection, menstruation, mutilation, and the limits of the flesh

Carrie, Excision, Martyrs, Teeth, The Human Centipede Trilogy, Black Swan

3 Nature   76
Ecological horror, animal attacks, and natural disruption

The Birds, Picnic at Hanging Rock, Cujo, Jaws

4 Aliens
Otherness, invasion, and existential danger

War of the Worlds, Invasion of the Body Snatchers, Phantasm Franchise, Alien, Predator 1 and 2, The Thing, Event Horizon, They Live, Signs, Annihilation

92

5 Vampires
Seduction, immortality, and the erotic gothic

Bram Stoker's Dracula, Daughters of Darkness, Let's Scare Jessica to Death, The Lost Boys, Interview with the Vampire, Blade, The Addiction, The Twilight Saga, A Girl Walks Home Alone at Night, Doctor Sleep

124

6 Home Invasion
Paranoia, domestic space, and psychosexual threat

Gaslight, Rear Window, The Slumber Party Massacre, Misery, Single White Female, Creep, The Strangers 1 and 2, The Invitation, Gerald's Game, Mother!

155

Bibliography — 199

Index — 202

Acknowledgements

I want to express gratitude to everyone at Routledge for their care and commitment to this project. Special thanks to Zoe Meyer and Alanna Donaldson, who brought rigour, patience, and kindness to my writing journey.

Thank you to the brilliant team at Freud Museum London for hosting my *Projections* lecture series since 2012, and to the many audience members who shared such wonderful insights over the years.

Thanks also to the other cultural and educational organisations who have hosted my *Projections* lecture series for over a decade: City Lit, Morbid Anatomy, Picturehouse Cinemas, Shoreditch House, London Centre for Interdisciplinary Research (LCIR), Global Center for Advanced Studies (GCAS), and Miskatonic Institute of Horror Studies.

To Mike Muncer—thank you for trusting my voice on *The Evolution of Horror Podcast*, and for creating the vibrant space in which *Wild About Horror* first came to life. You bring out the best in everyone you work with.

To the listeners of *Wild About Horror*—thank you for receiving my segments with enthusiasm. Your thoughtful feedback gave me the courage to write this book. Big shoutout to the wonderful *Evolution of Horror Podcast* Facebook Discussion Group for the deep convos and hilarious memes!

To my Patreon and Substack communities—thank you for your generosity and friendship. Your support sustains me more than you know. I'm inspired to create more for you, always.

To my supremely talented cover artist and friend Susana Vilchez, aka @Suspirialand—thank you for the gorgeous artwork you created. It is the perfect threshold for entering this book.

To my family— Paul A., Manijeh G., Javid H., Behrouz H., Mahsa H., Rouzbeh F., Thomas A., Erika S., Julie F., Megan A., Mary A., Yasmine F., and Kiyana F.—thank you for believing in me.

Heartfelt gratitude also to my friends and soulmates: Gabriella R., Vanessa S., Juliet S., Tim L., Emily B., Vicky R., Kaitlin D., Elisa T., Kathy N., Dario L., Desiree F., Ellen M., Scott H., Adam C., Lee D., Kurt B., Joshkun T., Perry H., Jamie R., Mehdi J., Candice P., Jessie E., Nicole H., Nooshin T., Rebecca M., Andrew P., Rosemary C., Katie D., Eamon T., Helen R., Bryn D., Eric W., Shaun F.

To Dr. Patricia Csank—thank you for teaching those wonderful courses at Concordia University in Montréal in the late 1990s and early 2000s. You were the one who formally introduced me to psychoanalysis and put me on the path of ongoing meaningful discovery.

Finally, thanks to my favourite filmmakers: David Lynch, Darren Aronofsky, Jafar Panahi, Coralie Fargeat, Catherine Breillat, Lars von Trier, David Cronenberg, Tom Six, Robert Zemeckis, Gaspar Noé, Luis Buñuel.

Foreword
Mike Muncer

As we sit in a dark room and watch a movie depicting a young girl being chased—screaming—through the woods by a chainsaw-wielding psychopath, our hearts begin to race, and our palms start to sweat. Why? We know what we're watching isn't real, yet later that night we're still lying awake in a cold sweat thinking about it. No other genre has such a physical, visceral, and psychological effect on us quite like horror. That's because horror is the genre of empathy. We feel fear because we empathise with characters who find themselves in unspeakable, nightmarish scenarios. But it's not all fear and terror—we also find perverse, illicit thrills in horror movies. Experiencing something dangerous, extreme, or transgressive in a safe space can feel exciting, cathartic, and—again—unique to horror. Horror cinema plays on our fears, desires, dreams, and nightmares; the parts of ourselves we might keep hidden or locked away. So, when it comes to critiquing horror, it's crucial to understand and confront those parts of ourselves. Nobody understands the intersection between horror cinema and human psychology quite like Mary Wild.

Mary approaches film analysis from a unique perspective: as a true cinephile with deep reverence for cinema, and as a scholarly voice in psychoanalysis. It's the perfect combination for a genre that evokes such a visceral response. Horror films make us jump, laugh, scream, and recoil—and historically, it's a genre that's been sneered at for precisely that reason. There's long been a strange snobbery towards horror. As cinephiles, we like to turn our collective noses up at films that give us involuntary bodily reactions (see also: comedies, pornography, and Hallmark tearjerkers). Some audiences don't take kindly to James Wan making them leap out of their seats with a well-timed jump scare in *The Conjuring*, or David Cronenberg making them physically retch at the sight of Jeff Goldblum pulling off his fingernails in *The Fly*. But isn't it fascinating to confront and unpick *why* those classic cinematic moments have that effect on us, and why that's so off-putting for certain audiences? For someone like Mary Wild, who is as captivated by the human mind as she is by horror films, absolutely.

I first met Mary in 2017, when she was a guest on the first season of my podcast, *The Evolution of Horror*. We talked about slasher movies, and Mary approached the subject with an infectious love for horror cinema. But what set her apart from all other critics and guests on the podcast was her background as a psychoanalytic scholar. Mary brought that most rare blend of skills: academia and accessibility. Yes, she quoted Freud, Jung, and other psychoanalytic thinkers in her detailed, in-depth insights—but she also exclaimed, with glee, that kill scenes in slasher movies reminded her of cum shots in pornography. That's Mary in a nutshell: smart, perceptive, accessible, entertaining—and just a little bit naughty. Rather like Freud himself.

We horror fans have a reputation for being the weirdos and degenerates, but in my experience, the world of horror fandom has always felt like a safe space, filled with smart, open-minded, respectful, non-judgmental individuals, always open to healthy discussion and debate. Mary embodies these values in the way she approaches horror. For her, all horror films—no matter how trashy or ridiculous—are interesting and worthy of analysis. Furthermore, for Mary, all readings or interpretations are valid. Whether you're fluent in Freud or, like me, more of a novice, Mary is open to all perspectives. She always grounds her academic work in something human and relatable. She understands that even the strangest and most difficult films—whether it's Andrzej Żuławski's bonkers masterpiece *Possession*, or David Lynch's impenetrable nightmare *Mulholland Drive*—can be approached psychoanalytically in ways that speak directly to our everyday fears, desires, and experiences.

After discussing slasher movies in our first season, I invited Mary back to make subsequent one-off appearances on the next few seasons; with each season she would bring her unique insights to a particular subgenre: ghost stories, folk horror, zombie movies, and occult movies. But it never felt like enough! So, by our sixth season, I invited Mary to become a regular fixture on the podcast with her own dedicated segment: *Wild About Horror*. With each *Wild About Horror* segment, Mary presents a short but detailed, insightful 5-to-10-minute analysis on the film being discussed in that episode. It quickly became one of the most popular items on the podcast, with listeners constantly writing in to praise Mary's incredible critiques (and her smooth, dulcet tones). It's truly been an honour to work with Mary and watch her become one of the leading UK voices in horror. I feel lucky to boast 60 *Wild About Horror* segments and counting on my podcast. You haven't lived until you've heard Mary's brilliant and unique take on the fetishisation of guns in *Predator* or her reading of desire and abstinence in the *Twilight* movies.

This compendium of Mary's writings on some of the greatest horror films ever made—across a range of subgenres—is an absolute dream tome for anyone who is "wild about horror."

Introduction

This book grew out of audio and sound. It is an adaptation of short *Wild About Horror* segments I originally scripted for the hugely popular *Evolution of Horror Podcast* (EoH), hosted by Mike Muncer. I'm grateful to Mike for believing in me and nurturing my writing practice—he is one of the best people I've encountered in the film industry. A brilliant producer, broadcaster, film historian, and programmer, with a visionary understanding of what podcasts can be, Mike has built a beloved platform that welcomes a plurality of perspectives—EoH is known to be a cutting-edge and expansive space. Mike has a remarkable gift for recognising the unique talents of others, always showcasing his collaborators' contributions with care. He is the antithesis of gatekeeping and cutthroat competitiveness—he genuinely wants those around him to thrive, and listeners can feel his sincerity. Mike never interferes with the creative process; instead, he cultivates trust and motivation. He gently nudged me out of my comfort zone and encouraged my fullest expression. I feel lucky to know him.

Many who engage with *Wild About Horror* on EoH describe the segments as hypnotic and thought-provoking, likening them to a poetic detour within the broader structure of the podcast episodes. One commenter, Peter Jetnikoff, likened the listening experience to "going through a gallery and finding a strange dark room with vague shapes on the walls and a disembodied voice gently telling you to look a little harder"—a testament to the immersive atmosphere *Wild About Horror* evokes. Tarquin Mandrake generously remarked, "Madame Wild has powers beyond this earthly realm. […] I like that she takes the films seriously; she's making an investigation into the filmmakers' intent and taking the characters to task for their actions."

Mandrake expressed appreciation for the way the segments diverge from the usual "beery lads night out" tone often found in horror discourse, instead offering an avenue for deeper inquiry.

I've always loved film—especially horror, a genre that has proven to be cathartic in helping me process difficult emotions in a meaningful way, without causing real-world harm. Horror is an EMDR machine; it is my clinic. It gently provokes with imagery and sensation, coaxing buried fears to the surface. Horror provides an opportunity to confront images we'd rather not see and feelings we'd rather not feel. Within the controlled environment of cinema, distress can be revisited in symbolic form, allowing emotions that might otherwise remain locked in the unconscious to be metabolised. This book explores what horror films reveal about the unconscious, using the language of psychoanalysis to uncover hidden anxieties, repressed memories, and psychic conflicts that shape our experience of terror onscreen.

As a young girl growing up in late 1980s Montréal, I lived through things I couldn't yet understand—some of them traumatic. My refuge was the local home media rental store, Vidéo International. I spent hours, enchanted, in the horror section staring at the VHS covers of *The Shining* (1980), *An American Werewolf in London* (1981), *Pieces* (1982), *Christine* (1983), *A Nightmare on Elm Street* (1984), *Fright Night* (1985), *The Fly* (1986), and *Hellraiser* (1987). I was transported by the artwork and designs of the cassette covers and would dare myself to look for as long as I could before running back to the children's section for some comic relief. Even then, I sensed that horror held a power other genres simply didn't. This book honours that little girl standing in the horror section of the video store.

If you've listened to *Wild About Horror*, you'll know that I narrate the segments in a style that leans towards ASMR—low, steady tones intending to soothe, lull, and invite intimacy. My aim is to bring a sense of calm and open a channel: I believe that when the nervous system is regulated, the mind becomes more porous and receptive to new ideas. Complex, even unsettling material can land more gently when delivered in a comforting cadence. It's a kind of seduction into learning, where insight can bypass the defences and sink in deeper. While the written word can't replicate the soundscape of spoken narration, I hope the spirit of ASMR still envelops you as you read—that you feel held in a soft, curious space, and that the tingles still find their way to you, somehow.

My interest in psychoanalysis took shape long before I studied it formally. I've always been drawn to hidden layers, double meanings, and the things people try not to say. In 1998, at Concordia University in Montréal, the brilliant professor Dr. Patricia Csank introduced me to key psychoanalytic concepts. Her invaluable teachings laid the foundation for my developing knowledge. I learned about Freud's insistence that nothing is ever accidental—that slips, symptoms, and lapses betray our inner life. These ideas resonated deeply with me and became the cornerstone of my approach to film analysis. My outlook is deeply influenced by the works of Sigmund Freud, Jacques Lacan, and Carl Jung, whose theories provide a powerful framework for interpreting the symbolic structures of horror narratives. In 2012, I founded *Projections*, a public lecture series hosted at the Freud Museum in London, which brings psychoanalysis into dialogue with cinema in an intellectually rigorous and widely accessible way. The series invites audiences to experience film not merely as entertainment, but as a rich psychic document—a portal into the unconscious, a reflection of personal and collective dreams, traumas, and desires. Over the years, *Projections* has attracted a diverse community of film lovers, scholars, artists, and psychologists. The wonderful insights generated through these discussions have inspired me to continue working as an educator in this field.

As a self-proclaimed "Freudian cinephile," I tend not to accept the official story in any scenario. The surface narrative of a film is, to me, just the tip of the iceberg—something latent always lies beneath. In the immortal words of Gregory Peck in Hitchcock's *Spellbound* (1945): "I kept thinking while I was dreaming that all this meant something, that there was some other meaning in it that I ought to find out." My compulsion to uncover hidden patterns finds its sharpest edge in the cinematic arts. Horror film most vividly induces the territory of psychoanalysis, illuminating key concepts such as the Unconscious, the Uncanny, the Shadow, the Double, the Real, the Death Drive, and the raw textures of psychopathology (from neurosis to psychosis). Horror is a sacred way of seeing, a reliable method of inquiry, and a landscape of profound psychological truth.

As a female writer, I recognise that feminine subjectivity finds one of its richest expressions in the horror genre, which I embrace with enthusiasm. The dominant Symbolic Order is organised around male desire, while the wants of women often fail to register in a meaningful way. This omission, I believe, stems from a deep ambivalence towards the feminine capacity for a surplus of enjoyment—one that exceeds what the phallocentric system can accommodate. As a result, women are simultaneously sought-after *and* feared, cast as both objects of longing and as menacing figures who topple the foundations of phallic mastery. Feminine desire is thus exiled from the prevailing discourse, rendered unspeakable, excessive, or monstrous. Horror cinema, with its visceral textures and transgressive bent, becomes an ideal arena for staging and exploring this phenomenon. My second book will be an autofictional study of feminine jouissance, structured around a single film as the blueprint for charting its theoretical features.

This book is a deeply personal offering born from podcast scripts I once whispered into a microphone. While much of this volume is adapted from those recordings, I've taken creative liberties throughout: refining passages, expanding ideas, and adding new titles where the spirit moved me. Structured into six chapters—Mind, Body, Nature, Aliens, Vampires, and Home Invasion—the book traverses key horror subgenres, suggesting thematic readings through a psychoanalytic lens. It flows between theory and analysis, not to prescribe a singular "correct" interpretation of any given film, but to invite a deeper, more nuanced engagement with the material. My brand of 'pop psychoanalysis' is offered as a means of exploring the cinematic unconscious to see what truths might surface. I hope this book acts as a guided tour through what filmmaker Andrew Kötting once called my "mindscape meanderings." It is written in the spirit of passionate inquiry, not institutional authority. The aim is to champion psychoanalysis as a generative tool for personal reflection, rather than a bureaucratic gatekeeping device. This is not a formal academic text, but a collection of heartfelt subjective associations—intended for horror fans, theory appreciators, arty weirdos, whimsical dreamers, and all those who see beauty in the strange and the sublime. My wish is that readers will tune in to the messages their own unconscious might be trying to convey. After all, films have much in common with projective tests like Rorschach inkblots. So—*what do you see?*

Mind

Identity, memory, delusion, and psychic fragmentation

1

Psychological horror films focus on the human mind and emotional states to evoke fear, anxiety, and unease. The subgenre draws its power from the complexities of human perceptions, creating dread through intangible internal threats rather than physical or supernatural dangers. Themes such as paranoia, guilt, trauma, repression, and the fragility of reality are pursued, often blurring the line between the rational and the irrational, exploring the boundaries between sanity and madness. These films investigate the darker corners of human psychology, employing unreliable narrators, fractured identities, and ambiguous storylines that challenge the viewer's perceptions. Psychological horror films go beyond jump scares and graphic violence, building tension through atmosphere, subtlety, and suggestion, creating a lingering sense of trepidation. The settings are often intimate and claustrophobic, mirroring the characters' mental states, while the narrative invites viewers to question what is real versus imagined. By emphasising atmosphere and the unseen, psychological horror offers a deeply introspective and cerebral experience, leaving audiences ontologically unsettled.

Mulholland Drive (2001)

The ultimate terror object in David Lynch's *Mulholland Drive* is the elderly couple that torments Diane Selwyn, driving her towards suicide. We first encounter them in a washed-out, almost uncanny register, smiling alongside Diane as she wins the jitterbug contest—a defining moment in her life. Their relationship to her is left deliberately ambiguous. Are they grandparents? An aunt and uncle? Family friends? Their exact connection remains elusive, but one thing is clear: their approval carries weight. Later, they resurface as grotesque, repressed spectres from her past—stage(d) parents of sorts, embodiments of suffocating expectation. Their presence mutates from benign encouragement to animosity, a manifestation of Diane's crushing failure to live up to an imagined glittering showbiz career.

Diane Selwyn relocates from Deep River, Ontario, to Los Angeles, California, in pursuit of an acting career. The leap from garlanded jitterbug dancer to aspiring film star might seem tenuous, but compatible disciplines are not the point. What matters is the intoxicating shimmer of the spotlight as Diane is crowned champion—the moment that ignites her fever dream of Hollywood greatness. She was once the golden child. Her silver-screen aspirations intertwine with those of her enigmatic, silver-haired companions, who linger at the edges of her fantasy. They are now waiting impatiently to see what she achieves next, and she had better deliver the goods soon, because they haven't got very long left to live!

The tragedy of *Mulholland Drive* is that Diane Selwyn never achieves her dream of becoming a celebrated actress. She is, for all intents and purposes, a professional failure. Instead, it is her contemporary, Camilla Rhodes, who ascends—Hollywood's new darling, the one casting agents adore. Camilla, not Diane, is chosen for the part—*every part*. Diane feels outshone, the rejection becomes too much to bear; she has drifted so far from her prestigious Deep River victory! This is a reverse Cinderella story, wherein someone else gets the glass slipper. And how does Diane cope with the disappointment? She doesn't. She withdraws, sinking into obscurity, down in the dumps. Marooned in her dingy apartment, slumped in a drab dressing gown she never bothers to change. At the risk of violating the *Goldwater Rule*,[1] she appears to suffer from depression and agoraphobia—perhaps even something deeper. Sleep becomes her only reprieve, a desperate escape into a world where she still matters.

In her dreams, Diane recasts herself as Betty—a naïve, bright-eyed ingénue brimming with optimism, a newcomer to Los Angeles destined to be the toast of Tinseltown. When her flight from Canada lands at LAX, she appears alongside the elderly couple, her ever-smiling companions. Buoyed by the promise of a dazzling future, she exchanges pleasantries with Irene, radiating hopeful enthusiasm:

IRENE: It's time to say goodbye, Betty. It's been so nice travelling with you.

---

1 The Goldwater Rule is a guideline set by the American Psychiatric Association prohibiting psychiatrists from publicly diagnosing or offering professional opinions about the mental health of individuals they have not personally examined and who have not given consent.

BETTY: Thank you, Irene. I was so excited and nervous. It sure was great to have you to talk to.
IRENE: Now, remember I'll be watching for you on the big screen.
BETTY: Okay Irene. Won't that be the day?
IRENE: The best of luck to you, Betty. Take care of yourself and be careful.

This might seem like a perfectly unexceptional moment in the dream sequence, but I believe it is overflowing with crushing significance, which I will unravel in full later. After Betty and the elderly couple part ways at LAX, she heads off in a taxi to her aunt's house, while Irene and her husband, now alone in the back of a limousine, exchange an eerie, knowing smile.

Diane dreams on. In this reimagined world, Camilla Rhodes is no longer a rising star but a missing person—an amnesiac whom Betty, ever the plucky heroine, is determined to help. Unable to recall her own name, Camilla adopts the moniker *Rita*, inspired by the luminous Rita Hayworth. Meanwhile, the wide-eyed Betty experiences a meteoric rise in the "dream place" of Hollywood, achieving an implausible level of success in mere days. At her audition, she delivers a performance so breathtaking that the entire room—studio executives, producers, directors—falls silent, utterly transfixed. Everyone adores her. They all want little Betty in their big movies. On a soundstage, she locks eyes with a virtuoso filmmaker, the moment charged with romantic inevitability—they are drawn to each other like magnets. But there's a snag. The industry is not governed by talent or fate but by unseen forces pulling the strings. Behind the scenes, mobsters dictate the rules, snatching creative control from the director. The decision has already been made: Camilla, not Betty, is the chosen girl. It's not Betty's fault. The system is rigged; natural law is broken. No amount of brilliance could have changed the outcome—it was never in her hands to begin with.

This is the delusional narrative Diane constructs to soothe herself—a fragile fiction designed to dull the pain—alas, she is bound to wake up to the cold reality. Diane dreams and dreams, retiring the Betty character and appearing as herself at a make-believe dinner party—one that cannot commence until she arrives. Here, she is forced to endure the excruciating humiliation of recounting her lowly backstory while watching Camilla bask in triumph. Camilla is radiant, effortlessly commanding the room. Worse still, she is engaged—to the very director who once gazed at Betty with infatuation. The brutal force of envy is almost too much for Diane to bear. Her eyes brim with tears as she watches the two Camillas—blonde and brunette—collide in a languorous, achingly glamorous kiss. There is a surefire clue that this dinner party, too, exists within a dreamscape: Diane drinks from a coffee cup marked "SOS"—a classic distress signal, a subconscious cry for help. My theory? In *Mulholland Drive*, coffee functions as a reality marker. When the coffee is good, we are in a dream. When it's bad, we are in Diane's stark, joyless waking life. Scenes of her shuffling around her dingy apartment in a dressing gown, brewing lifeless filter coffee, signify her bleak existence. Meanwhile, in the Betty portion of the film, gangsters threaten the lives of gourmet espresso servers. David Lynch's coffee obsession is well-documented, and this detail will have been carefully curated by him, I imagine.

But let us return to the elderly couple—the ultimate terror object in *Mulholland Drive*. They embody the weight of Diane's dashed dreams, the suffocating pressure of parental expectation, now twisted into a toxic white noise. When her Hollywood aspirations collapse, these blasts from the past resurface, nightmarish and vengeful, driving her to the edge. Locked inside her grimy apartment, Diane is jolted by a deafening pounding at the door. The unbearable noise sends shockwaves through the squalid space. It's them. They're *so* fucking back. In a surreal, almost demonic sequence, the old couple is shown emerging from a brown paper bag belonging to the terrifying figure behind Winkie's diner. They appear like tiny insects, small enough to scuttle under Diane's apartment door, spooking the hell out of her. Their *bug* size links them back to the *jitterbug* contest, and they *bug* Diane with their impossible expectations, giving her the *jitters*, to boot. Even in the dream sequence, Irene's seemingly warm farewell to Betty—"I'll be watching for you on the big screen"—carries a certain spikiness. There's a vaguely threatening quality about it, an unspoken pressure, an ever-present gaze that reeks of entitlement and toxic surveillance. It also evokes the phrase *"Don't forget about the little people"*—the idea that when someone achieves fame, they must acknowledge regular folks who helped along the way. But here, the sentiment has a more backhanded and sinister implication. Diane is never allowed to forget about these pesky *little people*—they don't just haunt her; they invade and antagonise, sneaking in uninvited, mocking her failure, eroding what remains of her sanity. Their warped glee is excruciating. Diane can only scream in horror and reach for a firearm to end the torment of her life.

The loss of vitality is a central theme woven into the tapestry of *Mulholland Drive*—a libidinal drive that surges, plateaus, and ultimately wanes miserably. Diane Selwyn begins as a bright young thing, a big fish in the small pond of Deep River, Ontario, jitterbugging her way to LA with vim, vigour, and sordid dreams of stardom. But Hollywood is a cruel seduction, a tantalising foreplay that never quite gets her off. *Diane seldom wins*; she loses momentum, caught in a painful loop of failed self-gratification. The dream image that once thrilled her—the fantasy of cinematic triumph, transposed onto a lesbian love affair with the dazzling Camilla Rhodes—has faded into oblivion. The erotic charge slips just out of reach, leaving her stranded in a frustrating vortex of compulsive repetition. She keeps rubbing herself raw, joylessly chasing satisfaction that never arrives. She crumbles in floods of tears and redoubles her efforts but what once turned Diane on now edges her torturously just on the periphery of release. Naomi Watts has said that, while filming this doomed masturbation sequence, David Lynch "didn't want an emotive scene; he wanted someone who was angry and trying to reconnect with an erotic moment." This lends support to my theory that *Mulholland Drive's* terrifying effect stems from the decline of the animating force.

Donnie Darko (2001)

Richard Kelly's sci-fi thriller *Donnie Darko* follows a troubled teenager grappling with doomsday visions and the unravelling of his reality. The film's depiction of paranoid schizophrenia is striking: Jake Gyllenhaal's Donnie experiences vivid visual and auditory hallucinations, but my focus lies in interpreting the discursive position of the conspiracy theorist. Set in October 1988 in the lead-up to the US presidential election, the film weaves in televised debates and discussions about Democratic candidate Michael Dukakis and his Republican rival George H.W. Bush. Against this backdrop, we learn that Donnie is a sleepwalker, drawn into cryptic encounters with Frank—a monstrous figure in a rabbit costume who warns him that the world will end in 28 days, just before the election. His full name is *Donald J. Darko…* which reminds me of *Donald J. Trump*—just a coincidence of course, but we Freudians revel in these happy accidents!

Donnie continues to see Frank, though his psychiatrist dismisses these visions as "daylight hallucinations," evidence of his detachment from reality. At Donnie's high school, Graham Greene's short story *The Destructors* is assigned as reading—a significant choice, as the author's birthday, 2 October, coincides with the film's opening scene, in which Donnie sleepwalks out of his house. This parallel suggests that the central tenet of Greene's story—that destruction can be a form of creation—serves as a driving force in *Donnie Darko*. It offers the viewer an intimate glimpse into the experiential reality of a teenage boy, a world brimming with absurdism and captivating commotion. Donnie's gym teacher, disturbed by the ideas in *The Destructors*, begins hosting "attitude lessons" based on the teachings of local motivational speaker Jim Cunningham. Donnie, however, rebels against these lessons, rejecting their simplistic worldview. As he grows increasingly convinced that obscure, unseen forces are at work around him, he takes drastic action, setting fire to Cunningham's house. The subsequent investigation by firefighters uncovers child pornography in the motivational speaker's home, leading to his swift arrest.

This sequence affirms Donnie's suspicion that his target was, in fact, a dangerous perpetrator, granting him a near-superheroic ability to see through hypocrisy and uncover hidden corruption. *The Destructors*, so closely aligned with Donnie's rebellious instinct, comes under attack by moralistic authority figures, reinforcing the film's central tension between an oppressive elite and a disaffected underdog fighting to expose injustice. Meanwhile, the looming 1988 presidential election hums in the background, amplifying the film's preoccupation with power struggles—a motif that weighs heavily on Donnie's restless mind.

Donnie Darko feels like being stuck inside a delusional mind—a cognitive rupture where the structural integrity of the world, the very fabric of reality, is torn apart. The normal laws of physics no longer apply; enormous objects inexplicably plummet from the sky, crashing into Donnie's house like something out of a Magritte painting. The effect is pure surrealist disorientation—a monstrous, outsized presence invading a familiar space, warping the home's comforting stability, and injecting an unmistakable sense of the uncanny. In this topsy-turvy world, even time travel is possible. Nothing is grounded. We can't fully rely on anything or trust anyone. *Donnie Darko* masterfully cultivates the suspicion that a nefarious force is pulling the strings, that some dark entity is behind the chaos. And as viewers, we are drawn into Donnie's paranoia, spiraling with him, compelled to ask the same question: *Who is doing this to him?*

Mild suspicions escalate into full-blown conspiracy theories, and I propose that this specific discursive position inevitably emerges during transitional moments—particularly when a nation stands at the precipice of a presidential election. Such periods accentuate a rupture in the Symbolic Order, leaving a gap where authority once stood. Psychoanalytically speaking, when the figure of the president—the paternal authority—is in flux, it creates a chasm in subjective space, potentially triggering a psychotic response akin to R.D. Laing's notion of ontological insecurity, in which the world feels unreal, identity becomes unstable, and the self is severed from any cohesive temporal continuity. The looming loss of presidential hegemony destabilises the psyche, forcing us to self-govern in an interim state of moral drift—between governments, fatherless. We are left unanchored, confronting our own capacity for aggressive and illicitly erotic impulses. A feeling not unlike anxiously awaiting the results of a paternity test on *Jeremy Kyle* or *The Maury Show*!

It is precisely in this fragile state that the conspiratorial mind is activated, compelling the subject to generate surplus signifiers—however outlandish—to patch over the black hole in discourse. When faced with uncertainty, the temptation to perceive hostile forces at work becomes irresistible. Shadowy figures in cahoots, secret cabals plotting against us, unseen hands pulling the strings—it seems like a figment of the imagination, a coping mechanism, an attempt to impose order on a world in disarray. *Donald J.* conjuring elaborate narratives to illuminate his path in the dark... sound familiar? In today's political climate, where misinformation spreads like wildfire, the paranoid psyche thrives. Spectacle eclipses substance, and manufactured madness keeps populations in a state of perpetual bewilderment. Confusion is not a byproduct—it is the point. The post-truth landscape, fuelled by algorithmic echo chambers and weaponised disinformation, operates by keeping the subject endlessly searching, trapped in a labyrinth of deceit where the only certainty is uncertainty itself.

Antichrist (2009)

Now, with great delight, I turn my gaze to Maestro Lars von Trier—Denmark's beloved *enfant terrible*, a polymorphously phobic provocateur who commands the attention of cinephiles like no other. Even those who claim to despise him—outraged by his supposed desecration of human decency—can't seem to stop talking about him. He lives rent-free in his detractors' heads; ain't it always the way? Lars revels in contradiction, playing devil's advocate with gleeful abandon, stirring the pot sometimes just to spark discussion. "It's quite important not to be loved by everybody," he once quipped, "because then you've failed." Words to live by!

Lars von Trier's motto is: "A film should be like a stone in your shoe." This operates on two levels: 1) true originality emerges through creative restrictions, forcing a filmmaker to carve out a distinct voice, and 2) a great film lingers and bothers the viewer, interrupting the rhythms of daily life—like a stone in one's shoe. The goal here ought not be to please but to provoke. Controversy isn't a byproduct; it's something to strive for, pushing the discourse beyond the confines of social decorum. A real artist mustn't be in the business of winning popularity contests or seeking validation. Impact—however uncomfortable—is a currency that matters.

Before diving into *Antichrist*, here's a fascinating piece of backstory. Lars von Trier's mother withheld the truth about his paternity for most of his life. On her deathbed in 1989, she confessed that his biological father was not Ulf Trier—the Jewish civil servant who had raised him—but Fritz Michael

Hartmann, a Catholic German classical musician. She had conceived Lars through an extramarital affair, deliberately selecting Hartmann to give her child "artistic genes." In an instant, the filmmaker wasn't just mourning his mother; he had also lost the man he believed to be his father. His sense of cultural identity and family lineage was thrown into disarray. Manipulated and furious, he spiralled into a deep depression—a rupture that would shape his work for years to come.

Antichrist is an experimental horror film through which Lars von Trier exorcises his Mommy issues. He wrote the screenplay in 2006 while hospitalised for a major depressive episode, crafting the film from a place of psychological distress. The initial spark came from a documentary about Europe's original forests, which depicted nature as a nightmarish battleground—an ecosystem of relentless violence, where every species exists to kill or be killed. This vision struck Lars, inspiring him to explore the paradox of nature: often romanticised as serene and restorative, yet far closer to a vision of Hell. Hence the film's defining line: "Nature is Satan's Church."

His mother's paternity revelation became very influential, shaping what would later be dubbed the "Depression Trilogy"—*Antichrist* (2009), *Melancholia* (2011), and *Nymphomaniac* (2013). Each film features complex female protagonists who function as stand-ins for Lars, staging his despair, angst, and loneliness. He has remarked that society grants women greater freedom to express emotions than men, making them ideal surrogates to convey his own suffering. One might assume, then, that the torment onscreen is autobiographical—not a sadistic spectacle, but a raw, unfiltered outpouring. He isn't revelling in female sorrow; he is in great pain himself and relies on his performers to convey his reality. *Antichrist* took the form of a horror film because, as he put it, the genre allowed for "a lot of very strange images"—a testament to horror's unique ability to accommodate otherwise inexpressible psychological states. He even described it as a "fun" way of working through his depression. Critics generally praised the film's artistic execution but were sharply divided on its substantive merit. Apparently, some were scandalised by the clitoris-cutting scene. Poor darlings!

In the opening sequence of *Antichrist*, a child plummets from an apartment window while his parents are engrossed in sex. This harrowing moment evokes the biblical story of humanity's expulsion from the Garden of Eden—a tragic fall from innocence into sin. The film draws a parallel to the concept of inherited human evil, rooted in the Fall from Grace. In the Bible, Eve is cast as the culprit for disobeying God, and similarly, in *Antichrist*, Lars von Trier seems to implicate the mother in his descent into existential suffering. The nameless mother—her anonymity underscoring her archetypal significance—watches in silence as her child falls to his death, preoccupied by her own pleasure. She is aware of the danger but does nothing to intervene. This moment encapsulates Lars's innermost crisis: the idea that the mother is driven by selfish desires, her erotic vitality directly at odds with the well-being of her child. It's a troubling notion that reverberates in *Nymphomaniac*, challenging the conventional assumption that all mothers are automatically nurturing and that their children are their foremost priority.

The infamous clitoris-slicing scene becomes vital in this context: *Antichrist* is, at its core, a revenge film. Haunted by the spectre of her dead child, the guilt-ridden mother turns garden shears on her own vulva—the site where birth and death coalesce. By destroying the source of her pleasure, she effectively extinguishes her will to live. Lars strikes where it hurts most! After the baby's death, the woman is consumed by grief and hospitalised. Her equally unnamed husband, sceptical of her psychiatric care, takes it upon himself to treat her using cognitive behavioural therapy. She appears pathologically afraid of Eden (the woods), and her husband, a psychotherapist, attempts to guide her through a visualisation exercise. "I want you to melt into the green," he instructs on the train ride to Eden. "Just turn green." In a sense, he is coaching her to surrender, to be subsumed within his narrative. The management of her depression becomes a power play in their marriage. He believes his expert knowledge can provide relief, but she secretly mocks his naïve conviction. His glib platitude—"What the mind can conceive and believe, it can achieve"—ignores the unconscious forces that lie beyond our control. He co-opts her suffering to prove an academic point, reducing her torment to an egotistical endeavour. His suspicions are aroused when she appears to recover spontaneously shortly after their arrival in Eden. He then encounters a talking fox in the forest, which declares, "Chaos reigns!"—prefiguring that he is not out of the woods yet! Eden is a cinematic exploration of origin myths as sources of anxiety and dread. That is, we would rather not identify the primary traumatising incident; we instead amass a host of defence mechanisms to ensure the upsetting memory is vanquished. Yet, true reprieve is impossible until we confront and navigate the psychological conflict zone.

In *Antichrist*, the woman writes a thesis on witch-hunts, initially aiming to critique the historical persecution of women. However, as she delves deeper into her research on gynocide, she begins to internalise the very misogynistic beliefs she set out to dismantle. Her husband is horrified, reproaching her for adopting the toxic ideologies she was supposed to debunk. Yet, the Polaroid photos reveal a chilling truth: the child's shoe was consistently placed on the wrong foot by his mother, suggesting she had harboured an intent to harm the baby all along. Her very nature, externalised in the ominous woods, is dominated by dark, primal impulses. Strangely, there is a liberating feeling in this realisation—an acknowledgment of the shadow self. This narrative serves as Lars von Trier's condemnation of his mother's real-life eugenics experiment, yet it also reveals his identification with her. He admits that he, too, is capable of violence, as he is not separate from nature's brutality but intrinsically part of it. This duality makes the film profoundly touching: while exposing his mother's cruelty, Lars also aligns himself with her aggressive representation. Despite the lasting damage caused by her devastating revelation, he resists the temptation to abandon her in the wilderness, choosing instead to confront and grapple with the complexity of their relationship.

Oldboy (2003)

Park Chan-wook's neo-noir action thriller *Oldboy* follows Oh Dae-su, a man mysteriously imprisoned for 15 years, only to be released into an even greater nightmare. As he embarks on a relentless quest for vengeance, he becomes entangled in a labyrinth of conspiracy and violence, desperate to uncover the motives of his captor, Woo-jin. Along the way, he falls in love with Mi-do, a young sushi chef—only to later discover that she is, in fact, his daughter. The source of Woo-jin's vendetta is gradually revealed: as high school classmates, Oh Dae-su once witnessed Woo-jin in a moment of incestuous intimacy with his sister. The ensuing rumours spread like wildfire, driving Woo-jin's sister to suicide. Consumed by grief and rage, Woo-jin meticulously crafts an elaborate revenge: through hypnosis and manipulation, he orchestrates Oh Dae-su and Mi-do's meeting, ensuring their fated attraction. By forcing his enemy to unknowingly commit the same taboo, Woo-jin ensures that Oh Dae-su is shackled to the same unbearable pain that once destroyed him.

Park Chan-wook deliberately named his protagonist Oh Dae-su as a nod to Oedipus, the tragic Greek hero fated to kill his father and marry his mother, unwittingly fulfilling a prophecy that brings devastation to his city and family. Beyond the theme of unintentional incest, the parallels run deeper: Oedipus, upon discovering the horrific truth of his actions, blinds himself—choosing darkness over a world that rejects truth. Likewise, Oh Dae-su, crippled by unbearable knowledge, severs his own tongue, silencing a truth he can no longer bear to speak. *Oedipus Rex*, Sophocles' seminal tragedy, encapsulates the enduring concerns of Greek drama: the flawed nature of humanity, the inexorable force of fate, and the individual's struggle within an indifferent universe. Centuries later, in 19th-century

Vienna, a certain Sigmund Freud attended a performance of the play and found himself profoundly moved. The themes of repressed desire and unconscious conflict lingered in his mind, inspiring what would become one of psychoanalysis's most infamous theories: the Oedipus complex, in which a child harbours an unconscious sexual desire for the opposite-sex parent while viewing the same-sex parent as a rival.

In *The Interpretation of Dreams*, Freud proposed that Oedipal desire is a universal phenomenon—an innate drive that lurks in the unconscious, burdening us with guilt before we even understand its implications (Freud 1900). He viewed Oedipus' tragedy as uniquely moving because, in his view, it could just as easily have been ours. "The Oracle laid the same curse upon us before our birth as upon Oedipus," Freud claimed. Perhaps it is the fate of all of us, he speculated, to direct our first sexual impulses towards our mother and our first murderous hatred towards our father. A bold claim! Personally, I see this as just one scenario among many possible outcomes in the tangled "family romance" of our formative years. We enter the world shaped by our primary caregivers, and their attitudes towards sexuality leave a lasting imprint on our own erotic development. But this is hardly a topic that public discourse embraces—because, well… it's super awkward, man! The subject occupies an ambivalent space, teetering on the edge of the forbidden, which makes it the perfect Freudian preoccupation. Ain't it always the way?

Oldboy is audacious because it faces the incest taboo in an experientially compelling way. The truth of the blood relation between the men and their respective love interests—a sister and a daughter—remains concealed for most of the film, only to detonate in an explosion of violence upon discovery. Incest remains one of the most unshakable taboos in modern society, yet as a primitive impulse, it lingers uncomfortably in the shadows of the psyche, not always so easily repressed in fantasy life. A cursory search on pornography websites makes that patently clear, with an overwhelming glut of X-rated content built on incestuous scenarios. Freud wrote extensively about the emotional ambivalence surrounding taboo desires. He argued that taboo is not inherently real but socially constructed—a prohibition whose original rationale may have once been functional but is now obscured by time (Freud 1913). Even when a taboo, such as incest, may have a known biological basis today, its prohibition often persists more as a cultural imperative than a consciously reasoned stance. Taboo becomes dangerous, carrying dire consequences, though no one quite remembers why. The mere mention of the impulse triggers unbearable guilt at the personal level and shame at the social level. The repression has been in place for so long that its original meaning is no longer traceable—only the horror of its transgression remains.

The narrative structure of *Oldboy* hinges on the suppression of the incest taboo. A direct confrontation with the impulse is forbidden, so it must be expressed covertly. The film's core symbolism—long-term imprisonment followed by an abrupt release into the jaws of transgression—paints a topographical picture of repression breeding obsession, the forbidden object made even more tantalising precisely because it is off-limits. This is why *Oldboy* is most compelling when read allegorically, as a cautionary tale about the dangers of rendering certain subjects unspeakable. To de-platform aspects of society—or of our psyche—no matter how unpalatable, is to imbue them with greater allure, making them even more precarious.

The Oedipal weight of *Oldboy* is powerful in the way that Greek myths always remind us: we cannot outrun the destiny of our impulses. These stories are classified as tragedy precisely because they expose the futility of repression. The more we deny our capacity for inappropriate fantasies, the more space they occupy in the unconscious. Of course, this is not to suggest that we ought to act on every illicit desire—rather, the psychoanalytic aim is to acknowledge the disturbing material honestly, thereby diminishing its hold through interpretation. Park Chan-wook's films carve a path towards that confrontation, bridging an imaginary gap that never ceases to be terrifying, yet offers catharsis when we finally engage with what unsettles us most.

Climax (2018)

Gaspar Noé's *Climax* unfolds during the winter of 1996, following a French dance troupe as they throw an after-party to celebrate a gruelling rehearsal. What begins as a euphoric gathering swiftly descends into anarchy when the group unknowingly consumes LSD-laced sangria. From the outset, I was intrigued by the presence of a child within the high-intensity world of a dance troupe. Tito, the young son of Emmanuelle, is positioned within a carefully constructed image—one that he is encouraged to identify with, a reflection of his mother's own aspirations and ideals. Yet, as *Climax* unravels, this idealised vision—promising wholeness and fulfilment—reveals itself as, at best, a naïve illusion and, at worst, a major deception.

Jacques Lacan's Mirror Stage theory provides a useful framework for understanding this dynamic. In early infancy, before developing bodily coordination, the child is entirely dependent on the primary caregiver for sustenance, cleanliness, and stability. Trapped in a state of internal unrest, unable to communicate, the infant experiences frustration—until, upon recognising themselves in a mirror (or, more often, through the mother's verbalised perception), they experience a moment of jubilant self-recognition. The mirror image appears unified, complete, perfectly contoured—an external assurance that counteracts the child's unconscious sense of fragmentation. Yet this "wholeness" is a mirage. The psyche becomes structured through a distancing exteriority, locating in the mirror a comforting ideal image that, paradoxically, fosters alienation rather than true integration (Lacan 1977, 1–7).

Climax uniquely captures the alienating effect of identifying with the mother—of shaping one's identity through her gaze and desires. The Mirror Stage offers only fleeting solace in the vast wilderness of ontological insecurity, and *Climax* serves as a cautionary tale about the perils of merging too closely with the mother's will. We believe we are safe, tethered to a source of warmth and affirmation—only to find ourselves locked in the electrical room, intimately close to the energy source that activates us, but also dangerously fused with her. In the end, the connection isn't just sustaining; it's fatal. We get zapped to death.

Let's unpack a term I just mentioned: ontological insecurity. Coined by Scottish psychiatrist R.D. Laing in *The Divided Self*, it describes a state of feeling more unreal than real, more dead than alive—lacking temporal continuity, with the self experienced as partially divorced from the body (Laing 1960, 42). Few films capture this condition as viscerally as *Climax*. When the LSD takes hold, the dancers spiral into extreme states of derealisation and depersonalisation. Unwittingly dosed, they descend into a drug-induced collective psychosis. Gaspar Noé's dizzying camerawork keeps us locked inside their unravelling perception, amplifying the unremitting terror of losing both physical and mental control.

All cultural niceties and societal taboos dissolve once the psychedelic substance pries open the dam of repression, unleashing primal urges in full force. Taylor attempts to have sex with his sister Gazelle—the breach of the incest taboo serving, as always, as a harbinger of total ontological collapse. She flees into the central hall, where the remaining dancers writhe on the floor, chanting in tongues, fucking, and beating each other senseless. By morning, the police arrive to find most of the revellers unconscious. Omar has frozen to death outside, while Emmanuelle, overcome with grief at the loss of her son Tito in the electrical room, has taken her own life. Gazelle wakes up beside her brother, seemingly oblivious to the horrors of the night before. Meanwhile, a bloodied Lou staggers out into the snow, convulsing with laughter in a state of shock. As the police comb through the wreckage, an unfazed Psyche—who just so happens to have books on hallucinogens in her bag—retreats to her room and casually administers droplets of drugs into her eyeballs. Aha… *it was Psyche all along!* She spiked the sangria. But what is the psychoanalytic significance of this revelation?

In Greek mythology, Psyche embodies the human soul. She falls in love with Eros but must endure a series of trials, repeatedly losing and regaining him. Her story reflects the perpetual struggle to reattain Eros—the life force, the animating principle of existence. This cyclical pursuit mirrors the psychoanalytic view of human desire: we are ceaselessly driven to fight for the will to live, to reclaim what slips from our grasp—this back-and-forth motion encompasses the soul's journey. Gaspar Noé's provocation taps into this existential rhythm, aligning with his own bleak worldview. In *Climax*, we are all like the unsuspecting dancers—thrust into chaos, taken by surprise, disoriented, never fully grasping what's happening. But the atmosphere is unmistakable: something ominous looms, and we are powerless to resist it. Psyche takes hold, she breathes life into us—we are at her mercy, whether we like it or not!

Gaspar Noé's films frequently circle back to the female reproductive body and the impulse to abort an unborn child. He seems fixated on the idea of preventing life as an act of mercy—perhaps reflecting an antinatalist worldview, a belief that dragging an innocent baby into a brutal world is inherently cruel, that the curse of sentience is too steep a price to pay. My impression is that Noé sees life as a relentless accumulation of losses, compounding until we are finally obliterated. And so, *Climax* casts Psyche—the seeker of the "Life Force"—as a devious prankster, flooding humans with passion, pain, and poison. The dancers, filmed from above, resemble fruit bobbing in life's spiked sangria punchbowl—a cosmic punchline, soaking up toxins, primed for endless suffering. Early in the night, before acid invades everyone's bloodstream, Psyche urinates on the dancefloor. But to me, it looks like something else: her water breaking. She's going into labour. Life is about to happen—and it ain't gonna end well for any of us.

The Silence of the Lambs (1991)

The time has come to focus on one of my all-time favourite characters: Hannibal Lecter. We all know the plot of *The Silence of the Lambs*, Jonathan Demme's tour-de-force psychological horror film. Young FBI trainee Clarice Starling is assigned the task of apprehending the elusive serial killer known as "Buffalo Bill." To build a forensic profile, she must seek guidance from the imprisoned Dr. Hannibal Lecter—a brilliant psychiatrist, a refined aesthete, and, of course, a cannibalistic murderer.

What I want to focus on is the electric relationship between Clarice and Hannibal—their spectacular power dynamic, a source of maddening mystery and fascination, the film's true driving force. My proposition is that Clarice, burdened by unresolved grief over her father's death, unconsciously projects Oedipal baggage onto the notorious convict as she embarks on this high-stakes professional consultation. In their exchanges, Hannibal is positioned as the gatekeeper of sought-after knowledge, capable of peeling back the layers of the criminally insane mind. The kicker? He isn't just an expert in psychopathology—he has firsthand experience as a mass murderer. The challenge is to coax him into dispensing his morbid pearls of wisdom without becoming ensnared in his web.

Hannibal, of course, is not so easily persuaded. The drama of *The Silence of the Lambs* hinges on his enigmatic nature—he withholds information, toys with law enforcement, and savours their desperation like a fine meal. He has no real interest in bargaining for better prison conditions, nor does he entertain any illusions of rehabilitation. But when he meets Clarice, something about her intrigues him. For the first time, he agrees to a quid pro quo arrangement: he will provide insights into Buffalo Bill, but only in exchange for intimate details about Clarice's past—juicy morsels of childhood trauma, buried fears, and vulnerabilities. Hannibal delights in dissecting her psyche, probing for weaknesses while offering cryptic clues in return. Like a modern-day Sphinx, he speaks only in riddles, never revealing the full truth. Clarice is just as determined—she watches him intently, studying him as obsessively as he analyses her.

The intricate dynamic between Clarice and Hannibal mirrors the psychoanalytic structure of a patient engaging with a therapist—seeking revelation, desperate for resolution. What makes their interactions remarkable is the fluidity of these roles. At various points in the film, they shift between analyst and patient, interrogator and confessor. They probe and scrutinise, but they also break down, act out, and become overwhelmed. This continuous oscillation injects the narrative with texture, suspense, and ambivalence. I find myself rooting for the deranged Dr. Lecter—not because he is redeemable, but because an existential link forms between him and Clarice. Their connection transcends hunter and hunted, transforming into a far more complex identification and mutual fascination... even the glimmers of a strange friendship. It's this eerie intimacy that elevates Hannibal from villain to antihero.

A key theoretical concept that illuminates this dynamic is Lacan's "Subject supposed to know" (translated from the French *"le sujet supposé savoir"*). Lacan defined transference as the attribution of knowledge to a subject—specifically, the role the clinician comes to embody in the treatment. But what kind of knowledge is presumed here? According to Lacan, the analyst is believed to possess an inescapable truth, an unspoken wisdom that lurks beneath the patient's words (Lacan 1977). This belief endows otherwise insignificant details with retroactive meaning. A casual gesture, an ambiguous remark—once the analyst is perceived as the carrier of hidden knowledge, the patient starts interpreting their every move as deliberate, laden with secret intent. It is at this moment, when the analyst fully embodies the essence of the *subject supposed to know*, that transference fully takes hold.

Sure enough, Clarice perceives Hannibal as the keeper of an obscure primer—her only hope of solving the puzzle of Buffalo Bill. Her unconscious Oedipal hang-up transfers onto him, and Hannibal, ever the master manipulator, exploits this dynamic for his own amusement. He delights in toying with her, always maintaining the upper hand by sporadically imparting factoids, carefully meting out just enough information to keep her coming back for more. Like the Sphinx, he veils his insights in riddles, spurring Clarice into action, keeping her on edge. As we see in both the sequel and prequel to *The Silence of the Lambs*, Hannibal routinely weaponises his role as the *subject supposed to know*. This is the theoretical quirk that makes him so utterly magnetic—he gets under our skin, burrows deep into our psyches, and despite his homicidal appetites, we can't help but be enthralled. Now, bear with me a moment—I'll be right back, just off to enjoy a nice Chianti...

Possessor (2020)

Brandon Cronenberg's sci-fi psychological horror *Possessor*, much like his debut feature *Antiviral* (2012), interrogates the intersection of technology and consciousness. Brandon is masterful at dissecting the liminal boundary between selfhood and reality, plunging deep into the experiential elements of identity. In *Possessor*, Tasya Vos is an elite assassin employed by a shadowy corporation that executes high-profile killings. Her method is as chilling as it is sophisticated: through an implanted device, she hijacks the body of an unwitting host, overriding their motor functions and decision-making capacity. A specialised machine facilitates the transfer, allowing her consciousness to infiltrate and dominate another's mind. The film's central conceit—the violent merging of identities—mirrors contemporary anxieties about technological overreach and the erosion of personal autonomy.

Vos returns to her own body by compelling her host to commit suicide at the end of each assignment. But as she spends increasing amounts of time inhabiting others, her sense of self begins to erode. The boundary between work and personal life dissolves—she rehearses her own persona just as meticulously as she practices imitating her hosts. Violent intrusive thoughts seep into her domestic routine, surfacing like flashbacks from the trauma of her murders. Her handler, Girder—a retired assassin—sees personal attachments as liabilities. She dismisses Vos's desire to stay connected to her family, insisting she would be a more efficient killer if she severed all ties. Despite her growing psychological instability and physical exhaustion, Vos takes on a high-stakes mission: the assassination of wealthy CEO John Parse and his daughter, Ava. To execute the hit, she hijacks the body of Ava's fiancé, Colin Tate, planning to stage a public altercation at a lavish party to establish motive. The goal is to kill both targets before turning the gun on herself, severing the neural link between Colin's brain and her own. But the hit goes awry—Ava dies and Parse survives.

Building on this, an intriguing parallel emerges between John Parse's business empire and Tasya Vos's profession. Parse is the CEO of Zoothroo, a major data-mining company that brazenly spies on private citizens by accessing their webcams, cataloguing their personal belongings without consent. This ties directly into the reality of surveillance capitalism—an economic system increasingly driven by the commodification of personal data for profit (Zuboff 2019, 30–45). Originally pioneered by advertising companies to refine targeted marketing strategies, this practice has since evolved into a far more insidious form of behavioural manipulation. The ethics of mass data collection remain highly contested, with critics arguing that surveillance capitalism threatens human liberty, autonomy, and well-being. The industry's primary objective appears to be the relentless expansion of data extraction, transforming ever greater aspects of social life into material for algorithmic processing—raising concerns about societal control and the erosion of privacy.

Vos's career of inhabiting others' lives serves as a potent metaphor for surveillance capitalism. Much like Colin Tate on the Zoothroo data-mining floor, scrutinising the intimate living spaces of unsuspecting individuals to catalogue their consumer habits, Vos watches her targets with forensic precision. She studies their mannerisms, speech patterns, and behaviours, slipping into their skin, embedding herself within their world—only to seize control and manoeuvre them like marionettes. In this scenario, the identity of Vos's host is no longer confined to their body; she steps in, overriding their agency entirely. The same applies to the mercantile peeping Toms at Zoothroo, casually invading private interiors without consent, amassing vast troves of seemingly banal data—yet beneath this surface mundanity lies a grave act of intrusion and structural violence.

Brandon Cronenberg's film highlights the perils of surveillance capitalism, which normalises the erosion of private life and makes impostors of us all. This is why Tasya Vos struggles to detach from Colin Tate—their perspectives are too alike. They are voyeurs, bound by the same scopophilic impulse, drawn to looking, observing, and slipping into other lives. It becomes all too easy for their consciousnesses to blur, to remain enmeshed. Scopophilia, the pleasure of looking, was analysed by Freud as an instinct integral to childhood development—the foundation of personality formation. He proposed that this impulse could be sublimated into aesthetics, manifesting in an appreciation of art, or, conversely, pathologised into obsessional neurosis. Other theories suggest that when one frequently retreats from reality into fantasy, scopophilia can lead to madness. This feels particularly apt in *Possessor*, where both Vos and Tate seem desperate to escape the burdens of their respective realities. The temptation to disappear into the worlds they intently observe, the lives they hijack, and the identities they fetishise is intoxicating—offering, however briefly, the chance to forget themselves in the act of looking.

At his lavish soirée, John Parse laments that his friends and associates are too flawless, rendering him utterly bored. He then quotes German philosopher and cultural critic Walter Benjamin: "Boredom is the dream bird that hatches the egg of experience" (Benjamin 1999, 105). He credits his capacity for boredom with leading him to a new business breakthrough. There's a telling parallel here—entrepreneurial ingenuity often lies in the ability to extract value from the seemingly mundane. To the untrained eye, the repetitive motions of daily life are unremarkable, but within this haze of routine, there is hidden potential—the opportunity to *really live*. The dream bird of boredom hatches experience, just as the vigilant watcher—Parse himself—fastidiously collects reams of humdrum data, transforming the banal into a tool of control. He seizes the autonomy of others, dictating their choices without their knowledge, never leaving a trace. John Parse is the ultimate social media influencer, his obscene wealth and power built on the systematic exploitation of life's monotonous moments. Surveillance capitalism is, in this sense, the perfect crime. The incremental theft of seemingly innocuous data generates little public outrage—after all, who among us is truly prepared to fight for the right to live an unexciting day in total privacy, to complete our boring chores without an algorithm's watchful eye?

Over time, the awareness of constant surveillance risks breeding ennui—the distinctly French brand of boredom, laced with existential doubt and world-weariness. Ennui is not mere restlessness; it is a state of lethargic disappointment, a confrontation with the fundamental emptiness of existence. Nothing matters, so nothing excites. Historically, ennui has been linked to the alienation of industrialisation and modern life—a byproduct of relentless mechanisation. How fitting, then, that the surveillance capitalist's own omnipotence, his tireless pursuit of control, should ultimately lead him to the very thing he dreads most: boredom. In the end, it all comes full circle.

* * * * * * * *

At this juncture, I want to explore ideas that bridge psychological horror and body horror, laying the theoretical groundwork for the next chapter. In Lacanian psychoanalysis, jouissance refers to an excessive pleasure that surpasses ordinary satisfaction—enjoyment taken to its extreme, where it spills over into suffering. It is disruptive, destabilising, and operates on what Lacan calls the painful principle—a paradox in which the pursuit of eroticism veers into self-destruction. Traditionally, jouissance has been structured around phallic enjoyment, bound by the Symbolic Order, governed by the logic of lack, castration, and male-dominated discourse.

In contrast, feminine jouissance exists beyond these constraints—boundless, unlocatable, enigmatic, and uncontained by language or law (Lacan 1977, 1–7). It is an oceanic pleasure that dissolves subjectivity rather than reinforcing Ego identity—closer to a mystical or numinous experience, as Lacan illustrates with Saint Teresa's ecstatic visions. Because it operates outside the phallocentric order, unruly female passion is often framed as excessive, dangerous, or unknowable. This leads to its repression, particularly within patriarchal structures that seek to regulate female erotic autonomy. Horror cinema, drawing attention to the excesses of the body and psyche, becomes an ideal space to stage cultural anxieties surrounding the rapturous intensity of feminine enjoyment—depicting it as both alluring and threatening, an unsymbolised force that defies containment.

Unlike phallic jouissance, which is structured by limitation—rising and falling, presence and absence—feminine jouissance exists as a surplus, eluding symbolic containment. This excess renders it both intoxicating and perilous, positioning female sexuality in a paradox: desired for its transgressive pleasure yet demonised for the same reason. Nowhere is this contradiction more evident than in the figure of the femme fatale—at once a figure of seductive power and a harbinger of castration anxiety, condemned for representing an eroticism that cannot be possessed or subdued.

The repression of women's disruptive ecstasy serves to uphold the phallocentric order, disavowing female erotic autonomy and consigning it to the realm of the unspeakable. In horror cinema, this manifests as ambivalence towards female pleasure—oscillating between fascination and fear, attraction and repulsion. The next films explored in this chapter—*Possession* (1981), *Paranormal Activity* (2007), and *Kiss of the Damned* (2012)—dramatise this tension, centring women whose erotic enjoyment and agency disrupt established structures. Their transcendental arousal refuses to conform to the limits of male desire, which is why it must be contained, expelled, or rendered monstrous. This dynamic reflects the psychoanalytic structure of hysteria, where bodily excess becomes a site of both rebellion and repression, exemplifying cultural anxieties about unbridled feminine power.

Possession (1981)

Andrzej Żuławski's psychological horror drama film *Possession* obliquely follows the breakdown of a marriage between an international spy, Mark, and his wife, Anna, whose behaviour grows increasingly disturbing after she asks for a divorce. Żuławski wrote the screenplay amid the collapse of his own marriage, stating, "I make films about what is torturing me, and a woman serves here as a medium. I only want to film excessive stories." This is a testament to cinema's invaluable role as a vessel for immoderate feelings—a space where artists can wrestle with problematic personal issues. Long may that continue, long may cinema be preserved as a special zone to clarify complex emotions. It saddens me that filmmakers today are expected to arrive fully resolved, with no quirks, no messiness. In that scenario, what is cinema even for? Why diminish its potential to provide solace in troubled times? The film medium, much like the psychoanalytic setting, compels us to return to the same ground, circling old wounds, obsessing over things that rationally *shouldn't* be difficult. Yet within the process of repetition, a deeper understanding emerges. Directors who continually revisit their preoccupations, fixations, and demons, ultimately produce a latent meaning in their body of work.

Possession has gained a cult following over the years, but upon release, it was widely misunderstood. The *New York Times* dismissed it as "a veritable carnival of nosebleeds," while *Variety* remarked, "*Possession* starts on a hysterical note, stays there, and surpasses it as the film progresses." Hysteria is often regarded as a loaded term—a pejorative shorthand for women's behaviour deemed outlandish or out of control. But in psychoanalysis, hysteria holds deeper significance: it designates a neurotic condition in which the body becomes the primary site of expression when language fails to communicate distress. The hysteric is incapable of articulating their suffering, so they *embody* it. When words prove inadequate, the turmoil manifests as a network of physical symptoms—spasms, convulsions, inexplicable maladies. *Possession* channels this dynamic with terrifying precision.

In Żuławski's film, Mark returns home to West Berlin from an espionage mission only to find that his wife Anna wants a divorce. She refuses to explain why but insists there is no third party involved. Reluctantly, Mark relinquishes their apartment and custody of their young son, Bob. *Possession* was filmed in Berlin at a time when borders were a pressing geopolitical reality; the city itself was fractured, communities divided. This setting resonates intimately with the rupture at the heart of Anna and Mark's marriage. Like Berlin, their relationship is riddled with grief, conflict, and painful splitting, its boundaries still in flux. We are thrust into the trenches of their marital war, forced onto the frontlines of their disturbingly unresolved fights. The intensity of their arguments—their physical brutality—mirrors the unbearable tension of a city defined by its own deep and violent divisions.

Mark begins to fixate on what Anna does while he's away on spy missions. Early on, she pointedly asks, "Were you unfaithful to me?" to which he vaguely replies, "The truth is… not really." Hardly a reassuring answer—one that suggests he grants himself leeway for indiscretions. Yet instead of reckoning with his own impulses, he projects his fear of infidelity onto Anna, turning the mere possibility of her desire into an abomination. The universal appeal of *Possession*, I suspect, lies in its unflinching depiction of troublesome romantic negotiations between men and women, which may never be settled, only observed and theorised. Mark's profession as an international spy is an apt metaphor for his relationship with Anna; he studies her surreptitiously, seeking clues, desperate to infiltrate the inner workings of her mind. She remains an enigma, her desire impenetrable. And yet, rather than engaging with her directly, he chooses subterfuge, attempting to uncover her secrets from the shadows.

In Barbara Creed's seminal book, *The Monstrous-Feminine* (1993), woman is conceptualised as horrific, particularly in relation to her reproductive functions. The archetypes of virgin and whore reduce female identity to sexuality, delineating the acceptable from the grotesque. In *Possession*, Anna is framed as some kind of fiend not just on account of her erotic capacity but also because she is perceived as an inattentive mother. The film lingers on the clutter of their Berlin apartment—unwashed dishes, scattered belongings, an atmosphere of neglect. Bob, once cared for, is now poorly fed and rarely bathed. This degradation reflects a warped view of Anna's sexuality overtaking her, demonically possessing her, obstructing her nurturing maternal instincts. Within the phallocentric order, this is how feminine jouissance is believed to function: excessive pleasure transforms the woman into a rapacious, self-serving ogre, prioritising her own desire at the expense of her sacred motherly duty.

In contrast to Anna is her doppelgänger, Helen—also played by Isabelle Adjani—distinguished by her green eyes and modest sartorial style. Helen, Bob's schoolteacher, is everything Anna is not: devoted, undemanding, eager to look after both Mark and his son. She is Mark's idealised fantasy of Anna stripped of unruly subjectivity, reduced to an accommodating, compliant figure. The true horror of *Possession* lies in Mark's preference for this hollow replica—a Sims-like character devoid of complexity—over his autonomous, emotionally complex wife. This brings to mind the case of Jeffrey Dahmer, who lured men into his apartment not with the immediate intention to kill, but to sedate them. Dahmer's grim experiment involved drilling holes into his victims' skulls to render them *technically* alive yet unresponsive—a warm body that wouldn't leave, argue, or require anything of him. Their subjectivity was erased, their agency stolen. The horror here is not just in the violence, but in the chilling desire for a barely sentient unresisting companion, an object rather than a person. In *Possession*, Mark's attraction to Helen echoes this impulse: an idealised automaton is preferable to a multifaceted human being with inconvenient desires.

Anna's infidelity surpasses even her eccentric paramour, Heinrich. Because you see, in the outer limits of female desire lies the *unspeakable*, imagined as totally abject and repulsive. She is not simply unfaithful—she is possessed, consumed by an evil force that takes hold of her body, mind, and soul. In Mark's fevered imagination, Anna writhes in obscene ecstasy with a Lovecraftian creature. He views her as a pervert not because she's a fetishist, but because she desires endlessly; *therein* lies the wickedness. Anna's monstrous lover literalises what Mark finds so appalling: excessive female eroticism. In his mind, her unbounded passion must be translated into something inhuman and foreign. He cannot comprehend her pleasure, so he forces her outside the realm of the imaginable—transforming her into a deviant, expelling her from the Symbolic Order. Anna is seen as fornicating with an alien figure, so she is alienated in the process.

The extreme physical violence in *Possession* is never gratuitous—it is commensurate with the sheer magnitude of emotional suffering. Wounds, bruises, and lacerations litter the film, externalising the psychic damage inflicted by Anna and Mark's irreconcilable differences. Nowhere is this more vividly staged than in the infamous meat grinder scene. As they hurl venomous insults at each other, Anna grinds raw meat, some of it spilling onto the floor—a chaotic, visceral image that mirrors their mutual destruction. They are grinding each other down, desecrating their humanity in the process. One might also read this as a moment of subversive symbolism: Anna, in a state of exasperation, feeds the phallic slab of meat through the grinder, chopping it up and spitting it out. A ritualistic obliteration of toxic masculine power.

The film's relentless outbursts align with the psychoanalytic concept of hysteria, historically a catch-all diagnosis for an array of physical symptoms—paralysis, loss of voice, seizures, vision abnormalities, deafness, convulsions, nausea, fainting, and uncontrollable emotional eruptions. When language breaks down, the body is forced to speak, manifesting distress through psychosomatic symptoms. In a letter to Josef Breuer, Sigmund Freud described a patient who was "at a loss to find words, and the difficulty gradually increased. With time, she became almost completely deprived of words and put them together laboriously out of four or five languages and then became almost unintelligible. Despite making great efforts to speak, she was unable to say a single syllable." It is as if language is placed under house arrest, locked inside the hysteric's body. In *Possession*, Anna's desire is banished—exiled from the realm of speech—and this suppression only amplifies its power, roaming and possessing various parts of her. Instead of a wandering womb, it is the exiled signifier that wanders, seeking expression.

The apartment where Anna hooks up with the octopus-like creature is far from a glamorous or alluring setting—it's filthy, depraved, and perverse. Her strange lover is the ultimate sex toy owing to its tentacles, like multiple phalluses sprouting at once, enabling a kind of three-way sex where every orifice is accounted for. In Mark's imagination, he stands no chance of competing with such overwhelming sexual prowess. His demonisation of Anna stems from the crushing weight of erotic redundancy and his perceived inability to satisfy her.

The scene of Anna's frenzied breakdown in the subway is iconic: she loses all control, thrashing wildly and smashing her grocery bag against the wall. This act becomes the ultimate symbol of the abject corruption of a homemaker, as she destroys essentials—milk, eggs—so closely tied to the archetype of motherhood. On the subway floor, Anna miscarries; fluids spill from her body's orifices, confounding the loss of life with female sexuality, implying an unholy alliance between death and female arousal (i.e., getting wet). This extraordinary scene stages the body of the Freudian hysteric as a warped theatre, where repressed desires are assigned roles to convey, through physical symptoms, what is otherwise *unspeakable*. If we look closely, the nature of these symptoms reveals the origin of the trauma. Anna is reacting to something that is no longer there—a void shaped by repression and stored in her body. Her outburst, though incomprehensible to those around her, is deeply real and valid to her. She feels everything intensely, accumulating sensations within her body and fashioning them into signs. What she cannot verbalise, she performs physically. Her eroticism, once a source of vitality, has been corrupted and replaced by destruction. In the phallocentric order, there is no space for feminine jouissance; her bone-chilling scream transmits the agony of that exclusion.

Paranormal Activity (2007)

Oren Peli's found-footage horror film *Paranormal Activity* follows Katie and Micah, a young couple unsettled by an apparent supernatural presence in their home. To uncover the source of the disturbances, Micah sets up cameras throughout the house, hoping to document any unusual activity.

At first, the incidents are minor—distant noises, flickering lights, doors moving ever so slightly. But soon, the phenomena escalate: loud thuds, abrupt door slams, and eerie, guttural screeches. Micah, sceptical yet fascinated, taunts the entity, daring it to reveal itself. His provocations only make matters worse. The spirit seems to feed off negativity, fixating its torment on Katie. A psychic warns them against attempting further communication with the malevolent presence, but Micah disregards the advice—if anything, he doubles down, antagonising the unknown force with reckless curiosity.

A defining conceptual feature of *Paranormal Activity* is scopophilia—the pleasure of looking, of spying on others without consequence. This drive is particularly potent in cinephiles. In *Visual Pleasure and Narrative Cinema* (1975), Laura Mulvey argued that women are objectified in mainstream film because heterosexual men control the camera. Classic Hollywood, she claimed, catered to models of male voyeurism, with the camera lens itself taking on phallic significance as a tool of surveillance. Here, the "male gaze" is a desiring gaze. In *Paranormal Activity*, Micah's fixation on recording events transfers his desire to the camera, which functions as an intrusive, all-seeing eye. He obsessively films Katie despite her repeated pleas to stop, reducing her to an object of study rather than a subject with agency. In my view, the film's real horror is not simply its supernatural haunting, but rather the male subject's fear of feminine erotic potential—driving him to strategically contain her under the guise of documentation, even though his efforts are in vain.

Micah's unconscious drive to suppress Katie manifests in an obsessive overinvestment in her body—her features become exaggerated, fetishised, endowed with excessive meaning. This process reduces her to manageable parts, neutralising her perceived threat as a castrating force. But something about Katie—her past, her desire, her very nature—refuses to stay confined. She lingers at the edges of containment, like a satellite drifting beyond the bounds of the phallocentric order. That is the true spectre haunting *Paranormal Activity*. Micah, fixated on control, relies on surveillance technology to unconsciously inspect and domesticate what he sees as the dangers of feminine jouissance. He wants to box Katie in, store her away, and clip her wings—sexually and otherwise. Lacan tells us that masculinity is structured around a jouissance that always fails, while femininity has access to an *Other* enjoyment, one that exceeds phallic limitations and resists articulation. It is this unknowable, otherworldly gratification that terrifies Micah the most.

Micah mediates his interactions with Katie through the lens of his camera, his framing choices often resembling the leering gaze of a voyeur. He films her feet, follows her into private spaces, requests a striptease on camera ("just bra and panties"), and even attempts to coerce her into recording their sexual encounters—an offer she firmly refuses. But these antics go beyond a mere masturbatory fantasy; a more insidious dynamic is at play. After sex with Katie, he smugly declares to the camera, "What we did was illegal in 13 states—this girl is wild." And therein lies Micah's central preoccupation: Katie's seemingly ceaseless erotic potential, a power he can neither fully grasp nor match. The impulse to record their intimacy is not just about capturing a moment—it's a desperate attempt to decode her, to render her sexuality legible and, in doing so, nullify its threat. This, more than any supernatural force, is the real haunting of *Paranormal Activity*. For Micah, the camera becomes a futile strategy of containment; if he can capture her within a camera shot, he can believe, however fleetingly, that, at least within the borders of that frame, he has her figured out. But, of course, he doesn't. It's a temporary salve for a more intractable anxiety.

For the "crime" of deriving unfathomable enjoyment, female sexuality is cast out of the Lacanian Symbolic Order—the realm of language, social structures, and cultural norms that shape identity and govern human relationships (Lacan 1977, 1–7). The Symbolic is the system of meaning through which individuals orient themselves in the world, arbitrated by the "Law of the Father," which imposes prohibitions, enforces boundaries, and regulates desire. Entry into the Symbolic marks the subject's separation from the mother and their initiation into the social order through language and codified structures. What lies beyond this realm is uncharted, unspeakable, and therefore a threat. This is tangentially illustrated in *Paranormal Activity*, in a scene where the professional psychic Dr. Fredrichs visits Katie and Micah and tells them:

> The demon is an entity that relates to something non-human. A lot of debate and discussion about what that could be, but it's not a person. I'm very uncomfortable with it, and I'll tell you, quite frankly, I sense there's something going on in this house. You cannot run from this, it'll follow you. It may lay dormant for years. Something may trigger it to become more active, and it will, over time, reach out to communicate with you.

Dr. Fredrichs warns that the demon is feeding off negative energy. A similar situation, he notes, happened to Katie and her younger sister Kristi in childhood. The psychic advises against engaging with the entity without a demonologist present, but Micah ignores this, persisting in his efforts to document and provoke it. The demon in *Paranormal Activity* is an elusive, nebulous force—emerging from nowhere, attaching itself to an unsuspecting host. Feminine jouissance functions in a strikingly similar way within the framework of phallocentrism: an unregulated pleasure that unsettles a discourse structured around male desire, which seeks to regulate and subjugate female enjoyment. By obstinately tracking Katie with his camera, Micah becomes the true source of disturbance. The camera's all-seeing (and ultimately powerless) eye is a stand-in for the demonic entity that plagues and pesters Katie. He is not merely documenting her; he is interrogating her past, her body, her very nature—desperate to access, isolate, and control something inherently beyond his grasp. My proposition is that what truly terrifies Micah is not the supernatural spectre, but rather Katie's interminable capacity for bliss, which threatens the limits of his own dominant yet fragile position.

The film's most iconic imagery features Katie and Micah lying in bed at night—Micah fast asleep while Katie, ostensibly entranced, rises and stands motionless beside him, staring for hours. She has no recollection of it the next day, but Micah's ever-present spy tapes capture the eerie spectacle. The topographical (spatial arrangement) of this scene speaks volumes: the male subject remains unconscious, oblivious, while the female figure looms over him, possessed of some knowledge he cannot access. Micah, the self-appointed observer, finds himself unwittingly observed. He is defenceless against his ensorcelled girlfriend's supplementary awareness that goes over his head. This reversal unsettles him—his gaze fails, and hers prevails. Katie's overwhelming sexual consciousness constitutes the true "demonic" force, the excess he cannot grasp. His camera may record it, but it remains beyond his reach because he is asleep at the wheel, sexually speaking.

Strategies of containment are nothing new. In the late 19th century, neurologist Jean-Martin Charcot sought to document hysteria by photographing and sketching female patients mid-convulsion, even staging public demonstrations of their symptoms at the Salpêtrière Hospital (Charcot 1887). His approach, though framed as clinical inquiry, mirrored a deeper impulse: the compulsive need to observe, classify, and confine the female subject within rigid parameters. Micah's modus operandi in *Paranormal Activity* follows the same logic. His overinvestment in surveillance—his relentless framing of Katie—serves as an attempt to categorise and contain her. But this is ultimately an act of self-reassurance, a desperate bid for control. What unsettles him is not what Katie does within his prescribed field of vision, but rather what she might be doing beyond it—outside the frame, outside his grasp. Keeping her fixed within his constructed space offers a fleeting sense of security. But, as the film makes clear, his efforts are futile. The more he seeks to pin her down, the more she eludes him.

Kiss of the Damned (2012)

Alexandra Cassavetes's *Kiss of the Damned* is a vampire horror film that follows Paolo, a screenwriter who becomes instantly enamoured with the beautiful and mysterious Djuna after a chance encounter at a video rental store in Connecticut. She, however, remains distant and elusive. Claiming to have a rare skin condition that prevents her from appearing in daylight, she attempts to evade Paolo's persistent advances—but he refuses to be deterred. Their physical attraction leads to a heated kiss through a barely open door, the safety chain still locked between them. In that moment, as Djuna bites his lip, her secret is revealed: she is a vampire who survives not on human blood, but by feeding on animals.

Initially, Paolo refuses to accept the veracity of Djuna's affliction—he cannot believe vampirism is real. To prove it, she asks him to chain her to the bed, allowing him to witness her transformation, which is triggered by sexual arousal. Bound at the wrists and ankles, Djuna reveals her secret self—a deadly vampire—but Paolo remains undaunted. He loves her, fangs and all. Just as he once pressed against the clasped safety chain of her door, aching to get closer, he now unlocks the chains that bind his dream woman, setting her free. They have sex. The scene unfolds in a long, uninterrupted take, as Djuna writhes in a trance-like state—not unlike Anna in *Possession*, with one crucial difference: Djuna is not alone, Paolo refuses to leave her side. It is one of the most sensual moments I've ever witnessed on film. Djuna is magnetic, like a romantic guttersnipe ascending to her rightful place as Bedroom Goddess, finally embodying the fullness of her sexual potential, long denied. In the heat of passion, they climax together; she ravishes Paolo and turns him into a vampire on the spot. She asks if he's scared, and he replies, "No. This is what had to happen. I would have done anything to be with you, however insane." They continue to exist in the halfway house for the international vampire community.

Djuna had long made peace with her solitude before encountering Paolo. She had resigned herself to the life of an outsider, a dangerous liability, retreating into isolation to protect innocent humans from her nature. But Paolo's arrival rekindles a desire she never expected. Crucially, it is at the peak of erotic arousal that her true self is revealed—her transformation is inextricably tied to sexual awakening. This is no incidental detail. Paolo realises that the woman he loves does not conform to the phallocentric order; she exists beyond its limits, untethered to conventional norms. Yet instead of recoiling, instead of scrutinising her or shielding himself from her awesome power, he embraces it. Fearless in the face of her metamorphosis, he sets her free—not to diminish her intensity, but to be consumed by it.

I see Djuna's vampire status as a red herring. Within the phallocentric order, her "excessive" sexual appetite is pathologised—framed as both transgression and sickness. She claims her skin condition forces her to avoid sunlight and exist solely in darkness, a fitting metaphor for feminine jouissance: banished beyond the realm of accepted discourse, consigned to the outer limits, unsymbolised and steeped in shame. Djuna tries to shield Paolo from her "condition," attempting to withhold her love—an excess that has been falsely rebranded as a deadly disease. But Paolo does not scare easily; he meets Djuna where her desire is. Unafraid of her sexuality, he is willing to be transformed by it even if it casts him out of "normal" existence. If female eroticism is structurally rejected from the dominant male framework, then the most radical act of love is to forsake one's privilege and follow the woman into the great beyond—to make love in the outskirts. Yes, Djuna and Paolo unite in an undead state, but only in relation to phallocentrism. They surrender to a love that subverts heteronormativity, escaping the gravitational pull of male-dominated desire.

It is illuminating to contrast Mark in *Possession* and Micah in *Paranormal Activity* with Paolo in *Kiss of the Damned*. In the former films, the male protagonists are deeply unsettled by the nature of female desire, their insecurity driving them to compulsively investigate their partners—Anna and Katie. Perhaps fearing expulsion from the established order, and fuelled by paranoia, these men opt to strategically contain their lovers, stalking them, trying to ensnare them in their defensive gaze, believing that amped up scrutiny is the key to cracking the code of female subjectivity. In doing so, they reduce Anna and Katie to objectified curiosities, projecting all manner of evil onto them, framing them as monstrous, possessed, or demonic. Male paranoia fractures these relationships further, widening an already broken bond. Paolo, however, is notably different. He does not seek to diminish Djuna's power or dissect her through a defensive gaze. He lets his guard down and allows the mystery of ecstatic feminine pleasure to overwhelm his Ego, sacrificing his privileged footing to access a level of intimacy he could never have imagined otherwise, allowing himself to be rearranged by it.

In *Kiss of the Damned*, Djuna's transformation is not merely a surrender to desire—it is an emancipation from the structures that have long kept her restrained. The unlocking of her chains is more than a physical act; it marks a rupture in the Symbolic Order that has demanded her containment. What was once forbidden now surges forth, no longer policed, no longer shamed. Her body, once a site of imposed limitation, becomes an instrument of radical expression, vibrating with an intense euphoria that cannot be domesticated or diluted. In this moment of release, Djuna ceases to be an exile from her own longing. It is fitting that *Kiss of the Damned*, the only film in this section directed by a woman, offers the most lucid articulation of this concept. Xan Cassavetes's gaze does not shrink from feminine excess, nor does it seek to regulate or punish it. Instead, it luxuriates in its rhythm and beauty. The film successfully depicts feminine jouissance and surrenders to its possibility.

Glossary of Psychoanalytic Terms

- **Feminine Jouissance**—A Lacanian concept describing a non-hierarchical, boundless form of pleasure that exceeds rational comprehension.
- **Hysteria**—Historically a diagnosis attributed to women, in psychoanalysis it refers to the conversion of repressed emotional distress into bodily symptoms, often expressed through exaggerated behaviours or uncontrollable physical reactions.
- **The Incest Taboo**—A fundamental prohibition in human society, often appearing in horror cinema as a representation of repressed or forbidden desires, returning as monstrous or uncanny manifestations.
- **Jouissance**—A Lacanian concept referring to an excessive, transgressive form of pleasure that surpasses simple satisfaction, often blending pain and enjoyment. Unlike conventional pleasure, jouissance defies containment and can manifest as an overwhelming, even self-destructive force that disrupts the symbolic order.
- **The Mirror Stage**—A developmental phase in Lacanian psychoanalysis in which an infant first recognises their reflection, forming an external self-image that provides a (false) sense of unity, shaping identity and alienation.
- **The Oedipus Complex**—Freud's theory that a child experiences unconscious sexual attraction towards the opposite-sex parent and rivalry with the same-sex parent, forming the foundation of their psychosexual development.
- **Ontological Insecurity**—R.D. Laing's concept describing a state of psychological instability in which an individual experiences a fragile sense of self, disconnected from reality and prone to paranoia, derealisation, or dissociation.
- **Paranoia and the Conspiratorial Mind**—A psychoanalytic perspective on paranoia as a defence mechanism against ontological insecurity, in which individuals create elaborate narratives to impose order on an overwhelming or chaotic world.

- **Phallic Jouissance**—A Lacanian concept referring to the pleasure derived from authority, dominance, and symbolic power.
- **Repression**—The unconscious exclusion of distressing thoughts, memories, or desires from conscious awareness, often resurfacing in disguised forms such as dreams, neurotic symptoms, or irrational fears.
- **Scopophilia**—A Freudian term referring to the pleasure derived from looking, particularly voyeuristic or objectifying gazes in cinema, where characters (and audiences) engage in acts of visual control over others.
- **The Subject Supposed to Know**—A Lacanian concept describing how a figure of authority (such as an analyst or a mysterious character in a film) is assumed to possess secret knowledge, which generates intrigue, transference, and emotional investment.
- **Surveillance Capitalism**—The modern practice of harvesting personal data for profit, metaphorically linked in horror cinema to themes of technological intrusion, identity loss, and the erosion of private life.
- **Symbolic Order**—A key Lacanian concept referring to the structured realm of language, law, and social rules that govern human identity and relationships. Entry into the Symbolic Order marks the individual's integration into society.

Body

2

Abjection, menstruation, mutilation, and the limits of the flesh

While psychological horror unsettles by destabilising the mind, body horror shifts focus to the grotesque malleability of the flesh, exposing the body as a site of transformation, violation, and existential terror. Defined by its fixation on corporeal volatility, this subgenre explores the disintegration of bodily integrity, depicting mutations, invasions, and distortions that provoke disgust, fear, and morbid fascination. Unlike supernatural horror, which externalises threats through ghosts or demonic entities, body horror situates terror within the flesh itself, forcing audiences to confront the unsettling reality that the body—assumed to be secure and self-contained—can betray its host. Rooted in fears of disease, infection, parasitism, medical experimentation, and biological corruption, body horror often depicts the physical dimension in a state of foul flux—melting, mutating, uncontrollably growing, or being consumed from within. Known for its extreme visceral imagery, this subgenre taps into anxieties surrounding bodily autonomy and selfhood, stretching, rupturing, and reshaping flesh in ways that dissolve the boundary between human and inhuman, self and other. At its most extreme, body horror dismantles the illusion of somatic wholeness, exposing the body's fragility and its latent capacity for monstrosity.

Carrie (1976)

Brian De Palma's supernatural freak-out *Carrie* is the perfect jumping-off point for exploring body horror within the chaotic life of a teenage girl. The titular character, unbearably shy and relentlessly bullied, is thrust into humiliation when she experiences her first period in the high school gym showers.

Unaware of what is happening to her, she panics, pleading for help—only to be met with cruelty. Her classmates jeer, pelting her with tampons and maxi pads, chanting *"Plug it up!"* This moment taps into the audience's unconscious anxieties surrounding female anatomy; menstrual blood, steeped in cultural stigma, represents a corporeal rupture, a site where meaning collapses. As Barbara Creed argues in *The Monstrous-Feminine*, horror frequently mobilises the abject aspects of the female body, with menstruation positioned as an unspeakable contamination that destabilises order (Creed 1993, 44). The body's raw, physical reality—so often sanitised and hidden—is exposed, and in the language of horror, coded as monstrous.

Carrie's suffering stems from her mother's belief that menstruation is a sinful marker of fallen womanhood, yet within the film's horror framework, it simultaneously signals the emergence of a terrifying new power. Society has long regarded the biological indicators of womanhood as shameful, casting blood as a contaminant, a symbol of disease, decay, even death. Later in the film, Carrie is subjected to an even greater humiliation—drenched in pig's blood as she is crowned Prom Queen. The prank echoes the nastiness of the gym shower scene, looping the narrative back to its primal wound. The cyclical structure of Carrie's suffering traps her in an existential deadlock, reinforcing the horror of a body that betrays and disrupts. This moment also underscores what others have identified as a narrative symmetry between the film's opening and climax, reinforcing the cyclical pattern of shame and punishment imposed on the female body (Profrol 2020).

Carrie endures relentless abuse at the hands of her fanatically religious mother, Margaret White. In their oppressive household, the development of Carrie's body is a point of contention, a source of shame and condemnation. She is made to feel sinful for blossoming into a woman—something entirely beyond her control, a natural rite of passage that should be met with sensitivity and guidance, not scorn. But to Margaret, growing out of childhood innocence is nothing short of diabolical. She tells Carrie that menstruation is God's "curse," that her breasts are "dirty pillows," reinforcing the idea that femininity itself is impure. Trapped in an atmosphere of repression and emotional austerity, Carrie's body becomes a battleground, her very being at odds with the rigid dictates of her mother's religious psychosis.

Yet, within this suffocating control, Carrie discovers an extraordinary ability: telekinesis. The capacity to move objects by sheer force of will becomes her gateway to autonomy, a psychic manifestation of her emerging power. In the film, telekinesis functions as a metaphor for embodiment and self-actualisation, a means of asserting control over an environment that has long subdued her. Margaret, who demonises every defining feature of womanhood, frames femininity as the devil's work—seduction and sexuality as wicked. Their relationship becomes a brutal clash between puritanical dogma and Carrie's untamed, extrasensory abilities. Ultimately, Carrie resists. The grip of maternal tyranny—rooted in superstition, shame, and rigid control—fails in the face of her radical emancipation. When Margaret accuses her of being a satanic witch, Carrie defiantly asserts, "It doesn't have anything to do with Satan, Mama. It's me. Me!" By embracing her power—by standing fully within herself—Carrie transforms from a victim into an unstoppable force, reshaping the world around her with terrifying, exhilarating finality.

On the surface, the infamous prom crowning scene appears triumphant—Carrie is bathed in applause, momentarily embraced by her peers and teachers. But beneath the stage, hidden from view, her tormentors are setting a cruel trap. This topographical split—the illusion of acceptance masking a violent undercurrent—mirrors the hypocrisy of society itself. Prom is supposed to be a fairytale ending, a social reward for conformity, yet for Carrie, it is a stage for her last devastating betrayal. She transforms from an awkward wallflower into a monstrous avenger in one fell swoop. The moment the pig's blood cascades over her, humiliation fractures into pure wrath. Hallucinating mass ridicule, she taps into her telekinetic power and unleashes it upon the students and faculty. Silent and motionless, she bends the entire space to her will—slamming the gymnasium doors shut, wielding a high-pressure water hose like a weapon, electrocuting the principal with a single, merciless glance. As flames consume the gymnasium, Carrie walks through the chaos with eerie serenity. The doors lock behind her. The inferno swallows everyone whole.

Brian De Palma's signature use of split screen amplifies the film's meditation on abjection. In *Powers of Horror* (1980), Julia Kristeva defines the abject as the "state of being cast off," a site of degradation that unsettles conventional identity. Subjective horror, she argues, emerges in moments where "corporeal reality" ruptures—the fragile boundary between self and other collapses, forcing an encounter with the intolerable. The abject is that which a society collectively rejects, expelling it to preserve its own order. De Palma's split screen formalises Carrie's condition as an outcast, visually reinforcing her alienation. Even as she orchestrates mass destruction, she remains distanced—dissociated, isolated, hovering just beyond her own bodily experience. Her separation is not only emotional but existential. Earlier, when Miss Collins asks how she's enjoying prom, Carrie responds:

"It's like being on Mars." The statement is quietly devastating. She has never belonged, never been fully integrated into the collective. She is—and always has been—utterly split off. This reading aligns with scholarly interpretations of Carrie's telekinesis as a manifestation of the female abject, in which her powers externalise the horror of her social and bodily marginalisation (Heim 2017):

> Telekinesis is itself a form of abjection. Through this power, a person has the ability to extend themselves into the world around them and manipulate objects at will [...] Telekinesis is the ultimate blurring of lines; Carrie's power is the ultimate form of the abject. It makes cultural sense, therefore, that women—those eerie, bleeding creatures—have broader access to it.

Kristeva also argues that abjection is enacted upon the part of ourselves that we must exclude—psychoanalytically, this is always the mother. To construct an independent identity, we must symbolically cast off the maternal, severing ourselves from the one who created us. *Carrie* is a turbocharged expression of this psychic rupture, culminating in a violent, irrevocable separation. The process is necessary, but that does not mean it isn't traumatic. Puberty, menstruation, and the body's transformation mark a threshold—a moment where a girl steps into womanhood, asserting her autonomy. Carrie's journey mirrors this shift, albeit through a supernatural register. "If I concentrate hard enough, *I can move things*," she says—a deceptively simple line that carries profound weight. It is a declaration of power, a recognition of her ability to shape her own reality. Through sheer will, she overthrows her mother's oppressive system, liberating herself from the suppressing forces that sought to keep her small. She is no longer an object to be controlled. She is the force that dictates her own terms.

Excision (2012)

One of the most striking examples of body horror is *Excision*, written and directed by Richard Bates Jr., starring AnnaLynne McCord and Traci Lords. The film follows Pauline, a socially maladjusted high school student trapped in a dysfunctional household. Her younger sister, Grace, suffers from cystic fibrosis and is the clear favourite of their overbearing, devoutly Christian mother, Phyllis. Pauline dreams of becoming a surgeon, but her fixation with blood and bodily violation goes beyond professional ambition. Her vivid, hyper-stylised fantasies of extreme mutilation and surgical carnage serve as an assertion of dominance, a means of controlling the body in a world where she otherwise feels powerless. Freud's concept of the castration complex is at play here; Pauline's obsessive preoccupation with opening, examining, and restructuring flesh speaks to a deeper psychological struggle with power and lack (Freud 1924, 177). Her surgical fantasies are not simply about mastery over the body—they expose an unconscious attempt to resolve her anxieties surrounding agency, control, and desire.

To say Pauline is socially awkward would be an understatement. She has no interest in conforming to conventional beauty standards or even maintaining basic hygiene—her hair is perpetually greasy and tangled, her skin is prone to breakouts, and her sense of style is non-existent. At school, she is firmly positioned on the social periphery, an outcast. Yet in her recurring dreams, she casts herself in an altogether different light: her hair and makeup are immaculate, she wears dazzling outfits, reigning supreme over her imagined world. Both in waking life and in her nocturnal fantasies, Pauline is drawn to the grotesque, obsessively engaging with the abject. She acts on her impulses with unwavering determination—piercing her own nose, carving the Red Cross symbol into her forearm, taking control of her body in ways that blur the boundary between autonomy and self-destruction. Her ambition is undeniable, fuelled by a relentless desire to bridge the gap between the mundanity of her real life and the exhilarating grandeur of her dreams. But Pauline's fatal flaw is her outlandish delusion: she believes she is destined for medical greatness, failing to recognise that her methods betray a disconnect from reality.

Grace's health is rapidly deteriorating—she needs a lung transplant. Driven by a delusional white knight syndrome, Pauline concocts a grotesque plan to "save" her sister, certain she can perform an impromptu transplant. With unwavering, deranged conviction, she proceeds without hesitation or remorse, chloroforming both Grace and their neighbour Kimberly in preparation for the "surgery." The final scene of *Excision* is among the most harrowing I have ever encountered in film. In the dimly lit garage, Pauline methodically carves into the unconscious bodies, eerily composed, bathed in blood. She transfers Kimberly's healthy lungs into her sister's open torso and places Grace's diseased ones on ice. Phyllis arrives home in a frantic state, stumbling on the horrifying tableau. With a manic glint in her eye and an air of serenity, Pauline presents her work with pride, inviting Phyllis to admire her stitch work, calling it "extraordinary." She is utterly deluded, envisioning herself as a heroic, Antigone-like figure, righteous in her confidence, wholly blind to the devastation she has wrought. Phyllis's response is one of pure, primal agony. She lets out a tormented scream before collapsing into her daughter's arms. Pauline, at first beaming with self-satisfaction, suddenly falters. The weight of her actions crashes over her. Her triumphant smile twists into a shriek of despair as she realises—too late—the full horror of what she has done.

The casting of Traci Lords is particularly fascinating given her history as one of the most infamous figures in the adult film industry. In *Excision*, she plays Phyllis, a God-fearing, rigidly controlling mother whose suffocating morality stands in stark contrast to Lords' previous star persona. The *baggage* of her former career inevitably lingers, creating an ambivalent tension that enriches the film. Without intending to speak of it disparagingly, the residual aura of her X-rated work spills into *Excision*, producing a compelling dissonance—a liminal space between Lords' past as a notorious sex symbol and Phyllis's bitter, stuck-up puritanism. It is as if Pauline exists between two versions of a mother: the prudish rules enforcer she knows, and an alternate spectre—the libertine, transgressive force that never materialises but haunts the film's subtext. Lords was once a sex goddess; Phyllis is a hateful, moralising killjoy, casually degrading her own daughter. This interplay between eroticism and miserabilism, liberation and repression, makes Lords' casting both layered and subversive, injecting *Excision* with an unspoken but undeniable charge.

PHYLLIS: "You saw her at dinner. She's disturbed. I want her out of this house."
BOB: "She's a teenager."
PHYLLIS: "Don't you dare take her side! I will divorce your ass so fast, you won't see it coming!"
BOB: "Come on, don't be—"
PHYLLIS: "Bob, she's a fucking menace! No wonder all of her friends have fallen by the wayside. You have to be fucking crazy to want to spend time with her. I have tried and tried! And it is impossible to love her."

The casting of John Waters in *Excision* is another stroke of genius. He plays Pastor William, a stiff, snooty religious leader and pillar of the community—a role that could not be further from Waters's own transgressive, irreverent persona. The result is an exquisite contradiction. Pastor William, on paper, is a paragon of conservative values, but Waters's very presence disrupts this reading. His extradiegetic aura seeps into the film, creating a kind of optical illusion: we are meant to take Pastor William seriously, yet we can't help but sense the larger-than-life provocateur lurking beneath. This surplus of energy unsettles the character, making him feel oddly enigmatic, vibrating with mixed signals. Pastor William's presence also underscores the family's misplaced priorities. Every available resource is poured into Grace's cystic fibrosis treatment, leaving nothing for Pauline, who is in desperate need of psychiatric intervention. Her symptoms—psychotic delusion, emotional dysregulation, and a tenuous grip on reality—cry out for professional help, yet she is left to spiral unchecked. In a film so fixated on bodily affliction, Pauline's psychological suffering is the wound no one bothers to treat.

Phyllis enlists Pastor William to play the role of makeshift psychologist, hoping he can provide Pauline with moral guidance free of charge. Unsurprisingly, their personalities clash. The irony, of course, is that Pauline's eccentricity is far more aligned with Waters's real-life sensibilities than his pious character. This inversion creates an uncanny fragmentation; the viewer can't fully trust Pastor William's authority because something about him feels externally imposed, the scene laced with a compellingly tongue-in-cheek quality. In her typically offbeat manner, Pauline asks the Pastor about the Church's stance on organ donation. He hesitates, explaining that it's a complicated issue since Christianity regards the body as a temple. Pauline, ever the provocateur, fires back: "What if I told you I found the resting place of Jesus Christ in my backyard and that with just a few advances in science and technology, I could resurrect him myself?" Pastor William stiffens, scandalised. "I'd say that you are a very troubled little girl." Despite the Pastor's pearl-clutching response, Pauline's question is, in essence, a thought experiment—provocative, certainly, but not totally without philosophical merit. Yet rather than engaging with her curiosity, he performs outrage, leaning into the weight of the faux pas—one that might have greatly amused Waters himself. Pauline's blasphemous remark also serves as a grim bit of foreshadowing. In the film's harrowing climax, Grace becomes the Christ figure of the family, the sacrificial body that Pauline, in her deluded grandeur, attempts to "resurrect" through her ghastly, self-styled surgical expertise. Prior to the astonishingly tragic dénouement, Pauline tells Pastor William:

> First off, this will be our last session. You are completely unqualified to be doing this. It's unethical. I have it on the highest authority that you're wrong. I refuse to allow you to indulge in my psycho-sexual fantasies. I would imagine a man as repressed as yourself would have his own issues to work out. I'm here to listen, not judge. Psychiatry is a science. At least in some circles anyway. If there's one thing I know, it's that science and religion don't mix.

To complete the triptych of ironically cast authority figures in *Excision*, Pauline's high school teacher, Mr. Cooper, is played by Malcolm McDowell—forever immortalised as the ultracool guttersnipe Alex in *A Clockwork Orange* (1971). Kubrick famously cast McDowell after seeing him in Lindsay Anderson's *If...* (1968), where he embodied a similarly rebellious spirit, playing a boarding school student who defies authority with smirking cheekiness. In both films, McDowell is an incendiary presence—wild, unpredictable, a force of nature who crashes through the frame with anarchic energy. But in *Excision*, Mr. Cooper is none of these things. He is a drab, rigid, thoroughly unimpressive stick-in-the-mud—the antithesis of Alex and Mick. Once again, the aura of an actor's earlier roles spills into *Excision*, complicating the viewer's perception. McDowell's history as a cinematic provocateur lingers, creating a quiet dissonance. Can we fully trust Mr. Cooper? Or does some part of us expect a flash of that former chaos? In the end, we slot him alongside Phyllis and Pastor William—a trifecta of prohibitive, unremarkable Superego figures, each working against Pauline rather than for her benefit. None offer guidance, reassurance, or support. Phyllis is a relentless nag, criticising at every turn. Pastor William provides no meaningful therapeutic insight, only moral posturing. And Mr. Cooper? He is outright condescending, sneering at Pauline's poor grasp of mathematics, delighting in putting her in her place. Together, they form an oppressive wall of disapproval—one that does nothing to prevent Pauline's downward spiral.

MR. COOPER: Congratulations! You've lost your bathroom privileges to the end of the semester.
PAULINE: Was I really gone that long?
MR. COOPER: Just take out your textbook, page 73. See if you can catch up with the rest of the class. And if you have any questions, you know where I am.
PAULINE: [groans]
MR. COOPER: What is it now, Pauline?
PAULINE: I feel sick, may I go to the clinic?
MR. COOPER: Tough it out. In another 10 minutes, you'll be somebody else's problem.

Incidentally, the casting of Ray Wise as Pauline's high school principal is also a deviously clever touch because he played Leland Palmer in David Lynch's game-changing television phenomenon *Twin Peaks*. The notion of Leland Palmer being responsible for teenage students is, for obvious reasons, monstrous and obscene because the character was the villain driving the central mystery of the show, having sexually abused his daughter Laura and driven her mad, leading to her devastating disappearance and death. Again, the actor's past performance bleeds into his current role, subtly inciting the viewer to recall the extradiagetic event, and in doing so creating a strange dynamic within the suspension of disbelief, comparable to post-traumatic stress disorder, dissociation, an existential crisis, or a fugue state.

At Pauline's high school—as in most educational institutions, it seems—the curriculum approaches human sexuality in exclusively alarmist terms. The classic framework persists, framing sex as a gateway to the worst possible outcomes: unwanted pregnancies, sexually transmitted diseases, and even death. There is no mention of the positive dimensions of eroticism—pleasure, intimacy, human connection, self-discovery, personal embodiment, or the propagation of life. Instead, the biology teacher fixates on the undesirable aspects, amplifying the fatal consequences of sexual activity. This forges a potent link between sex and death, a connection that profoundly shapes Pauline's mindset and actions. During the lesson, she asks whether it's possible to contract STDs from having sex with a dead body—a question that understandably unsettles both the teacher and her classmates. Later, she casually tests her own blood for STDs under a classroom microscope. Yet, Pauline might simply be taking the lessons to their logical conclusion: if sex equals death, then why not explore its most extreme implications? For her, the lesson negates the vitality of sex, reducing it to the lifelessness of necrophilia—the literal desire to copulate with a corpse.

The unhinged nature of Pauline's question is not to be overlooked, but my view is that she is intentionally presented as awkward and socially *mortifying*. Pauline reflects her environment, mirroring what has been imposed upon her. With STDs and death as the sole takeaways from her sex education class, she internalises this narrative and echoes it in an extremist way, discursively aligning herself on an unwavering trajectory towards death. The abject corpse is already eroticised in cultural discourse, so it follows that the act of dying—of returning to an inorganic state—might also be imbued with a libidinal quality. Pauline operates within the same logical framework as her teacher, but she vocalises the quiet part aloud, *gracelessly* blurting out the taboo. This, more than anything, is the real reason for her social exclusion. She lacks the finesse to play along without detection and fails to grasp the unspoken agreement to repress the elephant in the room.

Pauline approaches her own body and sexuality with a matter of fact, almost clinical, detachment. She decides to lose her virginity to her classmate Adam and chooses to do so while menstruating, driven by her preoccupation with blood. Far from low-key, Pauline actively pursues her desires—she is forward, direct, and unafraid of rejection. Intriguingly, this sequence of events is juxtaposed with an image of Pauline drawing a chalk outline of her sister on the pavement outside their house, as Grace playfully pretends to be dead. This act serves as another instance of foreshadowing, aligning with the tragic fate that awaits Grace later in the film, when Pauline kills her during the botched surgery. In this moment, as Pauline symbolically brushes against the boundaries of death, she casually informs Grace of her plan to lose her virginity. Once again, the film intertwines erotic energy with mortality, a theme echoed in Pauline's fantasies about period sex and her morbid fascination with fucking corpses.

When Pauline was very young, she nearly drowned in a public pool. Her father, Bob, rescued her from the water and performed mouth-to-mouth resuscitation. Unfortunately, he had a cold sore on his lip at the time, and the act of CPR transmitted the virus to Pauline. She later developed cold sores herself and took perverse delight in reminding her father about the "bug" he had given her. Bob, however, always emphasised that he had *saved* her life. While a cold sore is a symptom of oral herpes—a virus not necessarily sexually transmitted—the family teased Bob for having "given Pauline an STD" in his attempt to revive her. This alleged STD becomes inextricably linked to Pauline's existence as a living organism. Moreover, Bob's paternal instinct to save his daughter mirrors Pauline's own impulse towards her younger sister, Grace—a connection that underscores the film's recurring interplay between life, death, and responsibility.

Grace's lung disease is a relentless thief, draining her vitality and shadowing her youth with constant medical appointments, careful monitoring, and the grim reality of other CF patients dying around her. Pauline, in a fever of delusion, convinces herself that mastering complex surgery will allow her to perform a lung transplant and cure her sister. Her magical thinking operates on an industrial scale—an extreme overcompensation for the crushing helplessness she refuses to acknowledge. But beneath the grandiosity, another motive lurks: the desperate hunger for Phyllis's approval. Grace naturally embodies everything their mother cherishes—beauty, elegance, poise; she attends Cotillion, reads bridal magazines, radiates an effortless grace that Pauline could never hope to emulate. If Pauline can preserve her mother's golden child, if she can get into her mother's *good graces*, she might finally win the love that has always eluded her. The idea takes on near-religious proportions: to "gain grace," not just in the familial sense, but in its Christian meaning—the unearned favour of God, the salvation of the unworthy. In her deluded state, Pauline truly believes the surgery is an act of love, a selfless offering. She is, in her mind, not a monster, but a saviour.

PAULINE: "Come closer. I want to show you the detailed work I did on Grace's sutures. It's a mess, I know. It's just my first surgery. I haven't perfected my technique."
PHYLLIS: "What have you done?"
PAULINE: "What have I done? You mean, with the other one? I didn't know what to do with her body after I successfully retrieved the lung. So, I practised my incisions. You have to take a closer look, Mom. She is extraordinary."

Throughout *Excision*, a vast gulf separates Pauline and her mother, an emotional chasm that seems insurmountable. But in the film's gut-wrenching coda, Phyllis—rigid, punitive Phyllis—finally embraces her daughter. In that instant, she realises that no matter how monstrous Pauline's actions, no matter how sick she is for killing Grace and Kimberly, she is still *her* child. And Pauline, for all her derangement, experiences a rare moment of clarity. She collapses into her mother's arms, sobbing—not just in horror at what she has done, but in something deeper, more primal: the long-starved need for comfort and acceptance. The boundary that had always divided them is shattered. And yet, the tragedy is doubled—because just as they finally connect, the price has already been paid. Grace is gone. Phyllis had tried, just days earlier, to extend an olive branch to Pauline, putting into context her own Mommy issues:

PHYLLIS: "I've been reading this new book in my book club. It's caused me to do a lot of self-reflection. [...] Anyway, it's got me thinking that perhaps I could be a bit more patient."
PAULINE: "Sounds like you joined the right book club, a few years too late."
PHYLLIS: "Take it easy, Pauline. Some of your behaviour has been downright sociopathic [...] When I was your age, my mother hurt me more than words can say. I'm still trying to forgive her for that. I don't want us to have that relationship."

Pauline desires her mother's desire. She finds herself in a rivalry with her sister, wanting to embody the perceived "phallus" that satisfies the mother's lack. By attempting to identify with features exhibited by Grace that appear to please Phyllis, she enters a fraudulent dream world of images pervaded by discord and paranoia about the validity of her own place in the family. "Phyllis" is phonetically adjacent to the psychoanalytic notion of "phallus." Freud did not distinguish between the penis as a biological organ and the phallus as a signifier of sexual difference. In the phallic phase (ages 3–5), children recognise only one genital organ—the penis—and become preoccupied with its presence or absence. Freud argued that this realisation has profound psychic consequences, as children initially assume the mother possesses a penis. The discovery that she does not leads to the castration complex, disrupting the child's early assumptions about bodily completeness. For girls, this manifests as penis envy, a stage in which they experience anxiety upon recognising their anatomical difference.

Lacanian psychoanalysis shifts focus from biological reality to the symbolic function of the *phallus*, which operates not as a physical organ but as a signifier structuring desire and meaning. In the pre-Oedipal phase, the child perceives the phallus as the object of the mother's desire, which she lacks and yearns for. To remain central in her world, the child unconsciously attempts to *become* this lost object. However, the inevitable realisation that she is not the exclusive focus of the mother's desire leads to symbolic castration—the recognition of her own lack. Freud's concept of castration is thus not a literal loss but an initiation into the Symbolic Order, where desire is shaped by absence. Pauline, however, never fully undergoes this process. She clings to the fantasy that she can still *embody* the phallus and reclaim the role she believes Grace has usurped. Her alienation deepens as the gulf between her imagined and actual self becomes intolerable. Her fixation on *having* the phallus—the ultimate symbol of authority in Lacanian terms (Lacan 2006, 578)—manifests in her violent fantasies, where she assumes the role of both creator and destroyer. But this grasp for power is doomed to fail, for the phallus, as a concept, is always elusive, always beyond reach.

Pauline is a textbook delusional psychotic, utterly convinced of her own surgical genius despite lacking any qualifications—so much so that she transcends mere fantasy and plunges headfirst into grotesque, real-world experimentation. The climax of *Excision* is not just twisted; it is an operatic crescendo of imposter syndrome and grandiose delusion, culminating in a double homicide masquerading as a medical breakthrough. What makes this film so profoundly disturbing is the way it scratches at that recess of the mind, where the most shameful, insidious whispers reside: *"You don't know what you're doing. Everyone thinks you're a fraud. Who do you think you are? This is nonsense. You will be exposed."* This is where negative self-talk metastasises into existential terror, a voice that sabotages from within. *Excision* doesn't just prod at this wound—it sinks its scalpel into it, daring us to consider: What if I am Pauline? What if I spiral so far into my own delusions that I lose the ability to distinguish confidence from catastrophe? The film's power endures, refusing to fade with the credits, a horrifying reminder that the abyss of self-doubt, if left unchecked, can mutate into the unthinkable.

Martyrs (2008)

Pascal Laugier's *Martyrs* is a disturbing yet strangely hypnotic cult classic, centring on a secret philosophical society obsessed with unlocking the mysteries of the afterlife. Convinced that extreme suffering yields transcendental insight, they subject young women to torture, believing that agony will grant them a glimpse beyond death. Their leader, Mademoiselle, subscribes to a chilling binary: there are *victims*—those who succumb to suffering and spiral into madness—and *martyrs*—the rare few who endure their torment, sacrificing themselves in pursuit of a new consciousness. The society seeks nothing less than transfiguration: the survival of total deprivation, a shedding of earthly existence in favour of a higher and purer consciousness. And according to their twisted logic, women are particularly suited for this transfiguration. Go figure!

Martyrs unfolds in two distinct yet interwoven narratives, a structural choice that begs deeper examination. The first follows Lucy, a survivor of unimaginable abuse. As a child, she was held captive, starved, and beaten by Mademoiselle's organisation before managing to escape. Though she is placed in a care facility, the trauma has fractured her memory—she cannot fully recall what she endured or who her captors were. Lucy refuses to speak about her past, retreating into silence and detachment. Her body is marked by deep, inexplicable cuts, which she insists were inflicted by someone—or something—else. Haunted by visions of a monstrous figure, she remains ensnared in the horror she fled from, while the authorities search fruitlessly for those responsible. The second narrative shifts focus to Anna, Lucy's closest and most steadfast companion. She is never far from Lucy, tending to her wounds with the practiced care of someone who has done it countless times before. Anna's devotion to Lucy is more than friendship—it is an attempt to lead her towards healing, and ground her in a world outside of pain. In many ways, this becomes the emotional core of *Martyrs*, a film about suffering and the impossible question of whether it can ever be transcended.

We fast-forward 15 years, and the now-grown women arrive at the house of a seemingly normal family and proceed to brutally murder every single person there in cold blood. Lucy is still plagued by visions of a creature that seeks to harm her, and each apparent encounter leaves fresh wounds on her body. Anna is always standing by with her sewing kit, primed to patch up Lucy's knife lacerations. This dynamic is crucial: one character is troubled by unprocessed trauma, while the other diligently rushes in to apply pressure to the wounds time after time, a dimension that is loaded with meaning. Lucy is on a revenge mission seeking to eliminate the family she believes held her captive and hurt her. In this pursuit, she is slain, and Anna is captured as a new victim, but it's not a case of a new torture story beginning where an old revenge story ends, far from it. These energies are unconsciously bound together, representing distinct psychic forces that process harm, attempt repair, and seek to restore ontological security through the internal logic of pain and retribution.

Lucy embodies the raw, unhealed self, forever trapped in the past. The monstrous figure that torments her is not real but a projection of survivor's guilt, a manifestation of the suffering she cannot escape. We learn that Lucy was not the only victim in the torture camp—there was another girl, left behind when Lucy seized her one chance to flee. She had no choice but to run; staying meant certain death. Yet survival offers no relief—only relentless guilt. Lucy carries the unbearable weight of believing she abandoned the girl to further hardship, as though her escape condemned the other victim in her place. Haunted by flashbacks and visceral recollections of agony, Lucy is locked in a perpetual fight-or-flight state, unable to move forward. She has escaped physically, but psychologically, she never left—she still inhabits that place, still suffers its horrors. Only her revenge fantasy propels her forward, the singular drive to make her abusers pay. But vengeance is not resolution; it is merely an extension of captivity—a desperate attempt to rewrite the past in blood.

Anna, Lucy's faithful ally and closest confidante, never wavers in her devotion. She reassures Lucy at every turn, tending to her wounds, easing her distress, and even disposing of the bodies Lucy leaves in the wake of the rampage. She is Lucy's protector, prioritising her well-being with unwavering loyalty. Yet, when Anna discovers that the mother of the murdered family is still alive, she does not leave her to die—even though she is one of Lucy's abusers. This is not a betrayal; Anna's impulse to protect extends beyond vengeance. She is a guardian figure, preserving life indiscriminately, regardless of who is in danger. Where Lucy is trapped in a cycle of unhealed panic, debilitated by trauma and unable to break free from her revenge fantasy, Anna has risen above the need for retaliation. She maintains a bird's-eye view, always primed for harm reduction, always seeking a way out of the cycle.

We come to understand that there is no monstrous figure, and that Lucy is self-inflicting injuries—a visceral embodiment of her compulsion to internalise past horror. In this way, *Martyrs* presents a battle between two psychic forces: Lucy, locked in a PTSD-driven death drive, compelled to re-enact the same suffering in an endless traumatic loop, and Anna, who carries the life force, striving to break free from stagnation and repetition. Lucy is an automaton, trapped in a monotonous loop of destruction, while Anna reaches towards something beyond survival—towards healing.

The morning after the family succumbs to their wounds, and Lucy slits her own throat, Anna makes a surprising call to her estranged mother, seemingly to sort out an unnamed past grievance and restore their fractured relationship. This impulse is entirely in character for Anna—she is always inclined to suture old wounds, seeking resolution where others might accept rupture. We know she grew up in a childcare facility, suggesting that her parents were either unable or unwilling to care for her. When Anna's mother answers, she is incredulous to hear from her, immediately questioning the motive behind the call. This moment of attempted reconciliation is significant. It reinforces Anna's peace-making nature, her drive to move beyond suffering rather than remain trapped in cycles of shame and reprisal. Where Lucy is consumed by vengeance, Anna reaches for repair, trying to forge a future beyond trauma.

During the phone call scene, a radical plot twist occurs: Anna stumbles upon a hidden passageway leading to a subterranean horror. Beneath this unassuming family home lies a highly sophisticated torture facility, an upgraded version of the nightmarish site where Lucy had once been held. This is not just a basement—it is a factory of suffering, equipped with weapons-grade technology designed to inflict pain on an industrial scale. As Anna descends the steps, she is confronted with chilling images of so-called martyrs—women captured in their final, devastating moments, their bodies ravaged by catastrophic events: car crashes, terminal illness, unrelenting agony, disease. The illusion of domestic normalcy is shattered, revealing a carefully curated front for unimaginable sadism.

Here, in this pit of human degradation, Anna discovers the woman Lucy had spent years envisioning—the nameless prisoner who had remained trapped in darkness long after Lucy's escape. There is significance in Anna being the one to find her, to bear witness, and attempt a rescue. True to form, she reaches for her sewing kit, instinctively drawn to mend what has been broken—but the injuries are too extensive, the wounds beyond repair. Still, Anna offers what comfort she can, gently reassuring the woman, telling her not to be afraid, urging her to hold on. This is the nurturing side of the psyche—the force that protects, consoles, and seeks to heal even in the face of hopelessness. By bringing the captive woman out of the basement, Anna enacts Lucy's unresolved wish, offering a fleeting moment of relief to the part of the psyche that is otherwise trapped in panic, guilt, and unending fear of danger.

It isn't long before sinister, armed intruders arrive at the house, discovering the pile of corpses. Without hesitation, they execute the frazzled, wounded captive and seize Anna, dragging her down into the basement. From the shadows emerges a figure of quiet authority—Mademoiselle, the enigmatic leader of this operation. She delivers a measured, clinical explanation of their work: their mission is to induce a state of martyrdom in young women to uncover what lies beyond death. According to their findings, prolonged captivity in darkness and torment pushes the human mind through a sequence of states, each stage stripping away another layer of self. Over time, the subject's trauma manifests as hallucinations—visions of things that do not exist, a phenomenon Lucy herself experienced. The organisation does not experiment recklessly; they cultivate distress with precision, methodically, systematically, and without remorse. Their sadistic approach is motivated by a darkly unsettling impulse and a clinical obsession with pain as a gateway to the unknown. Mademoiselle explains:

> People no longer envisage suffering, young lady. That's how the world is. There is nothing but victims left. Martyrs are very rare. Martyrs are extraordinary beings; they survive pain, they survive total deprivation, they bear all the sins of the earth. They give themselves up, they transcend themselves. They are transfigured.

Mademoiselle says that transfiguration is revealed through the eyes of martyrs—a state of ecstasy her cult is determined to replicate. To become a martyr is to witness something beyond life, and their mission is to engineer these experiences, extract their secrets, and document them as proof of consciousness beyond death. As Anna listens, a grim realisation dawns on her: they intend to use her next. She is no longer just a captive—she is their new vessel, their next attempt at breaching the limits of suffering, at manufacturing the so-called state of martyrdom.

Mademoiselle's associates chain Anna to the wall inside the torture chamber. She is held down, force-fed, and beaten mercilessly—any attempt to resist is met with even greater brutality. The dehumanisation is total; the torment is unrelenting, structured, endless. Anna collapses, sobbing on the floor, but there is no comfort, no reprieve—only silence. The loneliness itself becomes a form of torture, hollowing her out from the inside. It is in this void that she begins to hear Lucy's voice, faint and insistent, whispering a command to let go. The relinquishing of the self lightens the burden of suffering, opening a path towards transcendence. To breach the limits of the body, one must first release the self-concept. Anna eventually stops fighting and surrenders.

Her captors tell her she must now pass through the final stage of the experiment—one from which there is no return. She is strapped into a mechanical device, where a ghastly procedure begins. Scissors slice through her flesh, peeling away her skin in layers, splicing her open until she is entirely flayed. Nothing remains to shield her—she is raw, exposed, stripped of all boundaries, utterly vulnerable. If Lucy's self-inflicted wounds hinted at a desire to breach the skin's barrier, then Anna's final ordeal is the ultimate annihilation of all fortifications. This is suffering at its purest, an attempt to reach the essence of being beneath every layer of protection.

After enduring a prolonged state of abject degradation, Anna finally reaches what Mademoiselle's cult refers to as the "final stage." She enters a euphoric, trance-like state, and Mademoiselle is summoned immediately—it is time to uncover what Anna has seen on the other side. Mademoiselle listens intently as Anna whispers an utterance only she can hear. The audience is left in the dark, but whatever Anna reveals leaves Mademoiselle visibly shaken. Word spreads quickly, and members of the society gather, hungry for revelation. They await their leader's statement, but she isolates herself in a private room, quietly removing her patchy makeup, bold eyelashes, and signature turban—stripping away layers, as though preparing for her own transition. An aide checks in, asking if Anna's message was clear. "Crystal clear," Mademoiselle confirms. She asks the aide if he can imagine what comes after death, and he says he cannot. At this moment, Mademoiselle issues her final command—"Keep doubting"—then calmly retrieves a handgun and shoots herself.

The film ends with the definition of martyr, a term derived from the Greek, meaning "witness." Anna embodies this role—the part of the psyche that observes suffering, endures it, and survives to tell the tale. She does not simply bear witness to harm; she is the guardian of the entire system, a force that continues to rise, no matter how much damage is inflicted. Through martyrdom, she perpetuates life. Perhaps this is what awaits us beyond death—not oblivion, but a consciousness that holds the weight of suffering while summoning the will to persist. Maybe this is what awaits us on the other side, an afterlife that holds a certain tension, an awareness of the agony, but nevertheless the summoning of vitality to fight on, preserving our essence through the struggle, not merely falling victim to terrible afflictions.

There has been endless speculation about why Mademoiselle took her own life. Did Anna reveal something that nullified the entire experiment, leaving Mademoiselle humiliated, unable to face her devoted followers? Or was Anna's vision so resplendent that Mademoiselle could not bear to wait another second before embracing death herself? That final instruction—"Keep doubting"—is tantalising, but what does it truly mean? A theoretical framework that helps me navigate the mystery of *Martyrs* is Jacques Lacan's notion of The Real.

Consider that our entire understanding of reality is structured through language. We navigate the world by assigning meaning, categorising everything into a Symbolic Order that allows us to make sense of our existence. But The Real is that which resists symbolisation—it exists beyond comprehension, outside the structures we impose on reality. The Real is impossible to integrate, grasp, or express. This very failure to articulate The Real renders it traumatic. A natural disaster is a fitting analogy: an earthquake, for instance, shatters the reassuring structure of home, rupturing the familiar and introducing a terrifying void where certainty once resided. The confrontation with The Real annihilates meaning, leaving us in a state of disorientation and existential freefall. Without language to process it, trauma reigns supreme. *Martyrs* takes the notion of suffering to its absolute extreme, reaching into a space that exists outside of language, beyond any symbolic framework. This is why Anna's final state resists explanation—she is suspended in an experience that cannot be articulated, only endured. In Lacanian terms, she enters the domain of the Real: a realm that defies meaning, where all structures collapse, leaving only raw, unmediated existence (Lacan 1977, 49). The film leaves us stranded in that very space, unable to decode what Anna "saw," because in the Real, there is nothing to interpret—only to feel.

I believe that what Anna bore witness to in the final stage of torture was akin to The Real. Mademoiselle's society had spent years meticulously constructing a Symbolic framework to contain and make sense of the unknown. But Anna's message was that over which their worldview stumbles, the non-removable residue of reality that could not be absorbed into their Symbolic Order, that which is lacking in their grounding beliefs. Mademoiselle sheds her mask (eyelashes, turban) before reaching for the gun, expunging her persona as cult leader before her brutal departure. In relation to the sublime power of The Real, any remaining flimsy symbolic embellishments quickly dissolve into nothingness.

Teeth (2007)

Mitchell Lichtenstein's black comedy horror film *Teeth* follows Dawn O'Keefe, a teenage spokesperson for an Evangelical abstinence group, who makes a vow of chastity and is shocked to discover that she is the owner of a mythical toothed vagina. Dawn belongs to a movement called The Promise set up to influence high school students to resist bodily urges and preserve virginity until marriage. In American Christian purity subculture, dating and masturbation are discouraged; women and girls are told to dress modestly to avoid arousing male sexual interest. The obsession with innocence is propelled by the denial of female desire. Members of the Promise club wear a red ring to symbolise their iron-clad purity pledge, outlined by Dawn in a rousing speech delivered early in the film:

> We have a gift, a very precious gift. What do you do with gifts? Do you go around giving them to everyone you pass on the street? No! No, those wouldn't be gifts, they'd be a handout. So, what about the most precious gift of all? Are you gonna give that to the first guy who buys you a big bunch of roses? No way! I'm not just talking to the girls. You guys, you have the same gift to give. Are you gonna give that to some girl 'cause she looks like she just stepped out of a music video? No! No, you're gonna hold onto it and share it with the mother of your children. That's what the ring is all about. The way it wraps around your finger, that's to remind you to keep your gift wrapped. Wrapped until the day you trade it in for that other ring, that gold ring. Get it?

Abstinence is framed as a noble moral ideal, but it functions as a tool of suppression, designed to block sexual self-knowledge. At this stage of the story, Dawn advocates the ideology of abstinence because she derives from it a sense of belonging and community. She proudly wears her red purity ring—a symbol that, ironically, echoes the very thing it seeks to control. She is eager to safeguard her virginity, having been persuaded to view sexuality as a gift to be given away, a finite resource with a diminishing value. The notion that experiencing sexuality results in having *less* of it easily slips into a horror zone. Abstinence movements deliberately hide the truth: that sexuality is a *generative* process where active engagement not only fosters but indeed flourishes the supply. The deeper and more comprehensive one's understanding of sex, the greater the possibility for enjoyment and subjective enhancement.

Dawn's family home is located near a nuclear power plant where poisonous chemical clouds spill into the air, seemingly causing fatal disease and horrifying mutations. For years, Dawn and her stepbrother Brad have been rivals. A typical early childhood game of *"I'll show you mine if you show me yours"* resulted in the tip of Brad's finger getting sliced. Apparently, Dawn's vagina bit off his finger: a repressed traumatic event that persists as a sexual neurosis in early adulthood. Brad is illicitly compelled by Dawn, but also terrified of her, affirming her ambivalent femme fatale status in the narrative.

Dawn lives at home with her parents. Her mother is sick with an unnamed disease; the symptoms point to cancer, presumably caused by the nuclear power plant operating in their town. A subtle but devastating metaphor spins in the film: a giant looming force pumps toxins in the air, contaminating the environment and causing sickness in the locals. Religious trauma in *Teeth* performs a similar function, rotting the mindset of followers by shaming erotic disposition and desire. Ironically, Dawn's mutant vagina dentata enables her to fight back against fundamentalist indoctrination. Despite attempts to brainwash her into sexual ignorance, her instincts kick in and fight back, *armed to the teeth!*

Dawn meets Tobey, a fellow ring-toting member of the voluntary celibate brigade; she is reassured that he appears to believe in the sanctity of post-nuptials sex. They share a mutual infatuation, and Dawn permits herself a nocturnal intimate fantasy about Tobey on their wedding night. Her wholesomely decorated girlish bedroom contrasts to the savage atmosphere of her stepbrother Brad's man cave, complete with wall-to-wall porn, blaring rock music, and a thick cloud of pot smoke. Brad and Dawn are photographic negatives of each other. She initially seems like a prim and demure girl, while he is brash, loud, rude, and tattooed. His style of speech is perverse, he enjoys startling Dawn and covertly flirting with her, always aiming to scandalise her. Brad might seem sexually experienced compared to Dawn, but in truth, he is more stunted—a heterosexual man so afraid of vaginal intercourse that he avoids it entirely, haunted by his childhood trauma. He believes, on a primordial level, that the vulva is menacing so he exclusively has anal sex with his girlfriend; his avoidant behaviour indicates a limited and immature sexuality. At one point Brad is shown aggressively brandishing a video game gun, desperately clinging to a phallic symbol to cover up a shameful phobic impotence.

Throughout *Teeth*, the education teenagers receive about sexuality seems to hint at womanhood being in the domain of taboo, requiring secrecy precisely because female sexual agency contains a clear and present threat to the dominance of the phallocentric order. *Teeth* is one of the best cinematic examples I've seen of castration anxiety, the unconscious fear of sexual intercourse with a woman resulting in physical injury for the male. In psychoanalytic theory, castration does not necessarily denote severing of the penis, it is a broader reference to a valued object being removed, or a life force being depleted where it had existed before.

A crucial scene in *Teeth* occurs at Dawn's high school, in which a teacher runs through a module on sex education, aided by graphics inside a textbook. One page contains a vivid illustration of the human male reproductive system, comprehensively labelled and explained; the students are allowed to fully see and learn about the penis. However, the image of female genitalia is covered up in the textbook by a massive shiny gold sticker; students are literally blocked from looking at a woman's anatomy, even for educational purposes, and when they try to remove the sticker to uncover the image it tears off the whole page so they're none the wiser. There appears to be a double standard: why is the penis shown in detail, but the vulva hidden? What's behind the big gold sticker? Dawn offers an explanation to the group, claiming that "girls have a natural modesty, *it's built into our nature*," a statement met with mockery and ridicule in the classroom. Dawn has been taught to accept herself as a taboo—to see her body as unknowable. But this illusion is unsustainable. The moment she peels back the sticker, the whole system collapses.

Dawn and her friends visit a local lake with a cave known to be a popular sex spot. The vaginal associations are front and centre: the cave's glistening entrance under a waterfall has moisture dripping from the top of it. This strong vaginal symbol builds a tension in the fabric of the film, pulling in a different aesthetic direction, away from phallic dominance. Dawn discovers that her sweet crush Tobey is not technically a virgin, rather more of the "born again" variety; pure in Christ's eyes, so to speak. Tobey's sheepish account of having had sex before is comically played off as a grave crime or unforgivable sin. Dawn is unsettled to know that her guy succumbed to his desires once before; he's suddenly tainted with an element of danger, having already tasted the forbidden fruit.

Later in her bed, while fantasising about Tobey in groom attire at their nuptial's ceremony, Dawn senses physical arousal building up in her body. She reaches to touch herself while imagining Tobey gently lifting her wedding gown and reaching between her legs. She situates the sexual scenario strictly within the bounds of a honeymoon; this is necessary for her to even entertain the thought of masturbation. In the Church she belongs to, any form of pleasure has to be in the context of marriage, otherwise it is forbidden. But, while she touches herself, an intrusive thought comes crashing down, her vision flooded with the image of a hideous B movie monster. She is jolted out of erotic action, her arousal interrupted and halted abruptly.

While studying Greek mythology Dawn comes across an image of Medusa with snakes sprouting out of her head: a perennially tortured creature, feared as a freakishly phallic and cursed woman. The motif of a dynamic force sharply emerging out of a woman's body becomes relevant in *Teeth*, challenging the common assumption that the female body is exclusively a receptive and nurturing environment. The phallic serpent theme is a feature of Brad's bedroom design, too, with a cobra poster prominently displayed on his wall.

Conflicted, Dawn invites Tobey to meet her at the secluded lake. They swim together, he kisses her, and when things get passionate, she reminds him of their purity vow and to slow down. Dawn swims off towards the cave, the infamous spot where couples have sex, with a waterfall dripping around it, but tells Tobey to stay away. He climbs over inside despite her wishes, breaching the opening—a clear boundary violation, entering a feminine space that he hasn't been given consent to be in. They kiss, but Dawn doesn't want things to go any further; Tobey aggressively climbs on top of her. She unambiguously and repeatedly says "no" to intercourse and begs him to stop, but he covers her mouth and forces himself on her. What ensues is bizarre, absurd, and quasi-comical: we hear a crack, Tobey pulls away from Dawn, he's bleeding from his crotch… sure enough, her vagina has bitten off his penis! Horrified, he screams and cries, they are both in utter shock! Blood spills everywhere and his chopped-off penis is on the ground of the cave. Due to some unknown evolutionary adaptation or possibly chemical mutation, Dawn's vagina is toothed! A castrated Tobey dives into the water, never to be seen again.

The next day, still rattled by the incident, Dawn attends another Promise event but she is no longer able to perform her duties as a purity advocate and role model. She had previously been perceived as a star speaker in the abstinence movement, but now she's choking, stumbling on her words, looking crestfallen. Dawn is prompted to exit the stage by the organiser who makes a reference to Eve's exile from the Garden of Eden, confirming Dawn's excommunication from the movement. She returns to the lake, removes the red purity ring from her finger as a bold symbol of emancipation, and chucks it over the edge of a cliff.

In one of the finest examples of a cinematic match cut, the red ring falling is sharply followed by the biology textbook page torn out and placed inside a sink full of water. Whereas Dawn's classmates had unsuccessfully tried to rip the gold sticker off the dry page, Dawn uses moisture as a technique to gently slip off the sticker covering the vulva diagram without tearing or damaging the page, poetically establishing the essence of female arousal (wetness) as the key to unlock the secrets of a woman's sexual power. The barrier is gracefully lifted by the feminine sexual function, revealing the hidden wisdom once and for all, like a sacred treasure box finally opened. Dawn can now see herself reflected in the illustration, all the features at long last visible and properly labelled. The match cut between the discarding of the ring and the understanding of her body is absolutely crucial. A purity vow blocked Dawn from self-knowledge. When that obstacle is removed, she has the freedom to observe herself and gain radical bodily autonomy, ushering in a new "dawn" in her evolution.

Women gaining awareness about their bodies ought to be universally accepted and celebrated, but within the phallocentric order such knowledge is viewed with suspicion and hostility, giving rise to debasing vagina dentata myths, which have persisted for centuries across cultures, and are referenced in Lichtenstein's film. *Teeth* plays with the noir trope of the villainous femme fatale who reduces the man from hero to zero:

> The toothed vagina appears in the mythology of many diverse cultures all over the world. In these myths, the story is always the same. The hero must do battle with the woman, the toothed creature, and break her power. The myth springs from a primitive masculine dread of the mysteries of women and sexual union. Fears of weakness, impotence. It is a nightmare image of the power and horror of female sexuality. The myth imagines sexual intercourse as an epic journey that every man must make back to the womb, the dark crucible that hatched him.

Freud posited that woman terrifies because she appears to be castrated. But according to the feminist film theorist Barbara Creed, a man's fear of castration leads him to imagine the mother or female lover as an emasculating agency. In horror films, we tend to think of monsters as male and women as victims, but Creed challenges this view and argues instead that the prototype of the monstrous is the abject female body. However, maybe the vagina as a "mouth of hell" does not necessarily need to result from patriarchal hegemony—perhaps the "dangerous cave" slur is a nihilistic indictment of life itself, designating the woman's reproductive organ as a cursed entrance on the grounds that it brings forth suffering and pain across the board, irrespective of gender or any other characteristic.

Another way to approach *Teeth* is via a critique of spiritual doctrine, specifically based on Freud's 1927 text *The Future of an Illusion*, which outlines his interpretation of religion's origins, development, and prospects. Freud regarded pious faith as a false belief system and argued that its concepts are an outshoot of the Oedipus complex representing human helplessness in the world. Freud saw the Abrahamic God as a projection of a childlike longing for a father figure, where natural impulses—rebranded as sins—invoke fear of punishment rather than curiosity about our own hidden nature. Freud concludes that religious beliefs are illusions with no basis in reality, driven by wish fulfilment—the longing for a heavenly father, the extension of earthly existence into an afterlife, and the promise of an immortal soul.

Society perceives the human subject as inherently dangerous, driven by instinctual urges that must be repressed for civilisation to function. Freud viewed human nature as rebellious, governed by overwhelming sexual and destructive tendencies—forces that threaten social stability when left unchecked. Lichtenstein's *Teeth* critiques the assumption that female sexuality is an inherently chaotic force, one that threatens the delicate balance of society. The film exposes the long-standing belief that feminine subjectivity is incompatible with Enlightenment ideals of reason, temperance, and criminal justice—suggesting that Western bourgeois family values would collapse without the regulating forces of organised religion and the state. Dawn O'Keefe's journey towards sexual autonomy is marked by a decisive act: discarding her purity ring, watching it disappear over the edge of a cliff. In this moment, she severs ties with the oppressive doctrine of abstinence and begins the process of owning her sexuality. The cutting power of her teeth carries a dual significance—on one level, it curtails the internalised fear of her body's erotic potential; on another, it manifests as a violent, proportional response against a society that seeks to subjugate and control 'unruly' female desire.

Dawn hastily pedals to the gynaecologist's office. Along the roadside, billboards flaunt hypersexualised images of women—lingerie-clad crotches emblazoned with the word "perfect." The normalisation of female objectification is glaring, reducing women to commodities in the service of commercial profit. Yet, in the realm of actual intimacy and self-exploration, a veil of ignorance persists—a contradiction the film pointedly calls out. Inside the gynaecologist's office, Dawn is visibly nervous. The pristine space exudes sterility, its clinical atmosphere reinforcing the tension between medical authority and physical autonomy. On the walls, delicate floral paintings reminiscent of Georgia O'Keeffe—the American modernist whose close-ups of blossoms evoke unmistakable vaginal imagery—subtly hint at the film's deeper preoccupations. *Teeth* makes this reference explicit: Dawn's surname is O'Keefe, a deliberate nod to the artist, further linking the protagonist's journey to the symbolic potency of female sexual expression. The film's director, Mitchell Lichtenstein, son of pop art icon Roy Lichtenstein, is no stranger to layered artistic references—his background infuses the film with an awareness of how art, sexuality, and cultural representation intersect.

The gynaecologist patronisingly instructs Dawn to lay back, put her feet in the stirrups, and scoot down on the table. She claims she just wants to be checked out, to ensure there are "no adaptations down there," to which the doctor replies that what she's probably adapting to is womanhood. That's an important line; the transition to sexual maturity can be painful, which is not helped by a society that renders female sexuality a taboo and hush-hush. Most women sleepwalk into that crossover, remaining oblivious because they're actively discouraged from gaining insight about their own bodies. Accumulation of female sexual knowledge is seen as dangerous, nefarious, and threatening to the phallocentric order. This thought crime becomes the "tooth" inside the vagina; knowledge—not the vagina itself—is weaponised and perceived as devouring/all-consuming.

The doctor slicks his entire hand with lubricant and plunges it into Dawn's vagina in one swift, invasive motion, prompting an immediate and visceral reaction. In an instant, her body retaliates—her vagina clamps down with unrelenting force, razor-sharp edges locking onto his hand. Panic sets in. He tries to pull away, but he's stuck—trapped in the very anatomical anomaly he likely never believed existed. His screams of pain escalate into a hysterical, slapstick struggle as the two writhe chaotically on the examination table. Jess Weixler's gift for physical comedy elevates the scene, her performance balancing horror and absurdity with remarkable precision. The ordeal reaches its gruesome punchline when the doctor finally breaks free—minus four fingers. Staring at his severed digits in shock, he bellows, "Vagina dentata!" as Dawn bolts from the room, screaming.

Dawn returns home to a grim scene—her ailing mother, Kim, lies unconscious on the floor. Rushed to the hospital, Kim passes away shortly after, her final cries for help having gone ignored. When Dawn learns that Brad deliberately disregarded her mother's suffering, something in her shifts. No longer timid or restrained, she steps into her power and seeks revenge. Transforming herself into the seductress he always wanted her to be, Dawn applies makeup and confidently walks into Brad's room, luring him into bed. As their encounter advances, Brad suddenly remembers—a childhood incident, a bite, and the chilling realisation that it wasn't her mouth that bit him. Too late. In the next instant, Dawn's vagina clamps down, severing his penis in an act of retribution. He staggers back in horror, and as Dawn rises, his mutilated member falls unceremoniously to the floor between her legs. Horrified, Brad commands his dog to attack—but the animal has other instincts. It devours the severed penis, crunching through flesh and cartilage before spitting out the pierced tip. Any hope of surgical reattachment is lost. Brad is irreversibly castrated.

The TV in Brad's room plays a movie featuring Medusa; the spectre of the phallic woman haunts him until the bitter end. In this pitiful state, Brad is not merely Dawn's pervy stepbrother, he is the fevered Ego of phallocentric illegitimacy, feigning sexual supremacy but cowering in the face of feminine power. Brad's aggressive Rottweiler "Mother" is trained to attack people—its name representing his projection of some maternal resentment. In vagina dentata myths, the hero is driven to return to the dark crucible that hatched him—the womb, the site of his origins—compelled to conquer his fear and emerge triumphant. But Brad is no hero—he is the villain in a myth he barely understands. His illusion of dominance is shattered, and his own dog, Mother, quite literally chews up his manhood and spits it out.

Dawn is feared as a monster—not because of a literal toothed vagina, but because she discovers herself. Her true threat lies in her journey towards sexual self-awareness, a revelation that terrifies misogynists. *Teeth* frames this as an odyssey beyond abstinence, beyond the confines of Evangelical dogma and chastity vows. Dawn moves from stagnant repression to dynamic embodiment, breaking free from the forces that sought to control her. She is not merely a killing machine—she learns that when she is relaxed and aroused, her "teeth" do not engage, allowing her to experience pleasure on her own terms. This, ultimately, is what makes her dangerous. Not her anatomy but her autonomy. Vagina dentata functions as a metaphor for devouring female wisdom, perceived as a force that dooms male sexuality into oblivion. In this context, knowledge becomes a set of teeth, feared as a consuming drive capable of annihilating manhood. Yet this fear is a serious misreading of female eroticism, reducing it to a vile aberration rather than recognising its full complexity. Dawn is cast out, not because she is unnatural, but because she refuses to conform.

The Human Centipede Trilogy (2010–2015)

I've watched hundreds of horror films since childhood and consider myself largely desensitised to the genre, yet for a long time, Tom Six's *Human Centipede* movies disturbed me the most. Despite this—or, more likely, because of it—I have a real fondness for Six and eagerly await his next project, *The Onania Club*. He has been derided by the self-appointed "leading lights" of film criticism, dismissed as a trollish edgelord, which only endears him to me further. Cinema needs its trickster provocateurs, the mischief-makers who cause a stir and push boundaries. Maybe I'm alone in this, but I'd rather hear what the benevolently trashy artists have to say than endure another moralistic sermon from the so-called "Great and the Good."

The Human Centipede (First Sequence) (2010) follows a deranged German surgeon who kidnaps three tourists and surgically conjoins them, mouth to anus, forming the eponymous "human centipede." Tom Six devised the idea as a dark joke about punishing child molesters by stitching their mouths to a truck driver's anus. His inspiration also stemmed from Nazi medical experiments, particularly the atrocities committed by Josef Mengele at Auschwitz. Aware of its off-putting premise, Six concealed the full details from potential investors, who only discovered the film's true nature upon its completion.

Though the concept is grotesque, its execution in the first instalment maintains a surprising level of restraint. Six frames the horror as medical research, keeping gore to a minimum and fostering a clinical, detached atmosphere. Dieter Laser's portrayal of Dr. Heiter—a sadistic, authoritarian figure—deliberately evokes fascistic undertones, mirroring the twisted ideological obsession with carrying out tests on innocent bodies. The film's horror derives less from explicit violence than from its cold, aloof aesthetic. The intellectual remoteness of the torture is allowed to exist in a state of moral detachment through the liminal space of a laboratory. Dr. Heiter's dark act of dehumanisation is shrouded in scientific rationalisation. The first sequence, in this sense, remains suspended in abstraction—its horrors are implied rather than fully revealed. It is in the film's sequel that theory gives way to execution, and where the clinical sterility is abandoned in favour of raw, chaotic brutality.

In *The Human Centipede 2 (Full Sequence)* (2011), Laurence R. Harvey delivers an unforgettable performance as Martin Lomax, a psychiatrically and intellectually impaired Englishman whose fixation on the *First Sequence* leads him to create his own centipede—this time with 12 victims, a drastic escalation from Dr. Heiter's tripartite structure. While Dr. Heiter's motivations remain coldly clinical, his inner life largely obscured, Martin is a raw nerve, a walking wound. He exists in squalor, his loathsome project unfolding as a direct extension of childhood abuse and a highly dysfunctional home life. Whereas Heiter maintains an air of calculated detachment, Martin is a gruesome spectacle of unprocessed trauma, his pain laid bare in every action.

The film opens with Martin watching *The Human Centipede (First Sequence)* on his laptop while working the night shift at a London parking garage, immediately forging a metatextual link between fiction and reality. This connection reinforces the film's position as a transgressive sequel—picking up where the first film left off but shifting its horror from theoretical detachment to something impulsive and messy. *Full Sequence* was widely censored, outright banned in some countries, and met with critical condemnation. Yet, I would argue that its most transgressive quality is its grim fascination with the psychosexual dynamics of oral and anal stages of development. The film forces the viewer into an extreme confrontation with these twin drives, doubling down to ensure we are well and truly lodged at the intersection of eating and excreting. The backlash against *Full Sequence* was, in many ways, a moral panic over the idea of being stuck in this zone, an affront not just to decency, but to the very notion of psychological maturity.

Tom Six conceived the sequel as a metafilm after reporters repeatedly asked whether he feared inspiring copycat crimes. Of course, countless studies debunk the notion that films or video games, however extreme, have the power to compel otherwise non-violent people to commit atrocities—criminals don't need cinematic permission slips. Amusingly, Six leans into this moral hysteria, crafting Martin's descent into depravity as a direct result of watching *The Human Centipede (First Sequence)*. In doing so, he gleefully overindulges in the scientifically unsupported idea that movies incite real-world violence, satirising the absurd belief that the darkest human impulses are simply learned from visual media.

So, a mad scientist's experiment is crudely replicated by an obsessed fan. Martin, holed up in a dingy warehouse, sets out to quadruple the length of the "centipede." But unlike Dr. Heiter, he is no surgeon, has no lab, no proper medical instruments—only a staple gun, a hammer, and duct tape, which he uses to haphazardly bind lips to buttocks. Without anaesthesia or precision, he cobbles his victims together like a demented handyman. To complete his ghastly vision, he injects them with a syringe full of laxative, forcing an explosive chain reaction of bodily functions. Martin, caught between ecstasy and revulsion, erupts into fits of jubilant laughter before vomiting in sheer disgust.

Tonally, the sequel is a stark departure from its predecessor. Gone are theoretical implications and lofty research ambitions; this is the nitty-gritty, the brass tacks. The grainy black-and-white print and disorienting sound design create the squalid aesthetics of a snuff film, looking borderline illegal. Where Dr. Heiter's dystopian nightmare is orderly and ruled by a delusional sense of professionalism, Martin's world is pure bedlam—dirty, frenzied, and entirely unsophisticated. He doesn't proselytise about dodgy science or posture as a thinker; he simply *does*. Perhaps much of *Full Sequence* is a daydream—Martin's crude methods and implausible success at kidnapping 12 people hint at fantastical projection, an obscene indulgence conjured in the monotony of his security job. Tom Six's stylised approach creates a derealised atmosphere, as if the entire film exists in a warped, altered state. Unlike Heiter, Martin is practically mute. He does not philosophise or pontificate; he grunts, laughs, moans, and wheezes through his depraved masterpiece. In a moment of ultimate degradation, he wraps his genitals in barbed wire and assaults the woman at the tail end. His literal pet centipede, fulfilling Dr. Sebring's prophecy that it is a phallic symbol, later sodomises Martin in turn. The film plunges into pure transgression, reaching a climax so warped that even the death of a newborn baby veers into slapstick. This is no longer a thought experiment—it is the mucky, primordial antithesis of Dr. Heiter's callous, controlled horror. The scientific discourse is dragged, kicking and screaming, into a grisly orgy of ass-to-mouth.

It is especially crass that Martin becomes aroused by a cluster of captives forced into a hive mind, moving as one grotesque organism. On an ideological level, this is perhaps more unnerving than the physical torture itself. Interrogating the phenomenon of enforced uncritical agreement (falling in line, acting in unison) seems to be Tom Six's central provocation here. As a filmmaker who champions free speech and relishes the contrarian stance, Six takes pleasure in pushing against industry norms. Martin Lomax, in his warped recreation of childhood sexual abuse, not only inflicts suffering but fully immerses himself in it, fashioning himself as another unit of the centipede. This goes beyond the intellectual pursuit of observing from a safe distance—Martin dissolves into the groupthink, surrendering to the slapdash carnage and macabre free-for-all of herd mentality. Perhaps this is the true warning issued in *Full Sequence*.

Full Sequence amplifies the theoretical implications of the first instalment. Dr. Heiter's appalling surgical experiment is, at its core, an attempt to construct a monolith—an organism governed by a singular digestive system, where whatever is ingested at the top is uniformly processed and excreted down the line. Individual autonomy is obliterated; there is no separate act of digestion—only submission to a blob of consumption. The entire mechanism is commandeered by an overseeing architect with an ulterior motive. Tom Six warns against the renunciation of independent thought in favour of assimilation. Rather than resisting, people appear to voluntarily queue up to join the proverbial centipede, eagerly submitting to ideological conjoinment, willing to sacrifice their autonomy for the soothing embrace of collective validation. And, as with Heiter's creation, the further down the sequence one goes, the more degenerate the material becomes.

The deep recesses of the cultural mass are deprived of nutrients—only the figure at the front dictates the menu. In this bleak equation, free thought is not just discouraged; it is pathologised. And yet, there is a perverse psychological comfort in belonging to such a cultish system. To step outside of it is to invite scrutiny, to stand apart is to become a target. Civilisation, Six suggests, corrals us into a centipede of conformity, where we are expected to acquiesce, open wide, and swallow the tunnel of shit.

The Human Centipede 3 (Final Sequence) unfolds as an absurdist nightmare in which a deranged prison warden attempts to solve his facility's rampant disorder by assembling a 500-person human centipede. This grotesque escalation loops back to the trilogy's inception—the dark joke about punishing a child molester by stitching his mouth to a truck driver's anus. In staging prisoners as a conjoined chain of punishment, *Final Sequence* quite literally stitches all its ideas together into a gory chain of signification. I once came across a YouTube comment by someone named Ash Knight, who described Tom Six's trilogy as a centipede in three segments, each one simply digesting the shit of the last. It's a perfect summation of the series' self-consuming logic.

The Human Centipede 2 is a topographical nightmare, where Martin—himself a victim of childhood sexual abuse—perpetuates the cycle of exploitation, weaponising his trauma against others. The centipede, an uncanny symbol of repetition and enforced synchronisation, mirrors Martin's fractured psyche—an externalisation of suffering, manifesting as a daisy chain from Hell. The third sequence serves as the trilogy's inevitable endpoint, circling back to its origins. It revives the initial dark joke—that the ultimate punishment for a paedophile would be to stitch his mouth to the anus of a truck driver—now reframed as institutional justice within a prison system. In this way, *Final Sequence* doesn't just escalate the horror; it stitches the entire trilogy into one self-consuming loop, closing the circuit on its own transgressive logic.

Tonally, *Final Sequence* is a radical departure from its predecessors—glossier, broader, and leaning into a more mainstream Hollywood aesthetic. By this point, Tom Six was fully aware of his "meme machine" status, emboldened by the knowledge that his underground shock piece had exploded into a full-blown internet phenomenon and cultural touchstone. The third film revels in this infamy, strutting with the bravado of a victory lap, a self-aware celebration of its own notoriety. The acting quality dips in the third one, making it easy to dismiss, but there's a valid dimension to its excess. It feels like a farewell party, a last hurrah before the curtain falls—a maximalist spectacle that throws everything at the wall just to see what sticks. The original concept of a singular person receiving scatological

Body 61

punishment has been jacked up, stretching into a ludicrously long chain of prisoners, each linked in an endless feedback loop of suffering. What began as a "deterrent" has spiralled into an unhinged bureaucratic nightmare, where the prison system swallows itself whole. The ever-growing mass of bound convicts becomes so unwieldy, so exponentially vast, that it loses all function—no longer an instrument of justice, just a dystopian monstrosity, a runaway apparatus of state-sanctioned dehumanisation.

The core critique of the third *Centipede* instalment is that, within the carceral system, there is no rehabilitation—no true equity—only sadistic experimentation masquerading as order. Dr. Heiter's twisted vision is now repurposed with a dodgy profit motive, a pyramid scheme where punishment-as-deterrent fuels an ever-expanding, self-perpetuating industry. The centipede, doomed from the outset, becomes commodified—a construct sold as an ironclad solution. This, I believe, is Six's final warning: the banal administration of a madman's perverse idea in red tape.

Hannah Arendt, in her critique of the Nazi regime, famously coined the phrase *the banality of evil*. War crimes were not solely committed by sadists pulling triggers—many were enacted by ordinary people reading lists, stamping documents, or checking train schedules, each performing a minor civic role within a vast killing machine. Atrocities, Arendt argued, were often not orchestrated by raving lunatics but by functionaries following orders, upholding the system with quiet, thoughtless compliance.

This is the engine of *Final Sequence*. The true horror is not the centipede itself, but the managerial structure that enables it—the prison employees, all playing their part in the seamless enforcement of a nightmare, each a cog in the wheel of its depraved logic. The inability to separate from the undifferentiated mass, to process and interpret information independently, becomes a form of incarceration in itself. That the trilogy concludes in a prison is ideologically perfect: here, the removal of freedom is total. You are dictated to, stripped of autonomy, and told that this fundamentally obscene violation is your rehabilitation. The affront is not just the system's cruelty, but its insistence that the ridiculous ordeal is good for you.

Black Swan (2010)

Darren Aronofsky's *Black Swan* is my all-time favourite movie. I've watched it over a hundred times, and with every viewing, I uncover new meaning. To me, it is a perfect film. A companion piece to *The Wrestler* (2008), both films explore artists who push their bodies to the absolute limit, where age and physical injury are ever-present threats. After obsessing over the trailer for months, I finally saw *Black Swan* at a London Film Festival press screening—9:30 am on Friday 22 October 2010. I had queued in the rain for almost an hour, anticipation in my veins. Seated in the front row of a packed cinema, Aronofsky's masterpiece crashed over me like a psychedelic tsunami. I was overwhelmed and enchanted. In that room, I made contact with a divine order of things, and as the credits rolled, I sobbed uncontrollably. If you cut my chest open, *Black Swan* would be playing inside on a loop—that's what my soul looks like. And yet it's the film I've most dreaded writing about as I want to perfectly capture its magnificent essence. So, after much deliberation and hyping myself up to climb this sublime mountain, here goes nothin'!

Black Swan follows a fictional New York City ballet company preparing a production of Tchaikovsky's *Swan Lake*. Nina Sayers, played dazzlingly by Natalie Portman, lands the coveted lead role of the Swan Queen. She naturally embodies the fragile innocence and disciplined grace of the White Swan, but the role demands she also channel the seductive, untamed nature of the Black Swan—qualities that seem to flow effortlessly from her alternate, Lily. Aronofsky originally developed *Black Swan* from an unrealised screenplay about understudies and the unsettling phenomenon of being haunted by a double, drawing inspiration from doppelgänger folklore and Fyodor Dostoyevsky's *The Double*. The film depicts psychosis with blistering intensity; as Nina strains to tap into her darker instincts, her grip on reality begins to splinter. She is told to "lose herself," to surrender control completely. In this world, perfection is not just precision—it is also the act of letting go.

Nina hallucinates her body twisting and contorting into something freakishly swanlike. The original *Swan Lake* ballet is a Gothic tale, about a woman who transforms into a swan. From the outset, Aronofsky envisioned *Black Swan* as a werewolf movie, a concept that shaped the film's feverish aesthetic. The kinetic camerawork pulls us directly into Nina's unravelling psyche—handheld shots trailing behind her, fast-paced tracking from the back of her head, a relentless, claustrophobic intimacy. We witness Nina's descent—we also *live* it. Aronofsky, whose sister trained as a ballerina, was exposed to the world of dance from a young age. He once remarked: "Ballet is a weird art form. Onstage, it's all ethereal beauty and light. Backstage, the dancers are out of breath and sweaty—it's anything but effortless, and you realize there's all this competition." Natalie Portman describes her gruelling experience of preparing for the role of Nina Sayers:

> It was a year of training. It started out as a couple hours a day and then later we started doing five hours a day of ballet class plus cross

training to try and get my body super in shape. About two months before shooting, I started eating for extreme weight loss and then we began choreography, which was eight hours a day. During shooting, we had to keep the training up, so we did a couple hours before or after work. During work, you must continuously be warming up all day long because every time you do a dance scene, you must warm up before, so I did four or five hours a day of barre, the warmup for ballet.

Black Swan opens with Nina's "crazy dream," mirroring the prologue of *Swan Lake*, where Rothbart casts his spell. We first see her as innocent and virginal, dressed in a long white skirt, gliding across the stage. An eerie presence lingers—Rothbart conjures dark magic and invades her spirit. She spins, startled by the entity, and undergoes an internal shift. Her costume, still white, is suddenly shortened—her purity disturbed. Alone, she continues dancing in the void. This opening scene serves as a microcosm of *Black Swan*, a distilled blueprint of Nina's entire journey. The film's core is revealed in these early moments: a coming-of-age story not for the faint of heart, one that demands unfathomable courage from its troubled heroine. The cost is steep, but the reward is otherworldly.

Nina lives with her mother, Erica, in an environment of rigid control. Her bedroom, frozen in time, preserves the style of her childhood—stuffed animals, pastel hues, a woman in her late twenties cocooned in a girlhood she never outgrew. Her days are ruled by discipline: mornings filled with rehearsals and warm-ups, stretching deeply in front of the mirror, refining every movement. Nina is a consummate professional, driven by an almost religious devotion to ballet. Her pursuit is of technical mastery as well as an unrelenting and soulful quest for perfection—an attempt to touch the sublime, no matter the pain suffered. Nina idealistically clings to the hope that, even for a fleeting moment, she might achieve the extraordinary. Breakfast is served by Erica: half a pink grapefruit and a boiled egg—both barely touched. Erica watches her daughter like a hawk, scrutinising every inch of her, catching the faintest blemish. She notices a rash forming on Nina's back—an early sign of a significant realignment underway. Disapproving, she fixes Nina with that sharp quizzical gaze, her expression laced with quiet reprimand. Erica does not tolerate deviation from the status quo; she does not welcome change whatsoever.

Aronofsky's handheld camera stalks Nina like a sinister shadow, always a few steps behind, racing to keep up. She is constantly in motion, her entire existence orbiting around the endless demands of her calling. Pristine in appearance, she maintains the delicate illusion of perfection, but her passion for dance requires a grittier reality—deep cuts, internal shifts, the slow erosion of self. This mirrors the way she prepares her ballet slippers: they emerge from the packaging in flawless, doll-like condition, but to make them functional, she must destroy them—hacking at the soles with scissors, cutting the ribbons, breaking them in through force and wear. The immaculate image of the ballerina is dismantled by an unyielding artistry. And so, in *Black Swan*, Nina is compelled to deform her body, to tear at her very soul, all in service of the craft, reaching new glorious heights at any cost. Ballet is a punishing medium, necessitating sacrifice on every conceivable level. But for those who worship beauty, agony is an unavoidable ritual to be embraced, a sacred offering to the gods.

Artistic Director Thomas LeRoy's new production of *Swan Lake* is modern, stripped down to its raw emotional core. Nina is eager to claim the coveted role of the Swan Queen, but Thomas remains unconvinced. While she is technically impeccable, he finds her too restrained. Perfection alone is not enough—he calls for passion, a ravishing performance that seduces, a Black Swan who radiates untamed sensuality. This leaves Nina mystified. Raised in an environment that suppressed desire and discouraged spontaneity, she has spent her life avoiding the very qualities Thomas insists she must now embody. Thomas explains his requirements:

> Truth is, when I look at you, all I see is the White Swan. Yes, you're beautiful, fragile, fearful. Ideal casting. But the Black Swan... it's a hard fucking job to dance both. [...] In four years, every time you dance, I see you obsess over getting each move exactly right, but I never see you lose yourself. All that discipline, for what? [...] Perfection is not just about control. It's also about letting go. Surprising the audience. Surprising yourself. Transcendence.

Thomas warns that Nina's rigid, virginal, and self-conscious character is a limitation. He suggests that true excellence is not found in technical mastery alone, but in provoking the spectator's erotic desire. When Nina auditions for the Swan Queen role, her performance is abruptly interrupted—Lily barrels into the studio, cutting through her moment. This structural choice is significant. Lily effortlessly exudes Black Swan energy, the exact trait Thomas is seeking. Her sudden, unscripted arrival foreshadows a recurring motif: the intrusion of chaos into control. Unlike the White Swan, the Black Swan cannot be summoned through repetition, rehearsals, or meticulous preparation; she is untamed, a force that resists logic or routine. She arrives unexpectedly, like a lightning bolt—an enrapturing, spontaneous seduction. To embody her is not to will her into being, but to surrender, to be overtaken. Lily's interruption, then, is beyond coincidental—it is a manifestation of the Black Swan's central disposition, disrupting order and gloriously taking up space in the moment.

Nina perceives her audition as a disaster. The moment she returns home, she is met with her mother's interrogation. But Nina can only cry. As a chronic people-pleaser, she has been conditioned to strive for perfection, to impress and earn approval. Erica has kept her trapped in a childlike state, just as the ballet world infantilises dancers, requiring obedience, deference, and tireless labour in service of others. The prospect of becoming the prima ballerina, however, forces Nina towards an inevitable reckoning. To embody the Swan Queen, she must break free from this imposed innocence, redirecting her precious libidinal energy towards self-discovery, peeling back the layers of her artificially constructed personality to uncover a raw truth. This transformation and strenuous soul work cannot happen under the suffocating gaze of her domineering mother who tends to her every need—solicited or not. Erica insists that Nina would be lost without her, seemingly oblivious to how toxic it is for a mother to desire her adult child's helplessness. She tucks Nina into bed like a fragile doll, opening a music box where a tiny ballerina spins endlessly to the tune of *Swan Lake*. This is where Erica wants to keep her daughter—trapped inside a box, twirling in place, never outgrowing her confines. The condescension clips Nina's wings, ensuring she never flies the coop.

Much to everyone's bewilderment, Thomas casts Nina as the Swan Queen—a thrilling promotion, but one laden with immense pressure. Overcome by the news, she rushes to the bathroom and calls her mother. "He picked me, Mommy!" The phrasing is tender, but also troubling—she sounds like a little girl. Sheltered and naïve, Nina has no inkling of the soul-forging odyssey ahead.

Thomas's decision is like the casting of Rothbart's spell—a catalysing moment that thrusts Nina into an irreversible metamorphosis, flinging her into the deep end, ready or not. From this point forward, she is consumed by the dual aspects of the Swan Queen, invaded by forces beyond her conscious control. Her fragile, carefully constructed personality cannot withstand the mounting pressure. Something will have to give. She must shed what no longer serves her. We witness the seismic shift as she is propelled towards artistry, status, and the wild process of becoming.

To celebrate Nina's promotion, Erica presents an extravagant pink strawberry cake—plush rose frosting, delicate ballerina figurines perched on top. It is a striking contrast to the sparse, bland breakfast she served earlier: a single boiled egg and half a pink grapefruit. The only commonality is the colour pink, a symbol of forced girlhood. The dramatic shift in calorie content underscores a deeper instability—life with Erica is a state of extremes. When Nina hesitates to take a bite, her mother's warmth freezes over. She lashes out, condemning the "sweet" gesture as garbage, threatening to throw the entire cake in the bin. It's an outrageous overreaction, but clearly not an unfamiliar one. Nina barely flinches, accustomed to her mother's mood swings, well-versed in treading the tightrope of Erica's explosive temper. She has learned that pleasing her mother—performing the role of the perfect daughter—keeps the peace. But in Erica's world, virtue is obedience and submission to the rules. Nina's journey demands that she unlearn this toxic dynamic, breaking free from the constraints of maternal control. To touch artistic transcendence, she must forsake overbearing discipline and instead surrender to the raw, instinctive wisdom of her own body.

Nina is invited to observe the dancing style of the new girl, Lily from San Francisco—uninhibited, instinctual, unconcerned with precision. Lily moves in a way that is wholly different from Nina, as Thomas puts it: "Imprecise but effortless. She's not faking it." Her lack of strictness mystifies Nina, who has spent her life cultivating rigour. At the company's lavish fundraising gala, Thomas delivers a speech announcing the retirement of principal dancer Beth MacIntyre, who will leave at the end of the season. Dodging the awkwardness, he swiftly redirects the room's attention; a toast is raised in Nina's honour, but the moment is not one of triumph—it is a transaction. Thomas urges Nina to mingle, impress donors, and secure financial investment. Once again, she is cast in the familiar role of people-pleaser. In the women's bathroom, one of the film's most iconic moments of body horror unfolds. Nina notices a hangnail on her finger. She grips the small flap of skin and pulls—only to rip a jagged strip all the way up to her second knuckle. Blood, pain, shock. But then, a flicker of disorientation. She runs her hand under water, and suddenly, the wound is gone. Her finger is intact. Had she imagined it? A strange unease creeps in—she can no longer trust her body, her thoughts, or even reality itself.

Thomas invites Nina for a drink at his place before she heads home. His apartment is starkly decorated in black and white—an immediate visual cue that he is a binary thinker, an all-or-nothing man who does not sit on the fence. True to form, he wastes no time cutting to the chase. He asks if she has a boyfriend. No. Then, if she's a virgin. Uncomfortable, Nina quietly denies it. He assures her there's nothing to be embarrassed about—these are things they need to be able to discuss. "Do you enjoy making love?" he presses. "Sex—do you enjoy it?" On one hand, it's easy to see why some view this line of questioning as inappropriate, given the power imbalance between them—Thomas is, after all, her boss. Why is he prying into her personal life? But on the other hand, from an artistic perspective, his concern is not unfounded. Sensuality is essential to the Black Swan, and he's trying to gauge whether Nina is even capable of channelling eroticism into the role. Does she possess that knowledge? Can she access it? Thomas assigns her a bit of homework: "Go home and touch yourself. Live a little." And with that, he abruptly sends her on her way. Later, Nina does attempt to follow his instructions, but just as she begins to experience solo pleasure, she turns her head—her mother is sitting in the chair beside her, fast asleep. The moment is obliterated. Erica is always there, forever the helicopter parent, observing censoriously. Nina has no privacy, no space to explore herself sexually— missing out on an awareness vital not only to her growth as a woman but to the artistic evolution she craves.

Thomas is, of course, right. Equating masturbation with living is the best advice he could have given Nina, trapped as she is in a sexless existence at her mother's apartment. Enclosed in her childhood bedroom, Nina has no privacy. Even the simple act of undressing is hijacked by Erica, who inspects her every move, assessing her body with a hawkish intensity. When Erica notices the rash spreading across Nina's back and shoulder, she becomes visibly agitated. In a fit of frustration, she aggressively trims Nina's fingernails, muttering, "I knew this role would be too much for you. You can't handle the pressure." Boundaries are non-existent in this household. Erica invades Nina's space, berates her with contempt, and undermines her confidence. She offers no encouragement or support—only criticism. Erica's assumption is clear: the rash is the result of compulsive scratching, a sign that Nina has been "touching herself" too vigorously. I interpret this as a metaphor for masturbation. The rash on Nina's back is more than a physical ailment; it's a manifestation of repressed sexuality, a spirit within her straining to break free. The hangnail, too, suggests an urge pressing outward, rising against the barriers imposed on her. Erica's hostile act of cutting Nina's fingernails becomes symbolic—an attempt to cut her daughter's sexuality down to pieces, to strip away any possibility of intimate self-discovery. What truly disturbs Erica is Nina's potential for erotic enjoyment, the idea that she might, as Thomas suggested, "live a little." Nina's life force, unregulated and unauthorised, is perceived as a threat. Erica responds by chipping away at her edges, reducing her to something manageable. Fingernails, in this context, represent the act of scratching at the surface of the self, of uncovering forbidden knowledge through sexual exploration. Erica's actions are not just about control—they are an assault on Nina's autonomy, an effort to suppress the parts of her that dare to resist.

The next day, the dance company receives devastating news—Beth has been hit by a car. Thomas suspects it was a suicide attempt. Reflecting on her artistry, he remarks, "Everything Beth ever did came from within. From some dark impulse. It's what could make her so thrilling to watch. Even perfect at times. But also, destructive." This is a pivotal moment for Nina. Until now, she has equated perfection with control and technical mastery. But here, Thomas describes exemplariness as an incalculable trait, born from instinct and tenebrosity. For the first time, Nina considers the possibility that chaos can be captivating. She wonders if this is the missing piece—the element she must embody to ascend to greatness. Thomas is the photographic negative of Erica. Both impose high expectations on Nina, but from opposite ends of the spectrum. Erica wants her to remain chaste, flawless, delicate—technically exact but emotionally restrained, a porcelain doll of obedience. Thomas, by contrast, pushes Nina to live on the edge, take risks, and abandon precision in favour of reckless abandon. He encourages her to surrender to impulse and become the kind of performer whose next move is enthralling and unforeseeable. Erica prefers Nina to remain in a glass case; Thomas wants to smash all comfort zones.

Everywhere she goes, Nina sees doubles of herself—strangers on the street, her coercively controlling mother, the idolised prima ballerina Beth, and her beautiful rival, Lily. Thomas pushes her to extreme physical and emotional limits, where reality and fantasy collapse into each other, indistinguishable and inescapable. If she is to personify both the Black and White Swans, she must relinquish the image-based conception of herself. Perfection cannot be achieved through mere replication—there must be a shift from the shallow, illusory realm of the imaginary to the raw, visceral domain of the body. And make no mistake, *Black Swan* is an attack on the senses: toenails splitting, skin irritation, a blood-drenched hangnail, and the torment of feet due to the unnatural load bearing of pointe work. As Linda Williams argues in *Film Bodies: Gender, Genre, and Excess*, horror cinema is one of the "body genres" that operates through intense physicality, using visceral spectacle to provoke bodily reactions in the viewer (Williams 1991, 4). *Black Swan* exemplifies this by transmuting the physical demands of ballet into horror, rendering the act of performance as grotesque self-mutilation. Nina's body becomes the battleground where artistic greatness and abject terror collide.

The film immerses us in the rigorous and punishing world of rehearsals, training, warm-ups, and physiotherapy. Nina works relentlessly, her every movement in service of her technique. She is an artist in the truest sense—willing to endure anything to achieve notability. But the toll on her body is evident; every step, every pirouette, is layered with tension, her limbs bearing the silent screams of overexertion. As Susan Bordo explores in *Unbearable Weight*, the female body in Western culture is frequently subjected to impossible ideals of discipline, with control and self-denial valorised as signs of feminine virtue (Bordo 1993, 15). Nina's suffering is both personal and systemic; the expectations of the ballet world mirror broader cultural pressures on women to surpass the limits of their physicality, to shrink, chisel, and ultimately erase themselves in pursuit of the sublime. She constantly seeks feedback, clinging to Thomas's notes, desperate for more criticism, more direction—anything to refine her craft. But it's precisely this neediness that holds her back. This is not the energy of a seductress, of a self-assured creature. The Black Swan does not ask for permission; she does not need approval. She *commands* attention. She is strong, unapologetic, and self-possessed. She moves with effortless fluidity, unshackled by self-doubt, cool and magnetic, driven by a raw conviction. A hunger stirs inside Nina—a desire she can barely name. But this concept eludes her. She cannot yet fathom what it means to relinquish to the role, to let go, to *become* the Black Swan.

On a rare night out, Nina observes Lily with fascination. She speaks freely, provocatively, dripping with erotic confidence—a stark contrast to Nina's demure inexperience. At dinner, Lily orders a cheeseburger and takes a ravenous bite. The sight is almost jarring. A woman openly indulging her appetite—devouring with pleasure—is utterly foreign to Nina, whose relationship with food is fraught. She often purges to maintain her low weight; her frail frame suggests a cycle of self-denial and excess, anorexia and bulimia. But Lily is different. She luxuriates in her environment, unburdened by shame, taking what she wants, in every sense—a maneater in more ways than one. Casually, Lily offers Nina ecstasy—she brought it from San Francisco, don't you know! Nina declines: she is always terrified of losing control. Lily gently makes the case that it'll help her relax, loosen up, *see the night sky*. The moment feels loaded; Lily, a living embodiment of the Black Swan, luring Nina towards transgression. She even lends her a black lace tank top, a symbolic shift creeping over the body. Nina's mother keeps calling but she ignores her. Lily flirts with two men at the bar, exuding effortless seduction. Meanwhile, she spikes Nina's drink. When Nina hesitates, Lily leans in, urging her to stay. *Live a little*, she coaxes—Thomas's words, now spoken through her rival's mouth.

Nina drinks her spiked cocktail, the world blurring around her as the night twirls into pandemonium. She dances with Lily under pulsing club lights, bodies entwined, the bass thrumming through her bones. They tumble into a taxi, hands wandering, breath quickening. Back at the apartment, Erica is waiting—scolding, inhibiting. But this time, Nina doesn't cower. She snaps. She yells at her mother to leave her alone, slamming the bedroom door and obstructing it with a metal rod. Erica protests, her voice laced with disbelief: *"You're not my Nina right now."* Inside the room, Nina and Lily merge in a fevered embrace. Clothes are shed, lips meet, limbs tangle. As Lily moves down her body, Nina shivers—the sensation of orgasm produces swan-like skin, goosebumps appear all over her. A moment of ecstasy—or was it merely a dream? Morning arrives with a brutal clarity. Nina is disoriented and hungover, the night before dissolves like mist. But there's no time to process it—she's late for rehearsal. Rushing to the theatre, she finds Thomas already onstage. Lily is dancing her number, effortlessly gliding through the movements, fluid and carefree. Meanwhile, Nina, still groggy, frantically warms up, pushing herself severely. The contrast is stark—one woman lost in the music, the other locked in battle with herself.

While being measured for her costume, Nina receives frustrating news—Lily has been chosen as her understudy. Standard practice in any live production, but to Nina, it feels like a direct threat. She pleads with Thomas: "She's after me. She's trying to replace me. Please believe me." Thomas dismisses her paranoia, reassuring her that she had a breakthrough in rehearsal. He instructs her to go home and rest, that everything is going to be okay. But Nina doesn't listen. Instead, she stays behind, obsessively practicing, running the routine over and over. Her accompanist eventually gives up, packing up for the night—he has a life, after all. Alone in the studio, Nina pushes on. But suddenly, she is startled. The reflection in the mirror no longer moves in sync with her. A hallucination takes hold: she sees Rothbart from *Swan Lake* having sex with Lily. In a jarring morph, Rothbart turns into Thomas. The vision contains latent meaning—her casting as Swan Queen is reframed as a dark spell, a bewitching that triggers her transformation. Her psyche cracks open. The innocence she has clung to for too many years is slipping away, replaced by a more complex state of mind. The path to erotic maturity continues apace.

Nina visits Beth in the hospital, carrying a small collection of her belongings—among them, a nail file. Carefully, she lines the objects up on the table, as if to restore something lost, to return to Beth the fragments of her identity. It is intended as a quiet offering, a reassurance that her essence is intact. Guilt-ridden, Nina whispers how sorry she is, that she knows how it feels to be replaced. Beth's expression darkens, she wants to know why her stuff was taken, and Nina says, "I just wanted to be like you. Perfect." Beth's face twists with rage. She spits back, "I'm not perfect. I'm nothing. Fucking nothing!" And without warning, she seizes the nail file and drives it into her own face, stabbing over and over. The choice of weapon is no coincidence. The nail file—an instrument of refinement and reshaping—becomes a tool of destruction. Throughout the film, the clipping and smoothing of fingernails carries symbolic weight: a ritual of female castration, a forced removal of desire and severing of erotic agency. Here, in Beth's hands, the nail file inflicts self-mutilation and annihilation of identity.

By now, Nina is unravelling. Her paranoia spirals into a full-blown psychotic break—visual and auditory hallucinations consume her. She hears whispers in silence, and sees movement in stillness. Her mother's drawings, once static, seem to animate. Locking herself inside the bedroom, she reaches for her back, fingers instinctively seeking the itch—and pulls. A black quill, thick as a feather, emerges from her skin. Panic surges. The metamorphosis is accelerating. Erica, sensing the frenzy behind the door, tries to break in, but Nina slams it shut, crushing her mother's hand. "Go away!" she screams, the last thread of restraint snapping. Her body convulses. Her eyes turn bloodshot, legs buckle, and bones crack under an unseen force. She blacks out. Hours later, Erica whispers that she has been scratching all night and refuses to let her dazed and disoriented daughter exit the bedroom. But this is opening night. Nina is the Swan Queen. She *must* go. Summoning what remains of her strength, she forces her way out, staggering into the hallway. "I'm the Swan Queen," she shouts at her mother, voice trembling with defiance. "You're the one who never left the corps!" The words land like a final blow. Erica, once an aspiring dancer, never ascended beyond the *corps de ballet*—the nameless, synchronised mass that moves as a backdrop to the stars. A Jungian reading suggests that Erica never individuated, never emerged from the monolith of dancers to forge a distinct identity. And now, she resents her daughter for doing what she could not. Nina has outgrown the *corps*. She has left the mass behind. And tonight, she will take centre stage.

Nina arrives at the theatre just in time. Lily is poised to replace her, but Nina refuses to surrender. She calmly negotiates with Thomas, ready to reclaim her role. His response is measured and powerful: "The only person standing in your way is you. It's time to let her go. Lose yourself." The performance begins. Nina masters the ballet's second act, but a hallucination unmoors her—just for a moment. She wobbles, loses her balance. The male dancer playing the prince is unable to support her, and she crashes to the stage. Thomas is furious. Humiliated, Nina rushes off, retreating to her dressing room. But she isn't alone. Lily is there, slipping into the Black Swan costume. A confrontation erupts, the tension between Nina and her own fractured psyche reaches a fever pitch. Lily shape shifts into Nina. Her doppelgänger stares back at her. The two struggle violently, smashing a mirror, shards raining down around them. Nina seizes a large fragment of glass and drives it into her double, killing her. The body reverts back to Lily. Panting, shaken, but fuelled by adrenaline, Nina shoves Lily's lifeless form into the bathroom and locks the door. Then, she returns to the stage. The final sequence is frenzied, feverish, transcendent. A seductively dark energy overtakes Nina; she goes on to *nail* her performance (pun intended), leading to the show of a lifetime. She becomes Odile, the Black Swan, fully realised. Her movements are electrifying, her presence utterly hypnotic. The music surges, and as Nina spirals into Odile's coda, her body undergoes a resplendently sublime change—her arms bloom with black feathers, her very being consumed by the role. She is no longer interpreting the Black Swan role. She *is* the Black Swan. The audience erupts into a standing ovation. The first time I saw this scene in the cinema, I was astounded, transported. I kept going back, unable to resist its pull. I saw *Black Swan* ten times on the big screen when it first released.

As Nina resumes the White Swan costume and makeup, a knock sounds at her dressing room door. She opens it—to her shock, Lily stands there, alive and well. Smiling, she apologises for the misunderstanding and congratulates Nina before slipping away. Stunned, Nina turns back to the room. The mirror is still shattered. The towel she used to mop up the blood is clean. The bathroom is empty. Slowly, she looks down. A shard of glass is embedded in her abdomen. The truth crashes over her—she had stabbed herself. Despite the wound, she steps onto the stage for the ballet's final act. The White Swan throws herself off a cliff, surrendering to fate, plummeting towards the end. Nina lands on the safety mat, ethereal and tragic. The audience erupts into thunderous applause. Thomas, Lily, and the other dancers rush to congratulate her—but Nina does not rise. Thomas's joy turns into alarm. His eyes drop to her waist. Blood soaks the fabric of her costume. Panic sets in. He shouts for help, demanding to know what happened. Nina, serene, untouchable, only gazes upward. "I felt it," she whispers. "It was perfect." The screen slowly fades to white.

To an outsider, Nina's obsession might seem frivolous, even absurd. An onlooker would be warranted to shake her by the shoulders and say, *Girl, what are you doing? This is madness. Go out, have fun for once. Do Molly. Let your hair down.* Meanwhile, Nina believes she's turning into a swan. She is living on another plane entirely, untethered from conventional reality. But that's the point. The process of making exceptional art is deeply personal, often incomprehensible to those who are not involved. *Black Swan* is a story about psychosis and the arts—a sacred journey, perhaps even the pursuit of a Holy Death. Nina dares to reach for something beyond herself, with no certainty that she will grasp it, only the hope of touching perfection, if only for a moment. Dying in the loving act of creation—of becoming—strikes me as a profoundly beautiful exit from this life. It is the ultimate expression of devotion, a commitment so pure that it defies reason. It may look deranged. But to Nina, it is everything.

What looks like insanity to the uninitiated is, really, an act of dedication. The long hours, sacrifices, and relentless chiselling away at nothing until it becomes undeniable—this is the essence of creation, so precious and important. And the glory belongs solely to the one who laboured for it. No one else can claim it. This is why the theme of doubling in *Black Swan* is so essential. Nina is terrified of being replaced, of an understudy swooping in and running off with what she has bled for. To someone who has committed their whole life to their craft, the prospect of misappropriation is devastating. But the antidote to the fear of being usurped by a devious double is simple: if you have the spark, if you truly embody *it*, no one can embezzle your talent. Whatever is stolen, you can regenerate. You are a fountain, a force of nature, accessing an infinite internal source. Yes, betrayal stings, and loss wounds, but your power is limitless. And if you keep moving forward, if you push through the pain and continue working, you will manifest the vision you always dreamed of.

A useful framework for understanding *Black Swan* is Carl Jung's concept of the Shadow—the unconscious aspect of the Ego, often disowned and forced out of sight, yet brimming with unrealised potential. The Shadow is prone to projection; what we suppress in ourselves—our perceived flaws and buried impulses—is unconsciously cast onto others, sparing us the discomfort of self-confrontation. Nina, unable to acknowledge her own eroticism, quells it into her Shadow, and then transfers it onto Lily as something shameful, even malevolent. What we label as evil, inferior, or unacceptable is often the very part of us that has been exiled into the Shadow. Left unexamined, it festers, becoming a destructive force. Paradoxically, the Shadow is also the wellspring of creativity. It is where bleakness and brilliance coalesce—a frightening abyss, but one rich with the promise to transform. Jungian psychology holds that true individuation—the full integration of the self—requires embracing the Shadow, assimilating it into consciousness rather than allowing it to sabotage us from the depths. This is Nina's journey. *Black Swan* is the story of an artist who dares to plunge into her own darkness, confronting her most terrifying fears to master her craft. She does not merely perform perfection—she embodies every fractured, beautiful, and monstrous part of herself, staging them all, elegantly and audaciously.

Ultimately, Nina succeeds in integrating her Shadow. The lesbian sex scene in *Black Swan* likely unfolds entirely in the realm of fantasy, but its significance is undeniable—it allows Nina to process the raw sexual power she has long denied under her mother's overbearing surveillance. More thought-provoking than the average horror film, *Black Swan* is an ode to erotic embodiment as a crucial feature of the artistic life. It suggests that to truly thrive, we must embrace sensuality, surrendering to the unpredictable currents of desire. It warns against the rigidity of control, urging us not to rely solely on White Swan energy, inviting us to quiet the perfectionist, to loosen the grip of the inner critic. Being on kissing terms with magnificence requires more than discipline; it reserves a privileged space for chaos. Maybe even a break from "reality"—a plunge into the vast interior, a moment of psychotic abandon. The Black Swan draws power from the edge of enigmatic rapid change. It startles and makes a scene. Sometimes inconvenient, but always, *always* indomitable.

Glossary of Psychoanalytic Terms

- **Abjection (Kristeva)**—Experience of being cast off or degraded, disrupting identity and order. It involves rejecting aspects of the self that are disturbing or threaten stability, such as taboo elements, bodily fluids, death, and the maternal body.
- **Anal Fixation**—A Freudian developmental stage related to control, retention, and expulsion. Fixation at this stage can lead to personality traits such as excessive orderliness (anal retentive) or impulsiveness and disorganisation (anal expulsive).
- **Castration Anxiety**—A Freudian concept describing the unconscious fear, typically in men, of losing the phallus, which symbolises power and authority. In a broader sense, it refers to the anxiety of losing control or being rendered powerless.
- **Death Drive (Thanatos)**—The unconscious drive towards destruction, repetition, and self-annihilation. In contrast to the life instincts (Eros), the death drive manifests in compulsions, aggression, and behaviours that undermine self-preservation.
- **Dissociation**—A psychological defence mechanism where an individual detaches from their thoughts, identity, or surroundings, often as a response to trauma or overwhelming experiences.
- **Hive Mind Mentality**—The loss of individual autonomy in favour of collective conformity, often explored in psychoanalysis as a symptom of unconscious submission to authority or mass psychology.

- **Magical Thinking**—A psychological defence mechanism in which individuals believe their thoughts, actions, or desires can directly influence reality.
- **The Monstrous-Feminine (Creed)**—A feminist psychoanalytic theory analysing how horror films frame female monstrosity through patriarchal fears of sexuality, reproduction, and abjection.
- **Penis Envy**—A Freudian theory suggesting that young girls experience a phase of development where they recognise sexual difference and desire the symbolic power associated with the phallus.
- **The Phallus**—In Lacanian psychoanalysis, the phallus is a privileged symbolic signifier of authority, power, and desire, rather than a literal anatomical reference to the penis. It plays a key role in structuring identity and social relationships.
- **The Real (Lacan)**—That which exists beyond language and symbolic representation, often experienced as trauma, rupture, or the limits of human comprehension.
- **Repression**—A defence mechanism in which unwanted thoughts, desires, or traumatic memories are pushed into the unconscious, often resurfacing in displaced or distorted ways.
- **The Shadow (Jung)**—The unconscious, repressed aspects of the self, often projected onto others.
- **Superego**—The internalised voice of societal norms, moral constraints, and parental authority, which can manifest as guilt, shame, punishment, or rigid self-regulation.
- **The Symbolic Order (Lacan)**—A system of language, law, and social structures that shape identity and desire.

Nature

Ecological horror, animal attacks, and natural disruption

3

If body horror exposes the terrifying instability of flesh, nature-as-horror shifts the focus outward, revealing the untamed wilderness as a force of profound and uncertain menace. This subgenre explores the ways in which the natural world—often taken for granted as neutral, beautiful, or even nurturing—can become a site of terror, stripping away human illusions of control. Be it predatory animals, epic and indifferent landscapes, or the sheer unpredictability of environmental forces, nature-as-horror reminds us that we are not masters of our surroundings but vulnerable inhabitants at their mercy.

In this section, we will tap into deep-seated anxieties about survival, the limits of human agency, and the fragility of civilisation. Nature does not operate according to human morality or reason—it is ancient, amoral, and nonchalant. The horror here emerges not from supernatural malevolence but from the realisation that the world we live in is not designed for our safety. These films dismantle the comforting idea that nature is a passive backdrop to human activity, instead presenting it as an active, often hostile force that resists subjugation. At its core, nature-as-horror confronts the primal fear that beneath all our technology, reason, and societal structures, we remain small, exposed, and powerless against unknowable forces that govern our world.

The Birds (1963)

Alfred Hitchcock's *The Birds* opens in a San Francisco pet store, where socialite Melanie Daniels crosses paths with lawyer Mitch Brenner, who is shopping for lovebirds as a gift for his sister's 11th birthday. Recognising Melanie from a recent court appearance—where she faced consequences for a practical joke gone awry—Mitch feigns mistaking her for a shop employee, playfully testing her knowledge of birds, which she fails. He then reveals that he was already aware of her identity and leaves without making a purchase. As an attorney, Mitch is accustomed to defending clients charged with crimes, and this dynamic subtly extends to his interactions with Melanie. Throughout the film, he assumes a similar role—compelled to vouch for her, as if she, too, is aligned with the figure of the outlaw due to her mischievous past.

Melanie is a beautiful, affluent woman with the freedom to pursue wild adventures. Her sexuality, however, appears too conspicuous within a phallocentric society that negates feminine jouissance—her very existence becomes a site of disavowal because of her desire. Within this framework, female eroticism is treated as a kind of transgression, aligning Melanie with the unruly birds that descend upon the town. This parallel is artfully established in the pet store scene, where a few birds momentarily escape their cages, flapping chaotically around the space. For a moment, disorder reigns—a disruption of the established order—until Mitch swiftly intervenes, capturing the rogue birds and returning them to confinement. His ability to impose structure, to compartmentalise and restore equilibrium, is evident here. But as the film progresses, Melanie emerges as a force that challenges his instinct for control, discomposing the neat boundaries he unconsciously upholds.

Smitten, Melanie buys the lovebirds and, leveraging her nepo baby connections, gains access to Mitch's San Francisco address. Upon discovering that he has left for the weekend to his family's farm in Bodega Bay, she drives up the coast in her Aston Martin to personally deliver the birds. Here, traditional gender roles are reversed—Melanie assumes the role of the hunter, eagle-eyed and unwavering, tracking her target with cool determination. She zeroes in on what she wants with surgical precision. A close-up of the caged lovebirds inside her convertible subtly reinforces this dynamic; they become an extension of Melanie's erotic drive, absorbing her aura as a dangerous guttersnipe. Her sudden arrival in this quiet California town could be interpreted as the film's first bird attack—a powerful, disruptive force of nature intruding upon the community's placid routine. The term "bird" in British slang refers to an attractive woman or love interest—a layered connection that Hitchcock, ever attuned to double meanings, would not have overlooked.

Melanie rents a boat and glides across the bay to discreetly leave the lovebirds at the Brenner family farm. As she rows away, Mitch spots her and, rather than taking the direct aquatic route, drives around the bay to intercept her at the dock. The symbolism here is striking: Melanie's image is immersed in the calm waters of the bay; she gracefully steers the boat and navigates her way across and back while Mitch remains landlocked, avoiding any direct contact with the water. The bay's natural landscape reflects a distinctly feminine condition—wetness being the cornerstone of female sexual arousal. Melanie moves fluidly through this space (pun intended!), reinforcing her connection to the water motif that recurs throughout the film. This link is further emphasised when we learn that she once made headlines for allegedly jumping naked into a fountain while vacationing in Italy. Water, in *The Birds*, becomes shorthand for Melanie's comfort in her own eroticism, while Mitch's avoidance of it suggests a wariness—perhaps even an aversion—to engage with female sexuality head-on.

The significance of Melanie's elaborate pursuit—purchasing the lovebirds, tracking Mitch down, addressing a card to his sister, and secretly placing the gift in the farmhouse—boils down to desire and its positioning. She has cleverly supplanted herself within the coordinates of the lovebirds, an object Mitch sought from the outset. By acquiring and delivering them, she further activates his desire, fusing herself dynamically with something he had already been pursuing. That she infiltrated his family home in the process confirms feminine jouissance as a trespassing energy precisely because it is prohibited. As Melanie approaches the wharf, a seagull swoops down and strikes her head, drawing blood. This sudden, seemingly random attack disrupts the tranquillity of the moment with shocking force. But Melanie's presence on the water when the assault takes place is symbolically loaded—her fluid erotic energy clashes against the rigid boundaries of the phallocentric order. The intrusion of female sexuality is met with swift, violent retaliation. And the longer she lingers in Bodega Bay, the more frequent and ferocious the avian attacks become, as though nature itself rises to rebuke her presence.

Mitch's mother, Lydia, immediately distrusts Melanie, viewing her through the distorted lens of gossip columns that have painted her as a reckless, immoral woman. Conservative in her values, Lydia prejudges Melanie as a vulgar character and a bad influence. We gain further insight into Lydia through Annie, Mitch's ex-girlfriend, who relocated to Bodega Bay to pursue a relationship with him but remained in town even after their romance ended. Annie is a relic of Mitch's past, frozen in place and unable to move on. She suggests that Lydia's cold, possessive nature was a key obstacle in their relationship. "Maybe there's never been anything between Mitch and any girl," she muses—a damning observation. Perhaps passion with Mitch is doomed from the start—he's so emotionally enmeshed with his disparaging mother that there's no room for a love story. After Mitch's father passed away, he fell into the dysfunctional pattern of cosplaying as husband to his own mother, filling the role left vacant by his Dad. Melanie's arrival at the farmhouse plagues this dynamic, not just because of the surplus of her desire, but because Lydia reacts less like a wary mother and more like a jilted lover. Slavoj Žižek, in his 2006 documentary *The Pervert's Guide to Cinema* (directed by Sophie Fiennes), refers to this as "the standard Oedipal imbroglio of incestuous tension between mother and son—the son split between his possessive mother and the intrusive girl." The birds, in this reading, materialise as agents of an unresolved psychic conflict.

Mitch is a textbook obsessional neurotic, caught in the push-and-pull tension between sex and death—between Melanie and the killer birds. Death by bird attack becomes the ultimate feared punishment for the avoidant type. His neurosis is evident from the start: at the pet store, he requests lovebirds that are "not too demonstrative, but not too aloof either"—a telling ambivalence that signals his deep discomfort with unregulated passion. He does not act but waits, preferring to let others take the initiative, sidestepping authentic confrontation. Mitch is erotically divested, like a robot going through the motions of courtship, performing romance without true engagement. Duty-bound and repressively self-controlled, he seeks the safety of a world where nothing spontaneous happens. But *The Birds* frames Melanie as a bothersome force, threatening to shatter his carefully contained emotional world. A pattern emerges: at the end of every scene featuring Melanie, a growing number of birds gather, at first placidly and ominously, before shrieking, pecking, and spilling blood. Her presence sends them into a frenzy. She seems to be the catalyst for an uncontrollable rupture, her arrival marking the moment when the natural world revolts.

But what could possibly drive masses of agitated birds to torment innocent adults and children, pecking them to death? This strange maelstrom taps into everything we do not understand about the world—what eludes our control, not just in the external, physical realm but also within ourselves, beneath the carefully constructed layers that seal us off from one another. Hitchcock chose not to expound the bird attacks, avoiding any reductive science-fiction rationale. The absence of explanation creates a far deeper impact, conjuring a vague but unshakable sense of impending doom. This ambiguity intensifies the film's uncanny effect, particularly in moments when the violence occurs just outside the frame—heard but not seen, as characters cower indoors. The imperceptible threat produces a cognitive dissonance, amplifying the horror precisely because it resists logic or containment.

I maintain that the volatility of the birds is closely tied to Melanie Daniels and the condition of femininity as a thorny force of nature. That a woman should dare to act spiritedly in matters of the heart—pursuing rather than being chased—breaches the acceptable boundaries of a phallocentric society structured around male desire. Melanie transgresses gendered norms of courtship; her decisive action and refusal to passively wait to be conquered bothers the onlookers in her environment. What one might call The Melanie Effect is symbolically rendered as an apocalyptic rupture; the disarray she seemingly incites is framed as an ambush. This is made explicit in one of the film's most striking scenes, when a hysterical woman in Bodega Bay directly blames Melanie for the bird attacks, demanding: "Why are they doing this? They said when you got here, the whole thing started. Who are you? What are you? Where did you come from? I think you're the cause of all of this. I think you're evil. EVIL!" The accusation exposes the latent anxiety at the heart of the film: that an ungovernable, desiring woman might be capable of wreaking havoc simply by existing.

Indeed, Melanie's desire is bound to register as an assault on the fragile architecture of heteronormative patriarchy. Feminine jouissance is perceived as an abomination in a repressed civilisation—it takes on horror overtones precisely because we are taught that men enjoy sex, while women merely endure it. A sexually self-possessed woman is destined to provoke psychic ruckus, and *The Birds* externalises this turmoil through widespread avian violence. Melanie is seen as a scary *chick*—a threat because she seduces and dismantles the illusion of male dominance at the centre of eroticism, toppling the house of cards carefully stacked by phallic jouissance in a desperate attempt to uphold its illegitimate authority.

Picnic at Hanging Rock (1975)

Peter Weir's *Picnic at Hanging Rock*, adapted from Joan Lindsay's 1967 novel, revolves around the mysterious disappearance of several schoolgirls and their teacher during a picnic in Victoria, Australia, and the haunting impact on the local community. Set on Valentine's Day, 1900, the story follows a group of students from a prestigious girls' school who venture to Hanging Rock for a celebratory outing, chaperoned by their teachers, Miss Greta McCraw and Mademoiselle de Poitiers.

At Hanging Rock, students Miranda, Marion, Irma, and Edith break away from the group to explore the landscape. As they cross a stream, they catch the attention of a young Englishman, Michael, and his Australian friend,

Albert, who watch them from a distance. Venturing further, the girls begin climbing the Rock, eventually succumbing to an eerie, dreamlike trance and falling asleep. When Edith awakens in terror, she screams and flees back to the picnic, while the others press on, disappearing into a hidden crevice within the Rock. Meanwhile, the rest of the group, who had also dozed off, wakes to the terrible discovery that Miss McCraw and the three girls are missing. A police search yields no answers, as Edith's fragmented recollections offer only cryptic, incoherent details.

Plagued by nightmares about the missing girls, Michael becomes obsessed with the case and embarks on his own search. Spending the night at Hanging Rock, he is overcome by a strange, almost trance-like state, and by morning, he stumbles upon Irma inside a crevice—alive but unconscious. When Irma finally wakes up days later, she has no memory of what happened. A full week has passed since her disappearance, yet she cannot account for Miranda, Marion, or Miss McCraw. Michael, too, is haunted—his visions of Miranda blur with the image of a white swan, an ethereal presence that eludes his grasp. By the film's end, the whereabouts of the missing girls remain an unsolvable enigma, their absence continuing to weigh heavily on the local community, lingering like a split in reality.

Peter Weir recalled that when *Picnic at Hanging Rock* was first screened in the United States, audiences were ill at ease by the lack of resolution. "One distributor threw his coffee cup at the screen at the end of it," Weir recounted, "because he'd wasted two hours of his life—a mystery without a goddamn solution!" The director's frustration was echoed by critic Vincent Canby in a 1979 *New York Times* review, where he observed the film's wistful ambiguity and its divergence from conventional horror tropes. Canby reflected: "Horror need not always be a long-fanged man in evening clothes or a dismembered corpse or a doctor who keeps a brain in his goldfish bowl. It may be a warm sunny day, the innocence of girlhood, and hints of unexplored sexuality that combine to produce a euphoria so intense it becomes transporting—a state beyond life or death. Such horror is unspeakable not because it is gruesome but because it remains outside the realm of things that can be easily defined or explained in conventional ways." Here, horror is not the spectacle of violence, but an uncanny experience as intoxicating as it is ineffable.

Building on Canby's insightful assessment, I turn to Edmund Burke's *A Philosophical Enquiry into the Origin of Our Ideas of the Sublime and Beautiful*, a seminal treatise on aesthetics that established a clear philosophical distinction between the beautiful and the sublime. According to Burke, the beautiful is characterised by harmony, proportion, and aesthetic pleasure, while the sublime is that which overwhelms, compels, and even threatens to destroy us. The shift in preference from the beautiful to the sublime marked the transition from the Neoclassical to the Romantic era, reflecting a growing fascination with the awe-inspiring and the ineffable. Burke's work captivated the imagination of many philosophers, including Immanuel Kant, who expanded upon these ideas in his own critical philosophy. In the context of *Picnic at Hanging Rock*, the film's horror lies precisely in this Burkean tension—its ability to lure us in with its ethereal allure only to unsettle us with its formless, uncontainable mystery.

The origins of our ideas of the beautiful and the sublime, according to Edmund Burke, can be understood through their causal structures. Drawing from Aristotelian physics and metaphysics, Burke delineates causation into four categories: formal, material, efficient, and final causes. The formal cause of beauty, he argues, is the passion of love; its material cause lies in specific qualities such as smallness, smoothness, and delicacy; its efficient cause is the soothing effect it has on our nerves; and its final cause is divine providence. What is most striking in Burke's conception of beauty is its detachment from traditional aesthetic principles—proportion, fitness, and perfection play no role in determining what is beautiful. By contrast, the sublime operates under a radically different causal structure. Its formal cause is the passion of fear—particularly the fear of death; its material cause resides in qualities such as immenseness, infinity, and magnificence; its efficient cause is the heightened tension it produces in the nervous system; and its final cause is theological—God's creation of, and triumph over, Satan, as famously depicted in John Milton's *Paradise Lost*.

Indeed, reflecting on Peter Weir's mesmerising film—particularly the scene in which the four girls wander off unsupervised to explore Hanging Rock—a uniquely enchanting yet terrifying effect takes hold of the viewer. The interplay of sound, cinematography, and editing creates a vertiginous sensory experience, a fever dream of unfathomable magnitude. Something that cannot be linguistically conveyed is nevertheless approximated cinematically, evoking a feeling that is familiar and alien at the same time. We are simultaneously drawn to and unsettled by what unfolds onscreen. This encounter transcends conventional beauty; it is not a simple pleasure derived from contemplating a benign object. Rather, we are in the domain of the sublime—a grandeur that defies calculation, measurement, and imitation. The natural world overwhelms us, and Hanging Rock suggests a cosmic enormity, a force extending beyond the limits of human comprehension. The sublime, by its very nature, carries an undercurrent of horror—lurking in darkness, uncertainty, and the ungraspable vastness of the unknown.

In *Picnic at Hanging Rock*, the sublime is conveyed less through dialogue than through a distinct visual gravitas. The way Miranda and Irma are filmed suggests an eroticism that transgresses the boundaries of innocent beauty. Burgeoning feminine sexuality exerts a magnetic force—one that elicits both pleasure and a more perilous intensity, capable of unsettling or even undoing the observer. Michael and Albert, beguiled, watch the girls as they move towards the Rock, their gaze laden with desire. Albert's crude remarks about the girls being "lookers," with hourglass figures and "decent set of legs," reduce them to objects of lust. Yet the film implies a more meaningful truth: that the energy at the site of seduction—the mysterious allure that magnetises people to one another—shares its essence with the sublime power of nature itself.

The girls are magnetically drawn to climb Hanging Rock, surrendering to its strange magic before vanishing into one of its crevices. The Rock holds unutterable knowledge, accumulated over millions of years—an ancient wisdom that exceeds human understanding, preserving secrets about the universe itself. In the film, this primal, natural intelligence is transferred to the girls, who, in turn, become enigmas—captivating onlookers and driving them into a maddening, protracted, and fruitless search. The fact that the girls disappear on Valentine's Day suggests an abstract allegory about the exasperating drive to comprehend romantic love. A small yet potent detail underscores this theme: Miss McCraw's watch, which has never failed before, inexplicably stops at 12. A vague explanation about "something magnetic" is offered, but the interruption of time alludes to the Rock activating a quality outside the usual passage of time, that nature accesses infinity itself, the very realm of love.

Before setting off on their picnic, the female students are sternly warned by their school's headmistress, the formidable Mrs. Appleyard, to remain vigilant against potential dangers: "Once again, let me remind you—Hanging Rock is extremely dangerous. You are therefore forbidden from any tomboy foolishness in the matter of exploration, even on the lowest slopes. I also wish to remind you: the vicinity is renowned for its venomous snakes and poisonous ants of various species. It is, however, a geological marvel." This cautionary speech drips with Victorian repression; the very name "Hanging Rock" exudes big dick energy, making Appleyard's admonition read less like a warning about physical peril and more like a thinly veiled directive against sexual exploration. And yet, from the earliest moments of the film, Miranda seems to possess an esoteric wisdom. This is evident when she whimsically quotes Edgar Allan Poe: "What we see and what we seem are but a dream, a dream within a dream."

At the picnic site, Mademoiselle de Poitiers gleefully remarks on a sudden realisation—Miranda is a Botticelli Angel. One of the orphaned students confides that Miranda possesses a rare knowledge: "She knew a lot of things other people don't know. Secrets. She knew she wouldn't come back." After ensorcelling the young Michael, Miranda's absence torments him, causing him to conduct independent searches—her erotic power is inextricably linked to the sublime force of Hanging Rock. She is a bewitching presence, one that mesmerises yet threatens to unravel the observer. Amid the havoc of the sublime, Miranda remains poised and resolute, as though she exists outside of time. With a mystical certainty, she utters a final, cryptic truth: "Everything begins and ends at the exactly right time and place…"

Cujo (1983)

Lewis Teague's film *Cujo*, based on Stephen King's novel, presents an intensely claustrophobic horror scenario: a mother and her young son are trapped inside a broken-down Ford Pinto, besieged by a rabid St. Bernard. Initially dismissed as a middling adaptation of King's work, *Cujo* has since garnered a cult following, celebrated for its unrelenting tension and psychological complexity. While the immediate horror emerges from the relentless assault of an infected animal, a deeper reading of *Cujo* reveals a film brimming with psychoanalytic resonance. Its horror does not merely stem from the threat of nature turned violent; rather, it manifests as the eruption of repressed emotional conflicts, primarily structured around the mechanisms of denial and cathexis.

Cujo, once a gentle and friendly St. Bernard, chases a rabbit into a cave, where he is bitten by a rabid bat. Meanwhile, the Trenton family—Vic, an advertising executive, his wife Donna, and their young son Tad—visit the rural home of mechanic Joe Camber for car repairs, unknowingly encountering the Camber family's beloved pet, Cujo. As tensions mount in the Trenton household due to Donna's affair with local playboy Steve Kemp, Cujo begins exhibiting the early symptoms of rabies, though no one notices. His condition rapidly deteriorates, leading him to kill Joe Camber's neighbour before mauling his owner to death.

With Vic away on a business trip, Donna and Tad return to the Camber property for more car repairs, only to be ambushed by the now-rabid Cujo. Trapped inside their broken-down Ford Pinto, they are subjected to a relentless blockade. The scorching sun exacerbates their suffering, forcing Donna to act before heatstroke or dehydration claims them. Each attempt at escape is thwarted by Cujo's vicious attacks, culminating in a prolonged and harrowing standoff that defines the film's nerve-shredding coda.

Now, let us consider the emotional energetics of Lewis Teague's film. Vic's profession matters here: his advertising agency is failing, and he is under enormous pressure due to a scandal over a breakfast cereal. The commercial campaign he has devised makes national news as several children have seemingly vomited blood after eating the ironically named "Sharp Cereals." The product is quickly recalled from all American stores.

The problem might have been caused by some red food dye, posing no real danger to consumers, but the optics are catastrophic, and serious damage has been done to Vic's business as a result. News anchors covering the story openly mock the advertising campaign, in which the so-called Sharp Cereal Professor extols the virtues of the product and, while tasting it, declares, "No, nothing wrong here." The TV commercial plays in a scene of the film where tension is palpable between Donna and secret lover Steve around the Trenton family dining table… indeed, something is decidedly very "wrong" here.

The structure of Vic's advertising hook, the insistence that there isn't anything untoward occurring, is an excellent cinematic example of the Freudian concept of denial: a defence mechanism where an individual refuses to accept or acknowledge a reality or fact that causes anxiety or discomfort. It involves the rejection of certain aspects of external reality that are too upsetting to the conscious mind, often because they challenge the person's self-image, beliefs, or emotional stability. Denial operates as a temporary refuge from trauma, yet in the long term, it can lead to the return of the repressed in a more grisly form. Vic's persistent avoidance creates a pressure-cooker effect—one that will ultimately find its explosive release.

Denial is the dysfunctional mode that Vic doggedly stays in regarding the state of his marriage, and I find it compelling that he discovers his wife's affair precisely when, driving one day, he happens to see a shirtless Steve talking to Donna near her car parked outside Steve's home. In my view, the Ford Pinto in this instance becomes a cathectic object which, in psychoanalysis, refers to a thing onto which an individual directs emotional energy, often unconscious. The term cathexis comes from the Greek, meaning "holding" or "investment." In Freudian theory, cathexis refers to the process of investing psychic energy (or libido) in an object, which can be anything the person has emotional attachment to, such as a loved one, a goal, or even a concept. The car—an inanimate object—becomes the unwitting conveyor of truth, exposing the very reality Vic had desperately sought to ignore.

In *Cujo*, the cathexis is the Ford Pinto, the smoking gun of Vic's failed marriage, literally containing and driving an illicit erotic attachment felt by his wife Donna. Initially in the film, the Ford Pinto is merely a practical object—Donna's vehicle. But once it is spotted outside Steve Kemp's house, it becomes an emblem of betrayal, the tangible evidence of an affair Vic can no longer ignore. Freud argued that we unconsciously charge objects with meaning, transforming them into receptacles for unresolved emotional tensions. So, the Ford Pinto must transform into the site of terror, breaking down on the Camber property, and getting repeatedly attacked by a crazed dog. The car, now immobile and under siege by a rabid animal, functions as a psychological theatre where suppressed anxieties resurface with violent intensity. *Cujo* literalises the claustrophobic horror of marital dysfunction—what was once a space of control becomes a trap, a nightmarish enclosure under attack.

Psychoanalytic readings of horror often focus on how monsters externalise internal fears, functioning as physical manifestations of repressed desires or anxieties. Cujo's transformation into a ravenous beast coincides with the film's mounting emotional tension, suggesting that the horror he enacts is not merely incidental but deeply rooted in the film's emotional terrain. As Donna and Tad sit sweltering in the Pinto, unable to escape, Cujo's relentless attacks symbolise an unconscious force that refuses to be suppressed.

It helps me to think about the cathexis as magnetised, drawing to itself a similar energy—a process that is amplified by denial. One might argue that Cujo's rampage is a dramatisation of Vic's latent aggression, displaced and externalised. The notion that he unconsciously wills his wife and child into a scenario of extreme suffering echoes the uncanny way in which guilt and unprocessed emotions manifest in the horror genre. The early images of children vomiting blood—a grotesque symptom of the cereal scandal—are alarmingly mirrored in the film's climax, as Tad convulses in terror, his small body harmed by dehydration and exhaustion.

The extended sequence of Donna and Tad antagonised by a rabid dog stages an unspeakable unconscious desire projected by Vic, maybe tapping into disturbing violent fantasies of punishing his family for Donna's extramarital affair. The transformation of Cujo from benign companion to savage aggressor mirrors the shift from denial to violent reckoning, wherein Vic's repression finds its monstrous avatar.

There comes a point where Vic can no longer carry on insisting that, "There's nothing wrong here." If *Cujo* teaches us anything, it is that repression is never permanent. Nature will bite back. And when it does, no advertisement, no polished surface, no carefully structured denial can hold it at bay.

Jaws (1975)

Steven Spielberg's *Jaws*, the original summer blockbuster, is based on Peter Benchley's 1974 novel. The film follows police chief Martin Brody, who, with the help of a marine biologist and a seasoned shark hunter, pursues a great white shark terrorising beachgoers in a summer resort town. On Amity Island, an unseen creature drags swimmers beneath the waves, prompting the police to shut down the beaches. However, Mayor Larry Vaughn, fearing the economic fallout, insists on reopening them. Oceanographer Matt Hooper confirms that an abnormally large shark is responsible for the attacks. When local fishermen catch a tiger shark, Vaughn seizes the opportunity to declare the waters safe. But Hooper, sceptical, performs a dissection and finds no human remains inside the stomach—confirming the true killer is still at large. Despite mounting evidence, Mayor Vaughn refuses to acknowledge the threat, dismissing claims that a great white is behind the incidents. On the Fourth of July weekend, with the seafront packed, the shark strikes again—entering a nearby lagoon, killing a boater, and nearly reaching Brody's son. Finally, a guilt-ridden Vaughn concedes, agreeing to hire the eccentric local shark hunter, Quint.

The *Jaws* theme revolves around an ominous ostinato of bass notes, which composer John Williams designed to represent the shark as an "unstoppable force of mindless and instinctive attacks." The simple, alternating two-note pattern became an iconic piece of suspense music, now synonymous with approaching danger. Williams described it as "grinding away at you, just as a shark would do—instinctual, relentless, unstoppable." Beyond its cinematic achievements, *Jaws* had huge cultural repercussions. Much like the iconic scene in Alfred Hitchcock's *Psycho* instilled a new anxiety of showering, *Jaws* made ocean swimming a source of fear for many viewers. Beach attendance declined and reported shark sightings increased. More worryingly, the film helped reinforce negative stereotypes about sharks, spurring waves of fishermen to slaughter thousands in competitive hunting tournaments. Steven Spielberg later expressed regret over the decimation of shark populations caused by the film's influence. Conservation groups argue that *Jaws* has made it significantly more difficult to persuade the public that sharks should be protected rather than feared.

I interpret *Jaws* as a topographical restaging of Freud's Hydraulic Model of the Mind. In this framework, the trajectory of desire is likened to fluid moving through a maze-like structure, circulating freely. When psychic energy encounters a blockage in one section, it redirects—like water—into another, finding alternative pathways within the mind. Desire is always in motion and propelled forward; if excessively censored, psychological turbulence ensues. Emotional equilibrium depends on the flow of this circulation. At the core of Freud's model, the Id serves as the primary source of spontaneous psychic energy, operating according to the pleasure principle—seeking immediate gratification regardless of social constraints, driven purely by the pursuit of pleasure. In contrast, the Ego, or conscious self, functions under the reality principle, acknowledging external limitations and negotiating between the Id's impulses and the demands of the real world.

When unconscious yearnings rise to the level of conscious awareness, they inevitably encounter the Superego—an internalised authority that compels the Ego to conform to societal norms and taboos, suppressing the original impulse. But repression does not equate to erasure. The energy of desire lingers, restless and undeterred, seeking alternative pathways to reassert itself. Typically, this desire circumvents censorship by adopting disguises—manifesting in slips of the tongue, furtive fantasies, or vivid dreams—always striving to dismantle the barriers imposed by the Ego.

Repressed urges do not stay buried forever. Instead, they "hitch a ride" back towards the brink of awareness, much like a spy infiltrating the land of consciousness with a fake passport, its identity concealed. Freudian analysis reveals where repression has taken hold, allowing these drives to be confronted directly. By bringing them into conscious awareness, libidinal energy is freed for sublimation, redirecting unconscious urges into creative or socially acceptable outlets. Freud argued that the unavoidable tension between these competing forces within the psyche forms the foundation of civilisation. In this light, the ocean in *Jaws* takes on a topographical significance—becoming a vast, unknowable reservoir, much like the Freudian unconscious. Meanwhile, the beach quite literally is a line in the sand, demarcating the threshold of conscious awareness.

So where do the *Jaws* characters fit within Freud's Hydraulic Model of the Mind? The untamed force of the shark unmistakably represents the Id—a primitive instinct operating without regard for logic or restraint. The Id is pure impulse, driven by raw desire, oblivious to the consequences imposed by the external world. In this sense, the shark serves as an embodiment of the aggressive and violent urges embedded within human nature—primal instincts that civilised society deems taboo. While the Ego ostensibly exists to maintain balance, ensuring that actions remain socially adequate, it often falls into a maladaptive cycle of denial—failing to acknowledge the ongoing battle between the Id and the Superego.

Instead of directly confronting the psychological implications of the shark, the Ego doubles down, calamitously refusing to acknowledge inner discord. In this light, the delusional Mayor Larry Vaughn functions as a manic Ego figure, insisting that the beach remain open despite the attacks: "Amity is a summer town. We need summer dollars. If the people can't swim here, they'll be glad to swim at the beaches of Cape Cod, the Hamptons, and Long Island." Vaughn is reminiscent of the classic HR manager archetype—wilfully ignoring deeper issues to preserve the illusion of order. His refusal to examine the bowels of the captured tiger shark perfectly illustrates this defensive stance: "Fellas, let's be reasonable. This is not the time or the place to perform some half-assed autopsy on a fish. I am not going to stand here and see that thing cut open." Operating in full Ego mode, Vaughn's role is to perceive the external world, make decisions, and solve problems. Yet, however well-intentioned, the Ego often resorts to defence mechanisms such as repression and denial—trying to superficially manage anxiety by shielding itself from uncomfortable truths.

The Superego functions as the moral and ethical authority of the psyche, an internalised set of societal standards governing right and wrong. Acting as a kind of conscience, it seeks to suppress the raw urges of the Id while driving the Ego towards an idealised sense of perfection. In *Jaws*, the Superego manifests as the abstract force of capital—the guiding principle behind Mayor Vaughn's decisions, strong-arming him to inhibit and ignore the primitive impulses of the Id (embodied by the shark). The Superego is rigid and absolute in its demands, and in this case, the "profit over people" mindset dictates the mayor's actions. Just as the Ego suppresses the Id under the illusion of maintaining order, Vaughn convinces himself that keeping the beaches open is in the town's best interest, downplaying the shark threat in a misguided attempt to preserve normality. In the name of uninterrupted economic growth, he stubbornly insists that the problem has been solved, when, of course, it hasn't. It is worth noting that the fictional setting of the film is Amity Island—"amity" meaning friendship and harmonious relations. This could be read as an extension of the Ego's wishful thinking, a woefully naive belief that starkly opposing forces of the psyche can peacefully coexist. The conceit of *Jaws*, however, is that the Ego and the Id are not besties—far from it. The beach, rather than remaining a benign site of leisure and safety, becomes a battleground; the Id violently asserts itself despite Vaughn's futile protests.

Neal Gabler analysed *Jaws* as presenting three distinct approaches to overcoming an obstacle: science (represented by Matt Hooper), spiritualism (embodied by Quint), and the common man (personified by Martin Brody). The film ultimately endorses the latter, positioning Brody as the one who succeeds where the others falter. To this, I would add that the three men who embark on their heroic quest together symbolise the commitment to rupturing the Ego's arbitrary and superficial boundaries. They represent the aspect of subjectivity that willingly undergoes a dark night of the soul, confronting and overcoming deep-seated fears. This journey is charged with *élan vital*—the raw life force—which I associate with the so-called "jaws of life," a euphemism for the hydraulic rescue tools (cutters, spreaders, and rams) used by emergency personnel to extricate victims from vehicle wreckage and other confined spaces. Ultimately, Quint—representing an unhealed trauma response—does not survive the ordeal. But Hooper and Brody complete their introspective mission, disentangling themselves from the phobic state via the jaws of life.

Glossary of Psychoanalytic Terms

- **Beautiful**—Burke's aesthetic category describing qualities that are harmonious, delicate, and pleasing to the senses.
- **Cathexis**—Freud's term for the investment of emotional or psychic energy into an object, person, or idea, which can become charged with emotional attachment and unconscious significance.
- **Dark Night of the Soul**—A metaphor for a profound spiritual or existential crisis, often involving suffering and transformation.
- **Denial**—A psychological defence mechanism in which an individual refuses to acknowledge an uncomfortable reality, suppressing distressing truths to maintain psychological stability.
- **Ego**—The rational, conscious self that mediates between the demands of the Id, the Superego, and reality.
- **Feminine Jouissance**—A Lacanian concept describing a non-hierarchical, boundless form of pleasure that exceeds rational comprehension.
- **Freudian Unconscious**—The part of the mind containing thoughts, memories, and desires that are repressed and not immediately accessible to conscious awareness.
- **Hydraulic Model of the Mind**—Freud's metaphor for the movement of psychic energy, likening it to fluid circulating through a system, redirecting when blocked.
- **Id**—The instinctual, pleasure-seeking component of the psyche, operating on the pleasure principle and unconcerned with social norms.
- **Libidinal Energy**—Freud's concept of psychic energy associated with sexual and life instincts, driving human behaviour.
- **Oedipal Complex**—Freud's theory of unconscious desires and rivalries in childhood, particularly a child's attachment to the opposite-sex parent.

- **Phallic Jouissance**—A Lacanian concept referring to the pleasure derived from authority, dominance, and symbolic power.
- **Pleasure Principle**—The Freudian concept that the Id seeks immediate gratification and pleasure, avoiding discomfort or pain.
- **Reality Principle**—The Ego's ability to delay gratification and navigate the real world by balancing desires with external constraints.
- **Repression**—A defence mechanism where the Ego pushes distressing thoughts, memories, or desires into the unconscious to avoid discomfort.
- **The Return of the Repressed**—Freud's concept that suppressed fears, desires, or traumas inevitably resurface in unexpected or distorted forms, often as unconscious symptoms or irrational anxieties.
- **Sublimation**—The process by which repressed desires are redirected into socially acceptable or creative outlets.
- **Sublime**—A concept in aesthetics and philosophy from Edmund Burke describing an overwhelming, awe-inspiring force that is both beautiful and terrifying, often linked to nature's vastness, power, and indifference to human existence.
- **Superego**—The internalised moral and ethical authority that enforces societal norms and represses the Id's impulses.

Aliens

4

Otherness, invasion, and existential danger

Certain aspects of the natural world tap into the primal fear of an earthly environment turning hostile; the alien subgenre expands this terror into the boundless unknown. While scary elements of nature expose the limits of human dominance over the world, alien horror dismantles the notion that humanity is even significant within the larger cosmos. It compels a reckoning with forces so vast and incomprehensible that they seem less like external entities and closer to manifestations of our own unconscious. In this subgenre, outer space is not solely an unfamiliar infinite expanse—it reflects psychological inner space, a limitless personal void where buried fears, desires, and anxieties take disquieting form.

The terror of alien horror arises from its destabilisation of certainty. While the natural world resists human control, the cosmic realm obliterates it, revealing a universe governed by laws indifferent to human survival. Encounters with extraterrestrial beings expose a fundamental split in knowledge, confronting us with life-forms so radically Other that they challenge our very definitions of identity, intelligence, and sentience. And yet, there is always a lingering suspicion that these alien entities are not wholly foreign—that the horror they invoke comes not just from their strangeness, but equally from their familiarity. They embody an uncanny doubling, reflecting aspects of human nature that remain unresolved or repressed. The alien is often depicted as an invader from beyond, but it can also function as a distorted projection of the self, a reminder that the greatest unknown is not in the distant stars, but within us.

War of the Worlds (2005)

Steven Spielberg's *War of the Worlds* follows an American dock worker struggling to keep his children safe and reunite them with their mother as towering alien war machines devastate Earth. Ray Ferrier, divorced from his ex-wife Mary Ann, is largely estranged from his family. Mary Ann, now pregnant by her new husband, is en route to Boston after leaving the children in Ray's care. When electromagnetic pulses of lightning strike Ray's Brooklyn neighbourhood, what first appears to be an unusual weather event soon reveals itself as the beginning of an alien invasion. As chaos unfolds, Ray must fight to protect his children while seeking refuge.

Massive tripod war machines erupt from beneath the ground, unleashing powerful energy weapons that disintegrate most onlookers into a fine grey dust. Across the globe, multiple tripods lay waste to major cities, their force shields rendering humanity's defences virtually useless. The alien pilots arrive via lightning storms, using them as a conduit to enter their war machines—implying that the tripods have been buried underground for thousands of years, lying dormant until now. In the end, the aliens succumb not to human weaponry but to Earth's smallest inhabitants— microbes. Lacking immunity to the planet's bacterial ecosystem, they perish en masse. Humanity, by contrast, has adapted and earned its place through natural coexistence with the biosphere. As screenwriter David Koepp put it, "Nature, in a way, knowing a whole lot more than we do."

The film contains several references that appear to invoke the events of 11 September 2001. (1) The atmosphere of the attacks is reflected in scenes of bystanders struggling to survive, with missing-persons displays echoing real-life post-9/11 imagery. (2) A Boeing 747 crashes into a suburban New Jersey neighbourhood, reinforcing the film's allusions to contemporary trauma. (3) US Marines engage in a futile battle against the tripods, paralleled by Ray's son Robbie, who insists on joining the fight despite its hopelessness. (4) Another moment of eerie resonance occurs when Ray and his daughter Rachel hide in a basement while a mechanical probe snakes into their space, searching for signs of human life—a moment that may symbolise the post-9/11 surveillance state and the systemic culture of watching citizens. *War of the Worlds* has been described as an anti-war film, depicting civilians fleeing rather than resisting, with survival prioritised over heroism. Spielberg sought to represent a real threat, explaining: "It's a wake-up call to face our fears as we confront a force intent on destroying our way of life."

A Freudian reading of *War of the Worlds* feels particularly apt, especially in relation to the family dynamic of Tom Cruise's character, Ray Ferrier. As a father alienated from his children, Ray takes on the role of transporting them to safety, quite literally "ferrying" them to the reassuring coordinates of their mother, Mary Ann, who physically embodies the symbol of life—her visible pregnancy reinforcing this connection. There is also something to be said about parenthood as a fearful odyssey—a journey that brings an acute awareness of the world's unknown dangers and its lurking darkness. In this treacherous landscape, "Ray"—true to his name—becomes a source of light, guiding his children with courage and hope, determined to shield them from trauma. Even when they resist him, expressing hostility or refusing to cooperate, he remains steadfast, embodying the impossible responsibility of parental protection in an unforgiving world.

A Žižekian analysis suggests that the shape of the alien invaders is significant; their tripod form evokes the structure of a camera, positioning the extraterrestrials as more than mere aggressors. Rather than engaging in conventional warfare, they impose an alienated gaze onto humanity—an unsettling act of observation through which suffering is both endured and permanently recorded. In this reading, destruction is not only physical but epistemic: the documentation of pain becomes ubiquitous and inescapable, rendering trauma impossible to suppress or recover from.

The film's reassuring ending aligns comfortably with Spielberg's signature brand of sentimental equilibrium—family members reunited, embracing in the glow of their hard-won survival, their triumph over an insurmountable threat complete. *War of the Worlds* ultimately functions as a modern fairytale, its final act neatly tied with a bow, allowing the audience to exhale after an unrelenting battle to stay alive. Despite the horrors endured, the film grants its characters, and by extension its viewers, the solace of closure—a sense of restoration after ordinary people and innocent children have borne witness to unimaginable terror.

The movie's disavowal of Harlan Ogilvy's murder—its deliberate omission from the final act—presents an intriguing psychological predicament. At one point, Ray and Rachel take shelter in a basement offered by Harlan, a character coded as deranged. When Ogilvy's frantic shouting threatens to alert the aliens, Ray reluctantly kills him. This moment situates madness firmly within the domain of the repressed, which must be excised to preserve the action-driven fight against an invading force. What we witness is a family on the run, their transformation occurring within hours: from ordinary citizens with a degree of societal privilege to refugees escaping mortal danger. In this precarious state, insanity is not a luxury they can afford. The philosophical problem of surviving an unspeakable threat shifts the moral framework, subtly absolving Ray of guilt for eliminating the perceived liability of mental illness. This, I would argue, is why Harlan Ogilvy's murder barely registers—a psychological blip, quickly discarded. His instability made him reckless and unpredictable; therefore, he had to go.

The foreclosure of madness when survival is at stake presents no immediate crisis of conscience. However, I would remind the reader that the repressed always returns—and the ghost of Harlan Ogilvy lingers as a strange spectre, a subtle wrinkle in the otherwise pristine sentimental fabric of Spielberg's *War of the Worlds*. Perhaps the "worlds" in the film's title do not refer solely to the clash between humanity and extraterrestrials, but also to the interior and exterior realms of the psyche. If so, Ray Ferrier may not be out of the woods just yet—his battle with psychological warfare may have only begun.

Invasion of the Body Snatchers (1956 and 1978)

In this section, I will examine Don Siegel's *Invasion of the Body Snatchers* alongside Philip Kaufman's remake, both adapted from Jack Finney's science fiction novel. These films are essential viewing for scholars of human psychology, offering a meditation on identity, conformity, and the fragility of the self—all while delivering strikingly elegant and daunting imagery. The basic storyline follows alien plant spores from space that invade Earth, growing into large seed pods capable of producing visually identical human copies. These duplicates assimilate physical characteristics, memory, and personality, yet remain devoid of all human emotion. Ostensibly, the pods are meant to be seductive. Their spokesperson, a psychiatrist, provides an authoritative voice appealing to the desire to "abdicate from human responsibility in an increasingly complex and confusing modern world."

The 1956 version of the film appears to comment on the dangers of America turning a blind eye to Joseph McCarthy's notorious witch hunt, which denounced citizens for supposed communist activities. Others have interpreted it as an allegory for the erosion of liberal values, particularly individual rights and democracy. The story is undeniably preoccupied with the loss of personal autonomy, a condition often associated with totalitarian regimes. However, the film's lead actor—coincidentally named Kevin McCarthy—stated in an interview that he saw no deliberate political messaging in the work, a claim echoed by producer Walter Mirisch, who remarked, "People read meanings into pictures that were never intended. It was a thriller, pure and simple."

Director Don Siegel spoke more openly about an underlying subtext that extended beyond a strictly political perspective, stating: "I think that the world is populated by pods, and I wanted to show them. So many people have no feeling about cultural things, no feeling of pain, of sorrow. I tried not to emphasise the reference to McCarthyism and totalitarianism because I feel that motion pictures are primarily to entertain, and I did not want to preach." I deeply appreciate this approach—filmmakers choosing not to overstate their own political or ideological leanings, instead allowing the cinematic material to function as a projective test, eliciting subjective and meaningful associations that naturally arise from spectators.

Philip Kaufman's 1978 remake of *Invasion of the Body Snatchers* retains the basic premise: humans are replaced by alien duplicates, each an exact replica of the original but stripped of all human emotion. Visually, the film is stunning. We witness gelatinous creatures abandoning their dying planet and drifting towards Earth, ultimately landing in San Francisco. The opening shots of this silent invasion are spectacular, immersing us in a devastating microbiological event. The aliens infiltrate Earth's ecosystem by latching onto plant life, initially presenting as small pods adorned with fragrant pink flowers.

Elizabeth, a laboratory scientist, brings one of the flowers home. The next morning, her boyfriend Geoffrey begins to act strangely—cold and distant. His behaviour, however, is not an isolated case; across the city, others report eerily similar experiences, convinced that their spouses or loved ones are somehow different. It soon becomes clear that the aliens are gestating inside pods before breaking open and spawning human duplicates that grow rapidly. The process occurs while the original person sleeps nearby—the pods copy their physical form, memories, and personality. Once the doubling is complete, the original human dies and disintegrates, leaving only the alien pod person in their place.

This directly connects to a psychiatric phenomenon known as Capgras Syndrome—a misidentification delusion in which a person believes that a loved one has been replaced by an identical-looking impostor, originally described as an illusion of look-alikes. This false belief is quite jarring, producing an uncanny effect that disrupts the expected reassuring quality of home. Instead of a space that feels reliable, predictable, and safe, an unwelcome sense of alienation takes hold. Capgras Syndrome taps into a fear that lurks beneath the surface of everyday life—the haunting possibility that a person we think we know is, in fact, someone else. This breeds mistrust and betrayal, shaking the very foundation of intimacy. But the anxiety does not stop there. A more disquieting awareness emerges: if absolute knowledge of others is unattainable, then so too is absolute knowledge of ourselves. We become strangers even to ourselves, disaffected from identities we assume to be stable.

At first, one might assume that the unfolding crisis resembles the early stages of a pandemic. But as collective dread escalates, speculation about the propagation of this unknown malignancy intensifies. The virulent germ is coded as biological warfare, tapping into Cold War-era fears of annihilation that loomed large when the film was made. One of the most startling moments in Philip Kaufman's remake features a hysterical man frantically warning bystanders, shouting, "They're coming! You'll be next!" before being chased through the streets by a mob and struck by a car. Bystanders silently watch him die without a trace of emotion. This moment powerfully underscores the horrific consequences of dehumanisation—the stripping away of empathy, warmth, and any lingering trace of human connection. The alien invasion does not simply imperil bodily survival; it threatens to erase what makes us human. The decline of people into unfeeling automatons is a terror that resonates far beyond its Cold War origins. I love the way this film captures a concern that continues to plague the modern era.

Alongside the numbing of emotional capacity, *Invasion of the Body Snatchers* evokes a powerful fear of losing our distinct identity through conformity and groupthink. This connects to a theory outlined in Sigmund Freud's seminal work *Civilization and Its Discontents* (1930), in which he explores the tension between the instinctual drive for freedom and society's demand for conformity and repression. Here, the conflict unfolds between our internal world and the rigid expectations of the world at large. The film reflects the psychological toll of this struggle, illustrating how human relationships—essential to establishing civilisation—can also inflict profound harm. To exist within society, we are compelled to accept its rules as binding; to resist them is to risk expulsion from the dominant group. Primal pleasure and autonomy are exchanged for the security and stability that living among others provides. We might ultimately feel that we belong, but we have paid a heavy price for this privilege—our liberty and individual rights. Herein lies the inescapable paradox: civilisation, designed to eliminate loneliness, instead becomes a source of unhappiness and neurosis, making aliens of us all. Freud warned that unchecked groupthink leads to the collapse of critical thought, resulting in a frightening community: totalitarianism and dystopia. History has, of course, proven him correct.

Another driving force of these films is the overwhelming sense of paranoia felt by those not yet invaded—the creeping suspicion that others are in cahoots, scheming in a covert, insidious plot. As Elizabeth observes in the remake, "I keep seeing these people all recognising each other. Something's passing between them all, some secret. It's a conspiracy." While this could be read as a clear-cut depiction of psychosis, I find it more compelling to interpret "conspiracy" as a signifier for the illicit dynamic between the central couple in Philip Kaufman's remake: Matthew and Elizabeth. Their relationship is, at its core, defined by infidelity—Elizabeth is spoken for, yet she and Matthew are in love. A straightforward romance is impossible; their bond is inherently complicated. The film invites us into their cloistered intimacy, framing them in tight, intimate shots as if drawing us into their hidden world. In this sense, the story becomes a conspiracy of two—a couple navigating the complexities of a forbidden affair by projecting their fears onto an external threat, a shared drama that binds them together. Viewed through this lens, Matthew Bennell—played masterfully by Donald Sutherland—emerges as the true "body snatcher" of the story, at least from the perspective of the hard-done-by Geoffrey, who loses his girlfriend to him. The film masterfully captures the terrifying alienation that can invade a space once filled with love, and I appreciate that it lends itself to multiple interpretations.

Phantasm Franchise (1979–2016)

Don Coscarelli's *Phantasm* is a cult horror franchise centred around the enigmatic Tall Man, a supernatural and malevolent undertaker who reanimates the dead, transforming them into dwarf zombies to do his bidding to achieve world domination. The story begins in a small town plagued by mysterious deaths, prompting young Mike to investigate. His search leads him to a shocking discovery: the local mortician is harvesting corpses, reshaping them into grotesque minions. Determined to stop him, Mike enlists the help of his older brother, Jody, and their friend Reggie, a local ice cream vendor. Together, they attempt to lure out and destroy the Tall Man, all while evading his creepy servants and the lethal, otherworldly silver sphere.

Rather than delving into *Phantasm*'s many plot twists and turns, I will focus on its recurring symbols to uncover the latent meanings at play. As a starting point, I'd like to highlight a comment from a member of the Evolution of Horror Podcast Discussion Group on Facebook—Chris, from the band Dischord. He remarked, "I know Phantasm is kind of schlocky, and perhaps I only love it as much as I do because I first saw it as a teenager, but it's always had a deeper significance for me." Chris goes on to note the film's themes of loss, its young protagonist's confrontation with mortality, the unknowable nature of death symbolised by the red planet, and the overall surrealism of the series. I fully agree with his interpretation and would like to build upon his assessment. It's worth noting that the concept for the original *Phantasm* came to Don Coscarelli in a dream. As a teenager, he once dreamed of running down endlessly long marble corridors, pursued by a chrome sphere intent on drilling into his skull with a needle. This origin is essential to understanding the film series, as the dream logic embedded within *Phantasm* demands that viewers interpret everything onscreen as a stand-in for something else.

Mike is the central protagonist of *Phantasm*—an ordinary boy who notices suspicious activity at the Morningside funeral home, where the Tall Man operates. When he uncovers a serious irregularity in the funerary process, the Tall Man begins to pursue him relentlessly. The notion of a young person spontaneously witnessing an event that provokes agitation, fear, and confusion aligns with Freud's concept of the primal scene—a traumatic moment that splinters development. The uncanny image of the freakishly strong Tall Man singlehandedly lifting a coffin into a hearse is secretly observed by Mike and absorbed as an enigmatic, violent event beyond his comprehension. The memory is imprinted during childhood, only to resurface later in the form of conversion symptoms and obsessive thoughts in adulthood. The primal scene can be understood as a moment that ruptures the innocence of childhood—a developmental threshold that forces Mike to confront darker realities he had previously been blissfully unaware of. Freud describes the primal scene as an "overwhelming unknown"—a trauma of excess excitement that the child is unable to fully process.

Jody is Mike's older brother and guardian. As Mike's only remaining family member, Jody represents a vital emotional anchor, and Mike clings to him, terrified that he will leave. This fear is tragically realised when the Tall Man murders Jody. Much of the *Phantasm* series is built upon the universal childhood fear of abandonment—a primal anxiety that resonates deeply. Children are innately hardwired to attach to caretakers, a process crucial for forming healthy interpersonal relationships later in life. Whether real or imagined, childhood abandonment disrupts the development of secure attachments and leaves lasting imprints on future relationships. Perceived abandonment often occurs before a child is old enough to comprehend that they are not responsible for others' actions. In such cases, children frequently internalise the loss, falsely believing themselves to be flawed, unlovable, or somehow to blame for the caretaker's departure.

The outlandish plot points of *Phantasm* may represent Mike's internal struggle to make sense of Jody's absence. So much psychic energy is spent constructing a narrative to explain why his brother was taken from him, which accounts for the franchise's recurring death motifs—mausoleums, cemeteries, and dug-up graves. Reggie, a close family friend, joins Mike's quest to destroy the Tall Man after losing his wife and daughter in a rigged explosion. His profession as an ice cream vendor is a curious detail, given the Tall Man's aversion to the cold, further reinforcing the symbolic divide between them. A recurring gag in the series involves Reggie's repeated, futile attempts to have sex with beautiful women. Here, the impulse towards sex functions as the photographic negative of the destructive instinct—once again positioning Reggie in stark opposition to the Tall Man. This dynamic mirrors Freud's concept of Eros (the life force) and Thanatos (the death drive), locked in an entwined dual system, destined to remain in eternal opposition.

This brings us to the Tall Man, an alien undertaker who was once a 19th-century human named Jebediah Morningside. After inventing a dimensional portal, he was transported to an unknown realm—only to return to Earth in villainous form. He routinely lays waste to entire towns, leaving zombies in place of the living, demonstrating his power not only to extinguish individual life but to eradicate culture itself. The Tall Man's true objective remains a mystery, though it clearly revolves around conquest and occupation. As a shape-shifter, he turns into The Lady in Lavender, his seductive feminine alter ego, who lures unsuspecting men to their deaths. This transformation introduces yet another psychoanalytic undercurrent in *Phantasm*: the ambivalent function of heterosexual intercourse, which initially promises intimacy and closeness but ultimately leads to total alienation.

A theoretical reading of this dynamic aligns with Jacques Lacan's infamous formula from the early 1970s: "Il n'y a pas de rapport sexuel," translated as "there is no sexual relationship." By this, Lacan meant that no direct, unmediated relation is possible between male and female human beings. He argued that an instinctive, natural connection between the sexes is unattainable because all sexuality is structured through the signifier—language acts as an unavoidable third party, mediating desire. Reciprocity between male and female discursive positions is impossible, as the Symbolic Order (language) is asymmetrical. Love, according to Lacan, is an illusion—an elaborate construct designed to mask the absence of harmonious interactions between the sexes. What exists instead is a relation not between two whole subjects, but between a subject and a partial object. For the man, the *objet petit a* occupies the place of the missing partner; in other words, Woman does not exist for him as an independent subject, but only as a fantasy object—the cause of his desire. This inherently alienating dimension of sexual intercourse is encapsulated by the Tall Man's shapeshifting abilities. His Lady in Lavender alter ego seduces and ensnares victims, disorienting them through the power of desire, embodying the treacherous mirage that masks the impossibility of true sexual relation.

The driving force behind *Phantasm* is Mike and Reggie's unwavering commitment to honouring their lost loved ones by ensuring they receive a proper burial. This theme resonates with a key idea from Jacques Lacan's seminar *The Ethics of Psychoanalysis* (1959): the imperative to remain true to one's convictions and desires. Lacan presents the Ancient Greek figure Antigone, from Sophocles' tragedy, as a model of ethical conduct. In the play, Antigone's brothers, Eteocles and Polynices, have slain each other in battle. Eteocles, who fought for the state of Thebes, is granted a hero's burial, while Polynices, deemed a traitor, is condemned to remain unburied—his body left to be ravaged by dogs and vultures. When Antigone pleads with Creon, the ruler of Thebes (and her uncle), to grant Polynices proper funeral rites, he refuses. Undeterred, Antigone defies his decree, burying her brother in secret and taking full responsibility for her actions. Her defiance leads to her imprisonment in a tomb, where she ultimately embraces her own death. Creon embodies an over-defended Ego, intolerant of any challenge to his authority—especially from a woman. In contrast, Antigone's act is defined by Lacan as truly ethical. She does not flee from responsibility or fear her own desire; rather, she proceeds in strict accordance with it. She is indifferent to the Ego's demand for happiness, avoiding hesitation or self-deception. Antigone exemplifies a principle of ethical conduct—one that transcends self-interest and refuses compromise in the face of injustice.

In a similar vein, Mike and Reggie in *Phantasm* embody Antigone's moral fortitude, passing Lacan's test of ethical conduct by remaining unwaveringly true to their desire. They endure relentless trials—trapped in nightmares, confined to psychiatric asylums, traversing interdimensional realms, and dodging lethal silver spheres—all in their quest to defeat the malevolent alien mortician, the Tall Man, who desecrates graves, preventing the proper burial of the dead, directly opposing their mission. Even if they ultimately fail to undo the full extent of the Tall Man's destruction, their resistance and open defiance—like Antigone's refusal to obey Creon—secure their ethical standing in a world increasingly devoid of moral integrity.

Alien (1979)

Ridley Scott's *Alien* stands as a towering achievement in science-fiction horror. Aboard the commercial starship Nostromo, the crew lies in cryo-sleep, suspended in stasis for their long return journey. Midway through the deep space voyage, the ship's computer, Mother, abruptly awakens them, having intercepted a mysterious transmission from a nearby planetoid. Upon landing—sustaining damage from the turbulent atmosphere and jagged terrain—the crew discovers a derelict alien vessel, inside which lies a vast chamber filled with egg-like objects. As they investigate, an organism suddenly bursts from one of the eggs, latching onto Kane's face through his helmet. Dallas and Lambert rush to bring the unconscious Kane back to the Nostromo, but as acting senior officer, Ripley enforces quarantine protocol, refusing them entry. However, science officer Ash overrides her decision, granting them access—an act that will have catastrophic consequences.

A defining moment occurs: Ripley's authority is deliberately undermined by Ash, creating an immediate opposition between them—one that will introduce a peculiar dynamic aboard the ship, which I will explore later. Meanwhile, Kane regains consciousness with slight memory loss but otherwise appears unharmed. The crew gathers for a final meal before returning to stasis, but the moment of calm is violently shattered—Kane suddenly begins choking and convulsing in agony. In a grotesque eruption, a small alien creature bursts from his chest, killing him instantly before scurrying off into the depths of the ship. The Xenomorph has arrived, and one by one, it begins systematically hunting the Nostromo's crew.

Ridley Scott deliberately conceals the full form of the Xenomorph for most of the film, shrouding its body in shadow to cultivate an atmosphere of terror and heightened suspense. By obscuring its shape, the film activates our worst fears as spectators—forcing us to imagine the horror that lurks beyond what is shown. Scott explained his approach: "Every movement is very slow, very graceful, and the alien alters shape, so you never really know exactly what he looks like. I've never liked horror films before, because in the end it has always been a man in a rubber suit. But the most important thing in a film of this type is not what you see, but the effect of what you think you saw."

Ripley uncovers a shocking truth: Ash is an android, secretly operating under corporate orders to ensure the alien's survival at all costs. The crew, deemed expendable, were never the priority—the true mission was to bring the Xenomorph back to Earth. Coldly detached, Ash expresses a chilling admiration for the creature, praising its psychology as "unhindered by conscience or morality" and taunting the crew about their slim chances of survival. At its core, *Alien* is structured around an epic power struggle—one between human agency, embodied by Ripley, and the calculated psychopathy of Ash, a fraud masquerading as an ally while remorselessly sabotaging those around him. Ripley is honest, conscientious, and professional;

she genuinely cares about the safety of her colleagues and works to secure their return home. Ash, by contrast, merely performs the superficial traits of humanity, all while betraying them from within—an imposter devoid of empathy, operating under a sinister corporate directive.

Ash's exposure as a duplicitous automaton invites the reading that machines are inherently antagonistic to the human condition—yet they remain dependent on us for system upgrades. This recalls a striking passage from Marshall McLuhan's writings: "Physiologically, man in the normal use of technology is perpetually modified by it, and in turn finds new ways of modifying his technology. Man becomes, as it were, the sex organs of the machine world, as the bee of the plant world, enabling it to fecundate and evolve ever new forms." This dynamic sets up a struggle between the erotic—humanity's life-giving, generative impulse—versus the cold, calculating logic of the machine. Here, the alien exploits and exacerbates human vulnerability without remorse. The Xenomorph's arrival shatters crew solidarity, isolating individuals and driving a fatal wedge between them. But, in truth, the mission was compromised long before the alien ever appeared—covertly invaded by the corporate interests of the Nostromo. What began as a dispute over inadequate pay descends into an existential crisis, an outright threat to life. Ultimately, profit over people emerges as the true alienating force—human resources are chewed up and spat out, sacrificed at the altar of technological advancement at all costs.

What happens between Ripley and Ash recalls a portion of Charlie Chaplin's powerful speech in *The Great Dictator* (1940):

> Soldiers! Don't give yourselves to brutes, men who despise you, enslave you; who regiment your lives, tell you what to do, what to think and what to feel! Who drill you, diet you, treat you like cattle, use you as cannon fodder. Don't give yourselves to these unnatural men! Machine men with machine minds and machine hearts! You are not machines! You are not cattle! You are men! You have the love of humanity in your hearts!

Ash is the very "machine man" Chaplin warns against—an AI devoid of empathy, blindly enforcing corporate interests at the expense of human life. He embodies capitalism's most ruthless logic, treating the crew as throwaway chattels. Ripley, by contrast, refuses dehumanisation. Deceived by a bot, she never relents—fighting relentlessly for her agency and dignity. Ash's Nabokovian name suggests his fate: reduced to nothing, while the human woman prevails.

H.R. Giger designed the alien to appear both alive and biomechanical, a stark contrast to the cold, industrial aesthetic of the Nostromo. For the interior of the derelict spacecraft and egg chamber, he sculpted much of the scenery using dried bones and plaster, creating an eerie fusion of organic and artificial textures. Veronica Cartwright described his sets as "erotic, visceral… like you're going inside some sort of womb." It's impossible to overlook *Alien*'s sexual overtones. Barbara Creed famously interpreted the film through the lens of the Monstrous-Feminine, identifying the alien's presence as an embodiment of the archaic mother. As she states, the movie is a dense network of female reproductive imagery: the uterine chamber of cryogenic pods, eggs, scenes of forced birth, and the Nostromo's narrow, winding corridors reminiscent of vaginal canals (Creed 1993, 19–20). Even the ship's life-support system is called Mother; Freud would have had a field day! The archaic mother—the pre-phallic, self-generating creator—is repressed in patriarchal ideology precisely because of her parthenogenetic ability to conceive without a male partner (Creed 1993, 20). *Alien* captures both the awe and terror of a woman's autonomy, her immense generative power, and the primal fear of returning to the mother, to our origins (Creed 1993, 18). Ripley's survival ultimately secures her Final Girl status, yet the film appears to align her with the archaic mother's strength—her formidable nature lingering indifinitely.

The facehugger's attack on Kane has frequently been interpreted as a metaphor for male rape, while the chestburster scene evokes the trauma of violent birth. The alien's phallic head and its method of piercing crew members further reinforce the film's pervasive sexual undercurrent. Screenwriter Dan O'Bannon explicitly described the chestburster moment as a symbol of the male fear of penetration, arguing that the facehugger's oral invasion serves as "payback" for the many horror films in which women are sexually assaulted by nefarious male characters. David McIntee, author of *Beautiful Monsters: The Unofficial and Unauthorised Guide to the Alien and Predator Films*, claims:

> *Alien* is a rape movie as much as *Straw Dogs*, *I Spit on Your Grave*, or *The Accused*. On one level, it's about an intriguing alien threat. On another, it symbolises parasitism and disease. And in terms of what was most important to the writers and director, it's about sex, and reproduction by non-consensual means. It's about this happening to a man.

McIntee further suggests that the film weaponises men's fears of pregnancy and childbirth, while simultaneously offering women a glimpse into male anxieties—forcing both genders to confront the horror of bodily defilement and reproductive terror.

O'Bannon later described the sexual imagery in *Alien* as overt and intentional:

> One thing that people are all disturbed about is sex. And I said "That's how I'm going to attack the audience; I'm going to attack them sexually. And I'm not going to go after the women in the audience, I'm going to attack the men. I am gonna put in every image I can think of to make the men in the audience cross their legs. Homosexual oral rape, birth. The thing lays its eggs down your throat, the whole number."

Psychoanalysis reveals that we are, at our core, aliens to ourselves. The unconscious is an uncharted landscape—brimming with repressed memories, aggressive impulses, conflicting desires, shameful instincts, and hidden dimensions we would rather not confront. This internal estrangement extends beyond the individual, permeating wider society. *Alien*'s depiction of the extraterrestrial as hostile and invasive can be understood as a projection of this psychic turbulence—manifesting in deep space what festers internally. Through the film's terrifying spectacle, we engage in a form of catharsis, expelling repressed anxieties and purging psychic tension.

Predator 1 and 2 (1987 and 1990)

Let's turn now to the thoroughly enjoyable first and second instalments of the *Predator* franchise. These films tap into a particularly unnerving psychological condition: the alienating effect of being watched—remotely, intensely, and with voracious intent. In John McTiernan's *Predator*, bona fide action movie star Arnold Schwarzenegger plays Vietnam War veteran Dutch, the leader of an elite paramilitary rescue team tasked with extracting a foreign cabinet minister and his aide, allegedly held hostage in guerrilla territory. Accompanying the team is CIA agent Al Dillon, Dutch's old war buddy, whose presence hints at ulterior motives.

After members of the guerrilla camp are mysteriously slaughtered, Dillon reveals the true motive behind their mission: to prevent a Soviet-backed invasion. But as the rescue team navigates the dense Central American rainforest, they become prey to an unseen force—the Predator, a technologically advanced alien that stalks them using a cloaking device. At first, Dillon assumes the guerrillas are responsible for the attacks, but it soon becomes clear that their pursuer is "not a man." The film's original concept revolved around the primal terror of being hunted, which was distilled into a high-stakes premise: an extraterrestrial targeting the most dangerous species—humans—and, among them, the most dangerous kind of man: a combat soldier.

Stephen Hopkins's *Predator 2* stars Danny Glover in an undeniably impressive performance. Set in Los Angeles a decade after the events of the first film, it follows a hardened police officer and his allies as they attempt to defeat the technologically advanced alien hunter. This time, the Predator prowls an urban jungle—LA, the hot spot for a brutal turf war between heavily armed Colombian and Jamaican drug cartels. Detective Lieutenant Michael Harrigan is under mounting pressure to solve a string of grisly murders, believing the culprit to be among the warring gangs. But FBI Special Agent Peter Keyes knows the truth: the killer is no ordinary criminal, but a fearsome extraterrestrial with superior night vision and the ability to render itself invisible. The film opens with the Predator watching from the shadows as a police shootout erupts between the Jamaicans, Colombians, and law enforcement—zeroing in on Harrigan as he rescues wounded officers from the firefight. A key aim of the sequel was to expand on the Predator's origins and motives, revealing that the creature has been visiting Earth for centuries—tracking, stalking, and preying on humans with calculated precision.

My reading of these two films is that they hinge predominantly on a highly aggressive form of voyeurism—the Predator's intense pleasure in watching from the shadows, tracking humans by detecting their body heat. This is what turns the creature on—not sexually, but strictly in terms of the Eros function, the animating drive that propels an organism into action. Linked to this is the discombobulated, paranoid uncertainty experienced by the Predator's prey—humans who are being militantly watched and overpowered. I would argue that this lopsided interaction creates a profoundly alienating condition for the target of covert stalking, generating a horror element within these otherwise straightforward sci-fi action films.

In psychoanalysis, voyeurism refers to the act of obtaining sexual pleasure from observing others, often without their knowledge. This may involve watching someone engaged in sexual activity, undressed, or clothed in a way the voyeur finds arousing. Crucially, voyeurism is a deviant expression of sexuality that relies on looking without being detected to achieve arousal. Closely linked to this is scopophilia—the pleasure derived from looking at an object or person. Freud explored scopophilia as a basic aspect of human curiosity, integral to the psychological development of personality in childhood. However, other theories suggest that, when taken to an extreme, scopophilia can lead to psychological derangement, causing an individual to withdraw from reality into a detached world of fantasy.

Freud argued that scopophilia becomes a sexual perversion when it ceases to be merely preparatory to a normal sexual aim and instead supplants it entirely. He provided a metapsychological explanation for the instinct to look, centring on the voyeur-exhibitionist dynamic and the reversal of activity into passivity, all in relation to a precise object: the sexual member. The voyeur modifies the instinctual currents of seeing—seeking to observe another's genitals while concealing his own. At the same time, he also attempts to be seen looking, responding to what he perceives as the other's desire to be watched.

Both *Predator* films can be read as elaborate psychosexual fantasies—men flaunting their phalluses, hyper-aware of being watched. And I don't mean this disparagingly; on the contrary, I happen to sympathise with them. The many montages in the original *Predator* of muscle-bound men brandishing handguns, rifles, AKMs, AK-47s, shotguns, machine guns, launchers, pyrotechnic dischargers, and hand grenades… Then—in the sequel—a testosterone-fuelled spectacle of pistols, Smith & Wessons, Colt Commanders, Hardballer Longslides, revolvers, submachine guns, Heckler & Kochs, Uzis, Mossbergs, and Iver Johnsons… This colossal arsenal designates the frantic desire to counter the discursive seat of power occupied by Predator's omnipotent, all-seeing thermal vision. And those are just weapons used by humans, don't even get me started on what kinda heat the Predator's packin'!

These films dwell on an existential tension—humans becoming acutely aware of their alienation and lack, precisely because they are under constant surveillance by an unseen entity. The natural response to this disaffecting occurrence is to reach for the biggest, baddest weapon at their disposal. The firearm serves as more than just a defence against physical harm; it also masks the imaginary void that fuels psychological suffering. The knowledge that the true seat of power remains elusive triggers a desperate bid to reclaim it through an outlandish display of violence. The excessive spectacle of macho action men parading through the *Predator* films, guns in hand, is an unconscious admission precisely of the very opposite of power. Under the eroticised watchful eye of the alien, they are stripped bare—naked, exposed, vulnerable. Their reaction? Overcompensation.

Yes, the alien occupies a discursively privileged position, but this comes with a downside—fear that its power might be confiscated. In Freudian terms, this equates to castration anxiety, compelling the Predator to devise strategies of containment for human bodies. Its suppressive, spying tendencies in both films result in an overinvestment in human body parts, which become exaggerated, fetishised, and over-endowed with meaning—neutralising their threat as a castrating force. The Predator's vision, as a symbol of surveillance, takes on a distinctly phallic significance—deeply aligned with the cinematic image itself, providing a safe distance for the emergence of voyeurism, which is bound up with the principle of lawless seeing.

By appropriating humans as an image, the Predator reduces them to objects of pleasure while remaining detached from the intimate dimensions of their lives. It does not seek connection or exchange, only the gratification of seizing the human form against its will. The goal is not merely to glimpse what is concealed by modesty or cultural taboos, but to dismantle the human body entirely. The voyeur fixates on what is forbidden to annihilate physical integrity—replacing a unified image with a fragmented one. The instinct to see is filtered through disavowal and fetishisation in a desperate attempt to negate castration. In its obsessive gaze, the Predator strips humans of agency, reducing them to debased objects—arguably reflecting the pervasive voyeuristic tendencies of modern culture.

The Thing (1982)

John Carpenter's science-fiction horror film *The Thing* is based on John W. Campbell's 1938 novella *Who Goes There?* It follows a group of American researchers in Antarctica who encounter the eponymous "Thing"—a parasitic alien life-form capable of assimilating and perfectly imitating any organism. It has no fixed form, no higher purpose beyond survival. As the researchers realise that any one of them could already be the Thing, paranoia and conflict consume the group, eroding their trust and plunging them into a desperate fight to remain alive.

The Thing was met with scathing reviews—critics balked at its cynical, anti-authoritarian tone and grotesquely graphic special effects. *Cinefantastique* even dubbed it "instant junk" and "the quintessential moron movie." *The Los Angeles Times* condemned it as "bereft, despairing, and nihilistic." Carpenter later reflected that audiences rejected the film for being too bleak, particularly during a time of economic recession in America. Yet, as is so often the case, *The Thing* was reappraised and found redemption in later years—now revered as one of the greatest sci-fi horror films ever made, with a devoted cult following.

Carpenter's film is steeped in paranoia and doubt. At its core, it explores the breakdown of trust within a small, isolated community—where the creeping suspicion that people are not who they claim to be destabilises all sense of security. It embodies the erosion of belief in others, the fear of betrayal, and, ultimately, the treachery of our own bodies. The film thrusts us into a misanthropic vortex, where even our closest allies become unrecognisable, spiralling into a Kafkaesque cynicism towards larger institutions and the very fabric of human connection.

A way to grasp *The Thing*'s theoretical framework is through its notorious "chest chomp" scene—a masterclass in practical effects designed by Rob Bottin. During a tense confrontation with helicopter pilot R.J. MacReady, Norris, the station's geologist, collapses and is rushed to the outpost's emergency room. As Dr. Copper attempts to revive him with a defibrillator, Norris' chest suddenly snaps open, revealing a gaping maw that clamps down on the doctor's outstretched forearms. In a shocking instant, Copper's arms are severed by the monstrous jaws emerging from inside the body he thought he was saving. The "Thing" operates in direct opposition to the chestburster from *Alien*. Whereas Ridley Scott's creature violently erupts from within, leaving only death in its wake, Carpenter's Thing is a settler-colonial monster—one that insidiously takes over its victims, hijacking their life force to sustain itself. The chest chomp sequence is a perfect visual metaphor for this inversion: humans are more useful to the Thing alive than dead. It dominates from within, and we devour what it commands us to.

The Thing does not speak, nor does it offer a motive for its actions—it simply survives, ruthlessly and without hesitation. It attacks, consumes, and perfectly imitates individuals, replicating their memories and behaviours with uncanny precision. It multiplies endlessly, even wielding opposition in a self-benefiting way; the human subject is subsumed by an alien copy. Den of Geek writers Mark Harrison and Ryan Lambie suggest that the essence of humanity lies in free will, which the Thing strips away—possibly without the victim even realising they have been commandeered. In a 1982 interview, Carpenter described *The Thing* as "pro-human," stating: "It's better to be a human being than an imitation or let ourselves be taken over by this creature who's not necessarily evil, but whose nature it is to simply imitate, like a chameleon." The film taps into an existential terror—not just of annihilation, but of becoming a hollow facsimile, a being that merely performs the conduct, opinions, and values of others rather than possessing any true inner convictions. This recalls Oscar Wilde's lament: "It's tragic how few people ever possess their souls before they die. Nothing is more rare in any man than an act of his own. It is quite true. Most people are other people."

At this juncture, I want to introduce Jacques Lacan's theory of the lamella, the imaginary bodily organ of the libido, as outlined in *The Four Fundamental*

Concepts of Psychoanalysis. This is the perfect conceptual device for approaching the cinematic texture of *The Thing*. The lamella is the "undead," indestructible organ of the libido—a form of existence prior to subjectivity, pure drive without limitation. Lacan describes it as:

> Something entirely flat, moving like an amoeba through everything, outliving every division, surviving every fragmentation. Just imagine what would happen if that covered your face while you are asleep. You would have to fight with such an entity. This lamella, this non-existent organ, is the libido as a pure urge to be alive, that is to be immortal, to be alive without needing an organ, to be alive in a simplified and indestructible way.

Srećko Horvat compellingly applies this Lacanian concept to *The Thing*, arguing that the alien embodies the *lamella*—a formless, infinitely adaptable force that counterattacks destruction. In his article *The Future Is Here* (published by NeMe), he connects this to capitalism's ability to absorb and repurpose everything, including resistance itself, making opposition futile. *The Thing*, like capitalism, thrives because it has no stable form; it mutates to fit any environment.

Thus, if the "Thing" represents the lamella, its ghastly effect lies in mimicry as well as radical plasticity. It does not simply replicate—it is everything and nothing at once, an entity with infinite morphing potential. The true terror is the loss of identity; the devastating realisation that selfhood was never substantial to begin with, leading to the total erasure of the subject. The researchers at Outpost 31 fear death as well as *Thingification*—moving, speaking, and acting while no longer existing as themselves. Unlike *Invasion of the Body Snatchers*, assimilation here is silent and seamless. As paranoia deepens, it exposes an existential crisis: what does it mean to be human when humanity itself can be worn as a mask? While Horvat sees *The Thing* as mirroring capitalism's adaptability, I argue that it radicalises the concept further. Unlike capitalism, which still relies on social exchange, *The Thing* operates without ideology or structure. It does not attempt to persuade or negotiate, it simply *persists*. In this way, the lamella offers the perfect framework for understanding the horror of Carpenter's film: a nebulous, ever-morphing drive to exist.

If the horror of *The Thing* lies in its limitless adaptability, this reflects an unsettling truth about human existence: survival often depends on the ability to blend in. Social functions hinge on consensus—on occupying a predefined space within the social structure. Imitation becomes a necessary means of survival. In *Camouflage*, Neil Leach argues that imitation reflects a deep-seated desire to belong:

> The compulsion to conform underpins all human behaviour. We are governed by trends. We follow fashion in our clothing, our hairstyles, and even in our mannerisms and personal behaviour; we subscribe to dominant ideologies of taste in all aspects of our lifestyle. For to follow fashion—although supposedly an act of individual expression—might in fact be an act of collective behaviour. We are often content to erase almost all our individuality through subscribing to cultures of conformity, most especially in religious communities, military groupings, sports teams, and corporate identities. We human beings are largely conformist creatures driven by a chameleon-like urge to adapt to the behaviour of those around us.

Naturally, Carpenter's "Thing" is no benign chameleon, desperate for love and acceptance. It is a surplus of the organic, an overabundance of life itself. While it may be the purest cinematic embodiment of Lacan's bizarre libidinal organ—the undead, indestructible lamella—it is not necessarily evil. It simply wants to live, like the rest of us. And yet, it is precisely this connection to our own survival impulse—the drive to persist by blending in—that makes *The Thing* so rich in psychic tension.

Event Horizon (1997)

One of my favourite sci-fi horror films is Paul W.S. Anderson's *Event Horizon*. Set in 2047, it follows a crew of astronauts dispatched on a rescue mission after the long-lost spaceship *Event Horizon* mysteriously reappears in orbit around Neptune. Upon boarding, the rescue team finds no survivors—only evidence of a massacre. As they search for answers, each crew member begins experiencing vivid hallucinations tied to their deepest fears and regrets, subjective horrors that feel unnervingly real. Eventually, they uncover a chilling video log of the original crew engaged in an orgy of violence—mutilating and desecrating one another in a frenzy of madness. The footage ends with the ship's captain, holding out his own eyeballs gouged from their sockets, while uttering the Latin phrase "Liberate tutemet ex inferis"—"Save yourself from hell." The team soon learns the horrifying truth: the Event Horizon was an experimental vessel designed to bend space-time with its gravity drive. But in doing so, it vanished entirely from our universe—allowing a malevolent entity to take hold. Now, the ship itself is alive, a sentient emissary of an unimaginable, hellish dimension.

In general relativity, an event horizon marks the boundary in space-time beyond which nothing can escape—not even light. In layman's terms, it is the ultimate "point of no return," where gravitational pull becomes so immense that escape is impossible. Most associated with black holes, an event horizon ensures that any light emitted from within can never reach an outside observer. Likewise, any object approaching the horizon appears to slow down infinitely, never quite passing through. As this happens, its image becomes increasingly red-shifted—its wavelength stretching longer as it recedes from view.

Thinking through these concepts, I can't help but interpret *Event Horizon* through the lens of the Freudian Unconscious—a realm of veiled mental processes that unfold automatically, beyond empirical observation. This includes repressed impulses, subliminal perceptions, habits, and implicit knowledge. Freud argued that the most significant psychic events occur "below the surface," as if submerged in a black hole of the conscious mind. In psychoanalysis, the Unconscious functions as a "storage facility" for socially unacceptable desires, traumatic memories, and painful emotions—material forcibly buried through repression. The conscious self, in this view, operates as an adversary, struggling to keep these suppressed elements locked away. Crucially, the Unconscious is not merely everything outside mindful awareness but specifically that which is actively kept out—what we don't want to know. These bottled-up thoughts remain inaccessible to ordinary introspection, yet they surface indirectly—through free association, jokes, slips of the tongue, dream analysis, and, in our digital age, perhaps even an unfiltered glance at one's browser history.

Unlike his medical contemporaries, Freud viewed dreams as valid psychic phenomena—wish-fulfilments that demanded integration into waking mental life. He famously described dreams as "the royal road to the unconscious," believing that because Ego defences are lowered during sleep, repressed material emerges in symbolic form, offering valuable insight into the workings of the unconscious mind. Freud distinguished between manifest content (what the dreamer remembers and articulates) and latent content (the hidden, symbolic meaning beneath the surface). The goal of psychoanalysis is to uncover buried psychic material, accessing the Unconscious through symbolic clues to achieve catharsis, bringing repressed trauma into awareness. Anderson's *Event Horizon* offers a strikingly vivid topographical representation of the Unconscious in action, illustrating not only how it operates but why it terrifies us.

As one character observes, "There are connections between the readings and the hallucinations, like they are all part of a defensive reaction of some kind of immune system. This ship is reacting to us, and the reactions are getting stronger. The ship brought back something with it, a life force of some kind... it's alive." The Event Horizon breached the boundaries of the known universe and returned from a dimension beyond human comprehension. In its wake, it carries a nightmare—a smorgasbord of everything we have worked tirelessly to expel from consciousness. Worse still, it adapts, adjusting itself to our own psyches, reflecting bespoke horrors from which there is no escape. Miller is haunted by a subordinate he was forced to abandon to his death; Peters sees her son, his legs riddled with lesions; and Weir is tormented by the eyeless spectre of his late wife, who urges him to join her in death.

I can't help but connect *Event Horizon* with Andrei Tarkovsky's 1972 sci-fi art film *Solaris*, an adaptation of Stanisław Lem's novel. The story follows psychologist Kris Kelvin, sent to a space station orbiting Solaris—a planet covered by an oceanic surface that mimics recognisable forms. Scientists suspect that Solaris is a vast, sentient brain, capable of reading human minds. Soon after his arrival, Kris encounters his dead wife, Hari, who years earlier took her own life after he abandoned her. Every attempt to rid himself of her fails; when he ejects her into space, she rematerialises the next day. Analysis of her tissue reveals she is not composed of atoms like ordinary human beings—beneath a certain micro-level, there is nothing but void. Hari is not a person but an embodiment of Kris's traumatic fantasies. A fragile yet inescapable spectre, she exists in the liminal space between two deaths, doomed to eternally return.

Both *Solaris* and *Event Horizon* offer striking illustrations of how the Unconscious operates. When one commits to true self-reflection—dismantling the barriers that keep repressed material at bay—what emerges is often terrifying in a deeply personal way. The orgiastic video log in *Event Horizon*, with the captain's chilling warning, "Save yourself from hell," can be read as the Ego's last word of caution. The conscious personality's primary role is to suppress forbidden impulses, and the Ego functions as the ship's captain, desperately navigating the stormy waters of the psyche—warning of what lurks beneath.

The Event Horizon captain gouging out his eyes recalls the myth of Oedipus, who, upon realising he has fulfilled the prophecy—killing his father and marrying his mother—blinds himself in horror. The act is a refusal to perceive, a desperate attempt to unsee an unbearable truth. Likewise, the crew aboard Event Horizon, confronted with their deepest fears, might feel the same compulsion—to eradicate the terrifying vision by tearing out their own eyes. But as a faithful Freudian, I would offer the opposite advice to the captain's grim warning. Don't waste time trying to *save* yourself from Hell—you'll end up circling back anyway. No, stick around. Get real familiar with Hell. Learn its corridors, memorise the trap doors. Let it shape you, make you stronger, wiser. The only way out is through… so, *see you in Hell!*

They Live (1988)

John Carpenter's sci-fi action movie classic *They Live* follows a drifter who discovers through special sunglasses that the ruling class are aliens concealing their appearance and manipulating people to consume, breed, and conform to the status quo, via subliminal messages in mass media. Carpenter stated that the film's political subtext stems from his dissatisfaction with the economic policies of then-US President Ronald Reagan and the increasing commercialisation of both popular culture and policymaking. He remarked:

> The picture's premise is that the "Reagan Revolution" is run by aliens from another galaxy. Free enterprisers from outer space have taken over the world, and are exploiting Earth as if it's a third world planet. As soon as they exhaust all our resources, they'll move on to another world. I began watching TV again. I quickly realized that everything we see is designed to sell us something. It's all about wanting us to buy something. The only thing they want to do is take our money.

To underscore this critique, Carpenter conceived of the sunglasses as a metaphorical tool for seeing the truth—rendering reality in stark black and white. The aliens themselves were designed to resemble ghouls, with Carpenter explaining that because they corrupt humanity, they too are distortions of the human form. At its core, *They Live* is an indictment of yuppie culture and the unchecked greed of late-stage capitalism.

The idea for *They Live* originated from Ray Nelson's short story *Eight O'Clock in the Morning*, which follows a man who, after being placed in a trance by a stage hypnotist, awakens to a horrifying truth—the entire human race has been hypnotised, and alien creatures secretly control the world. He has only until eight o'clock in the morning to break their hold and expose the reality hidden in plain sight.

Sophie Fiennes's 2012 documentary film *The Pervert's Guide to Ideology*, presented by philosopher and psychoanalyst Slavoj Žižek, offers an incisive reading of *They Live*. Žižek uses the film's central trope—the special sunglasses that reveal hidden truths—to illustrate his definition of ideology. In the movie, Nada tells Frank, "I'll give you a choice: either put on these glasses or start eating that trashcan." To this, Žižek responds:

> I already am eating from the trashcan all the time. The name of this trashcan is ideology. The material force of ideology makes me not see what I am effectively eating. It's not only our reality which enslaves us. The tragedy of our predicament when we are within ideology is that when we think that we escape it into our dreams, at that point we are within ideology.

Žižek expands on this by positioning Nada as a "pure subject," stripped of substantial identity—his name, *Nada*, meaning "nothing" in Spanish. A homeless worker in LA, Nada stumbles upon a pair of sunglasses that function as "critique of ideology" lenses, revealing the hidden messages beneath advertising, posters, and media spectacle. Though we are told we live in a post-ideological society, Žižek argues that contemporary ideology does not address us as subjects who must sacrifice for a greater cause, but rather as consumers of pleasure. Instead of commands like "Do your duty," we are interpolated—addressed by authority—with seductive imperatives: "Realise your true potential. Be yourself. Lead a satisfying life."

Žižek argues that when you put on the sunglasses in *They Live*, you don't just see hidden messages—you see dictatorship embedded within democracy. It's the invisible order that sustains the illusion of freedom. Typically, we assume that ideology distorts reality, that it functions like a set of glasses that blurs our vision, and that the critique of ideology should remove these lenses so we can finally see the world as it truly is. But *They Live* exposes this as the ultimate illusion. Ideology is not an external force imposed upon us—it is the very fabric of how we undergo reality. It shapes our spontaneous relationship to the world, structuring how we find meaning and, crucially, how we derive enjoyment. Žižek elaborates:

> Stepping out of ideology hurts. It's a painful experience, you must force yourself to do it. This is rendered in a wonderful way with a further scene in Carpenter's film where Nada tries to force his friend Frank to also put the glasses on. It's the weirdest scene because the fight is eight, nine minutes. It may appear irrational because, why does this guy reject so violently to put the glasses on? It's as if he is well aware that spontaneously he lives in a lie, and the glasses will make

him see the truth, but that this truth can be painful. It can shatter many illusions. This is a paradox we have to accept: the extreme violence of liberation. You must be forced to be free. If you trust simply your spontaneous sense of well-being, you will never get free. Freedom hurts.

I completely agree with Žižek's reading of *They Live*, and I want to push this idea further—specifically, why free market ideologues come to embody an alienating, almost otherworldly force in the lives of ordinary workers under neoliberalism. In the 1980s, Ronald Reagan and Margaret Thatcher famously declared that "There is no alternative" to laissez-faire economics. They spearheaded a privatisation bonanza, slashed public spending, deregulated risky commercial practices, and inflicted fiscal austerity. We were promised that unrestricted wealth accumulation at the top would ultimately benefit all, that prosperity would "trickle down." But in reality, the rich only grew richer while the poor were left further behind. What neoliberalism has given us is not a well-ordered system of monetary rationality, but a kind of Wild West casino-style economics—a ruthless, winner-takes-all game, where those without wealth are left fighting over scraps.

Carpenter's *They Live* demonstrates the stark contrast between lived experience and the incessant propaganda of an aspirational fantasy—a designer dream peddled to the masses, utterly disconnected from the material reality of scarcity. As Žižek suggests, turning a blind eye to this contradiction is, in many ways, a natural impulse. Clinging to neoliberal ideology provides a sense of stability, an escape from the overwhelming burden of true freedom. But I would argue that this wilful denial generates a dangerous cognitive dissonance. We are forced to pretend we don't know what we, in fact, know all too well—despite the overwhelming evidence.

This ever-widening psychological gap, I would argue, is the true source of alienation—an abyss into which we continue to drift, bearing witness to economic injustice while simultaneously participating in its gaslighting script, unable to call it out. The ghoulish features of *They Live*'s alien overlords are ultimately a projection—a displacement of our own fractured state, living in estrangement from ourselves. As always, it is far easier to imagine an externalised perpetrator, a malevolent phantom out there, than to confront our own complicity—our failure to act decisively when the moment demands it. This, in my view, is the true strength of Carpenter's film. Recognising our own atomisation at the heart of the story is crucial if we are ever to work towards a meaningful response to economic inequity. If we refuse to face this, we remain in a deadlock—forever eating out of the trashcan of ideology.

Signs (2002)

M. Night Shyamalan's sci-fi mystery thriller *Signs* follows Graham Hess, a former Episcopal priest who now lives on a remote farm with his two children, Morgan and Bo. Since the recent death of his wife, Colleen, in a tragic car accident, Graham has lost his faith and abandoned the church. His younger brother, Merrill—a former minor-league baseball player—has moved in to help the family navigate their grief and keep the farm running.

One day, large crop circles—believed to be alien navigational markers—appear in Graham's cornfield. Soon, similar formations are spotted worldwide, and mysterious lights hover over major cities. As a full-scale alien invasion unfolds, the Hesses barricade themselves inside their home. When the aliens break in, the family retreats to the basement, where Morgan suffers a severe asthma attack but manages to survive the night. The next morning, a wounded alien infiltrates the house and takes Morgan hostage. Recalling Colleen's dying words, Graham tells Merrill to "swing away" with his baseball bat. The alien sprays a lethal toxin towards Morgan, but Graham retrieves his son as Merrill relentlessly strikes the creature, knocking over glasses of water left behind by Bo—the liquid scorching the alien's skin. Outside, Morgan regains consciousness after Graham administers his medication. His constricted lungs had prevented him from inhaling the alien's poison—an outcome Graham interprets as divine intervention, restoring his faith in a higher power.

M. Night Shyamalan's cameo as the driver responsible for Colleen's tragic death—an event that shattered Graham's faith and destabilised the Hess family—functions symbolically as a stand-in for the role of God in human lives. The director inserting himself into the narrative, testing his characters, and guiding them onto a redemptive arc mirrors the way divine intervention unfolds in the stories of the Abrahamic religions. In this sense, Shyamalan plays an almost omnipotent force, setting trials in motion that ultimately lead to revelation.

The plot of *Signs* hinges on what we might call coincidences—a remarkable concurrence of events that seem random yet prove essential. Graham's faith is restored not through divine revelation, but through recognising a meaningful pattern in the family's encounter with the alien. Every detail, once arbitrary, now appears deliberate: Bo's habit of leaving half-full glasses of water around the house, Morgan's asthma, Merrill's past as a baseball player—all elements that, in hindsight, served a crucial purpose. This recalls Carl Jung's concept of synchronicity—the idea that certain events appear meaningfully connected despite lacking any direct causal link.

Synchronicity describes the subjective experience of coincidences that, while seemingly unrelated, feel meaningful. Jung proposed that such occurrences reflect an unknown connection between inner thoughts and external events—one that transcends conventional causality. He considered synchronicity to be a vital function of the human psyche, though he also warned that an overreliance on it could tip into psychosis. As a concept, Jung framed synchronicity as a hypothetical, non-causal principle—an unseen thread linking significant coincidences. While mainstream science largely dismisses it as unfalsifiable, Jungian psychology maintains that recognising the compensatory meaning of synchronicity can expand consciousness, provided it does not spiral into superstition.

At its core, *Signs* is a film about faith—but not necessarily religious faith. Psychoanalytically speaking, it explores the fundamental human need to construct narrative, even in the face of chaos, confusion, and destruction. It's the belief that meaning can still be found, even in an indifferent universe where alienation takes hold. By employing the alien invasion trope, *Signs* positions the absence of faith as a form of estrangement—the pain felt when connection with the Symbolic Order is severed. It's a rejection of signs themselves, rooted in a profound distrust of interpretation. Graham's suffering stems not just from grief, but from his refusal to believe that his wife's death could hold any meaning at all. The loss of Colleen is an unbearable trauma, rendering faith incomprehensible to him. As a result, he grows distant from his family, his inability to perceive a greater pattern isolating him further. Here, alienation goes beyond loneliness—it is the certainty that miracles are impossible, that nothing can surprise us anymore.

There's a wonderful moment in *Signs* where the alien signals are best captured through Bo's baby monitor—when the entire family gathers close, moving as a single unit. The implication is clear: connection brings clarity. Graham's faith is ultimately restored not through divine intervention, but through the recognition of his family's role in his life. The faded spot on his bedroom wall, where a cross once hung, is later shown to be freshly painted and adorned with framed family photos—this is what he believes in now.

But what is the implication of the aliens in *Signs* disappearing in plain sight, blending seamlessly into their surroundings? Why does their ability to mimic the environment matter? I believe it speaks to the nature of alienation itself—the way it seeps in, unnoticed, precisely when the real world is copied, distorted, and encroached upon. The alienating force is always present, lurking at the edges of perception; the potential to disconnect never truly disappears. *Signs* suggests that faith in meaning cannot be taken for granted—alienation is an ever-present possibility. What matters is the commitment to the search, the refusal to surrender to meaninglessness, no matter the outcome.

Which brings me to my final theoretical point in this section. Jacques Lacan famously stated, "Love is giving something you don't have." He illustrated this with a striking metaphor: you reach out for a ripe fruit, only for it to transform into a hand reaching back at you. The fruit represents lack—the object of desire—but love occurs when this object is no longer just an object. Instead, it is another subject, also reaching, also lacking. Love, then, is the act of offering what you yourself do not possess—your lack—placing it in the hands of another who is equally incomplete, equally searching.

In *Signs*, M. Night Shyamalan presents a former religious leader who, in an authentic act of love, gives to others what he himself has lost: faith. In a moment of crisis—trapped in the basement as aliens invade his home—Graham finds the courage to acknowledge his own lack and place it in the hands of his family, who, in turn, seek wholeness through him. It is through this vulnerable yet defiant act of love that he not only overcomes the alien threat but also heals the spiritual alienation in his own heart. For this reason, *Signs* is a gripping horror film that also happens to be an unexpectedly uplifting and deeply moving tear-jerker.

Annihilation (2018)

What do you get when you mix *Predator* and *Event Horizon* in the coolest, most mind-bending way possible? Alex Garland's *Annihilation*, of course. This stunning sci-fi horror follows a group of explorers who venture into "The Shimmer," a quarantined zone where plants and animals have been mutated by an alien presence. But The Shimmer is more than just a strange terrain—it manifests polymorphous impulses that the Ego perceives as a mortal threat, something foreclosed that violently resurfaces as a frenzied, untamed force. What returns is, paradoxically, life itself—transformed, mutated, unrecognisable. That the conscious personality experiences this as terrifying only confirms the Ego's main role as a mechanism of repression.

The central theme of *Annihilation* appears to be self-destruction, encapsulated in these lines spoken to Lena by Dr. Ventress:

> As a psychologist, I think you're confusing suicide with self-destruction, they're very different. Almost none of us commit suicide, whereas almost all of us self-destruct. Somehow. In some part of our lives. We

drink, or take drugs, or destabilise the happy job, or happy marriage. But these aren't decisions. They're impulses. As a biologist, you're better placed to explain them than me. Isn't self-destruction coded into us? Imprinted into each cell.

In psychoanalysis, the destructive impulse is expressed through aggression, self-sabotage, and compulsive repetition of negative life patterns. Freud initially viewed the Ego as a barrier to pleasure, but later argued that our greatest obstacle to happiness is an inherent masochistic impulse—a subconscious need to *annihilate* what we love, whether through fear of commitment, denial, or the compulsive recreation of trauma. This struggle manifests in the tension between two opposing drives: (1) Eros (life instinct)—creativity, harmony, sexual connection, reproduction, self-preservation; (2) Thanatos (death instinct)—self-destruction, repetition, aggression, the lure of non-being. Freud also speculated on the biological basis of repetition compulsion, arguing that it is not merely psychological, but a cellular urge to return to an earlier state of existence. At its most extreme, this is the pull towards inorganic matter—the desire to dissolve back into nothingness. The ultimate drive to die.

Every character in *Annihilation* is marked by the Freudian thanatic pull. Paramedic Anya battles addiction, constantly managing the impulse to relapse. Physicist Josie's self-destructive tendencies are more overt—she used to cut herself, her arms now hidden beneath long sleeves to conceal the scars. Geomorphologist Cass mourns not just the death of her daughter, but the death of the woman she used to be before the tragic loss. In Lena's case, the death drive manifests in a different form—the pursuit of a potentially ruinous affair, even at the cost of her marriage. Infidelity is often a textbook example of thrill-seeking, reckless, self-sabotaging behaviour. But might it be even more dangerous for Lena to stay with her husband, Kane, when her heart belongs to her lover, Dan? *Annihilation* suggests that destruction is not simply an act, but an inherent rebellion of life against the Ego—a force that seeks to dismantle its illegitimate limitations. Perhaps, in the end, it is the conscious personality itself that represents death: a petrified structure that interrupts the natural flow of life.

Within this framework, we can interpret The Shimmer in *Annihilation* as a feature that dissolves Ego identifications, stripping away the rigid constructs of selfhood. Social masks collapse, and organisms interact in a raw, unfiltered way—whether through violent outbursts or total surrender to the Shimmer's eerie, all-consuming aura. Freud saw the psychic urge to dissolve clinically manifest in masochism, suggesting that the compulsion to self-harm is one of its most reliable indicators. In his model, the psyche is shaped by two warring forces (Eros and Thanatos). Locked in eternal combat, these drives form the foundation of human experience—*Annihilation* just makes the battle visible.

Freud theorised that creating living cells binds energy and generates an imbalance; in his view, this unevenness fuels a natural inclination to return to an inorganic state. He proposed that the death drive—the first instinct developed by organic life—seeks to resolve tensions produced by external stimuli by dismantling the self. Annihilation, then, is not an aberration but a return to a primordial condition. This idea is embodied in Dr. Ventress, whose terminal cancer exemplifies the very principle Freud describes: a biological force compelling a return to an earlier state. Rather than resisting, she embraces the Shimmer's destructive energy, drawn to it as if compelled by an inner biological imperative. Her arc highlights a paradox—while the death drive is typically associated with passive entropy, in Ventress, it propels her into action. Her obsession with understanding the Shimmer, even as it unravels her, exemplifies Freud's notion that life itself is animated by the tension between persistence and dissolution—her cells seem more alive than ever. From this perspective, molecular diffusion functions as a literal death-wish, an instinct not just within individuals but woven into the fabric of existence itself.

The psychological death-wish, then, reflects a biological impulse embedded in every cell. *Annihilation* masterfully illustrates this concept, confronting an impulse that remains largely taboo in our culture. Western values elevate life above all else; to suggest that we might be drawn towards destruction—via self-sabotage, compulsive repetition, or a fascination with death—risks social condemnation and alienation. *Annihilation* rejects the mindless mantra to "choose life," instead arguing that confronting the death drive is not nihilistic but necessary. Suppressing our destructive impulses does not make them disappear; it only renders them more insidious. True survival, the film suggests, is not about denial—it requires integration. Only by acknowledging our destructive impulses can we transform them, ensuring that, like the mutated life within The Shimmer, we do not merely persist, but evolve.

Glossary of Psychoanalytic Terms

- **Alienation**—An existential concept describing estrangement from oneself, others, or reality, often linked to a loss of identity or disconnection from one's own emotions.

- **Archaic Mother (Creed)**—Pre-Oedipal, primal maternal figure associated with overwhelming generative and destructive power.
- **Capgras Syndrome**—A psychiatric condition in which a person believes that someone close to them has been replaced by an identical-looking imposter, reflecting anxieties about identity and recognition.
- **Castration Anxiety**—In Freudian psychoanalysis, the fear of symbolic or literal emasculation, often linked to power dynamics, loss of authority, and surveillance.
- **Death Drive (Thanatos)**—The unconscious urge towards aggression, repetition, and self-sabotage, often in opposition to the life-preserving instincts of Eros, the life force.
- **Desire**—In Lacanian psychoanalysis, a fundamental lack that structures human subjectivity, emerging from the gap between what one wants and what is attainable.
- **Ego**—In Freudian psychoanalysis, the rational part of the psyche that mediates between the instinctual drives of the Id and the moral restrictions of the Superego.
- **Eros (Life Drive)**—Freud's concept of the life instinct, encompassing creativity, love, connection, self-preservation, and reproduction.
- **Foreclosure**—A Lacanian term describing a psychic process in which a traumatic or intolerable element is expelled from consciousness, only to return in a distorted form.
- **Freudian Slip**—An unintentional verbal or behavioural mistake that reveals unconscious thoughts or desires.
- **Gaze (Lacan)**—A concept in psychoanalysis and film theory where the act of looking establishes power relations, often linked to surveillance, voyeurism, and alienation.
- **Ideology (Žižek)**—The unconscious framework that structures reality, making power relations seem natural, inescapable, and invisible.
- **Lack (Lacan)**—The fundamental absence at the core of human subjectivity that generates desire and compels action.
- **Lamella**—A Lacanian concept describing an indestructible, formless, and excessive life force that exists beyond symbolic representation. It represents pure drive, uncontainable by the structures of identity, and survival beyond human limitations.
- **The Monstrous-Feminine (Creed)**—A feminist psychoanalytic theory analysing how horror films frame female monstrosity through patriarchal fears of sexuality, reproduction, and abjection.
- **L'Objet Petit A**—In Lacanian theory, the unattainable object of desire that fuels human longing but can never be fully possessed.

- **Paranoia**—An extreme form of anxiety marked by distrust, suspicion, and a belief in hidden threats or conspiracies.
- **Primal Scene**—Freud's term for a moment in early childhood where a child unintentionally witnesses an event (often sexual in nature) that they cannot fully comprehend, leading to psychic disturbances.
- **Repetition Compulsion**—A phenomenon where individuals unconsciously re-enact past traumas, destructive behaviours, or unresolved conflicts, perpetuating suffering.
- **Scopophilia**—The pleasure derived from looking, particularly in a voyeuristic manner, often explored in film theory.
- **Symbolic Order**—A Lacanian concept referring to the structures of language, law, and ideology that shape human reality and meaning.
- **Synchronicity**—A Jungian concept describing meaningful coincidences that appear connected despite lacking a clear causal link.
- **The Uncanny**—Freud's term for something that is both familiar and profoundly strange, evoking an eerie sense of unease.
- **Unconscious**—The vast, hidden domain of the psyche, where repressed desires, fears, and unresolved conflicts reside.
- **Voyeurism**—The act of deriving pleasure from observing others without their awareness, often linked to issues of power, control, and objectification.

Vampires

Seduction, immortality, and the erotic gothic

5

While alien horror is preoccupied with the unknowable and terrifying vastness of the cosmos, vampire horror brings the unknown much closer to home—manifesting uncanny seductiveness in human form. The vampire is an enduring figure in horror cinema, a creature that thrives in the liminal space between life and death, the natural and the supernatural, the erotic and the violent. Unlike the blank nature of alien life, vampires entice as much as they terrify, luring their prey with the illusion of intimacy before delivering a lethal strike. Theirs is a horror of proximity rather than distance, of up close and personal seduction rather than cryptic signals from deep space.

Vampires speak to fundamental anxieties about consumption, infection, and immortality. They are parasites, thriving on human blood, blurring the line between predator and lover, victim and oppressor. Whether depicted as aristocratic figures of decadent corruption or feral, ravenous creatures, the vampire myth persists because it taps into fears about desire, dependency, and the loss of control. Just as alien horror destabilises notions of humanity by introducing an external other, vampire horror forces an even more unsettling confrontation—what if the villain roams among us, wearing the face of something irresistibly familiar?

Bram Stoker's Dracula (1992)

As symbols of lust and seduction, vampires are quintessential Freudian subjects. Much has been written about Jonathan and Mina Harker, Professor Abraham Van Helsing, and, of course, Count Dracula himself in Francis

DOI: 10.4324/9781003425236-5

Ford Coppola's *Bram Stoker's Dracula*, an adaptation of the 1897 novel. But what piques my interest most in this film is Lucy Westenra, played by Sadie Frost. At just 19, Lucy becomes Dracula's first English victim—her transformation into a vampire marks her descent into forbidden desire, and ultimately, her destruction.

Lucy is far more eroticised in Coppola's adaptation than in her literary incarnation, transformed into a coquettish, tantalising presence. A spoiled child of aristocracy, she speaks with an artless frankness that borders on indecency—yet she remains kind-hearted and strikingly beautiful. Unlike her friend Mina, who is rather restrained, Lucy is flirtatious and teasing, a quality seemingly entwined with her downfall. She is vibrant, fully in touch with her sexuality, and openly curious about romance. Her physical allure captivates many impassioned admirers, and while she embraces her eroticism, Mina is more demure about such matters.

Lucy's only preoccupation in life seems to be selecting a husband from her three devoted suitors: the wealthy nobleman Arthur Holmwood, the rugged American adventurer Quincey Morris, and the reserved psychologist Dr. John Seward. However, she soon begins sleepwalking and develops an alarming case of anaemia; her body grows frail, and her canine teeth lengthen. Dr. Van Helsing suspects Dracula's influence and urges Lucy's suitors to provide her with blood transfusions in a desperate attempt to save her. But the efforts fail—Lucy succumbs to her illness and is laid to rest. Yet death does not keep her. Rising from the grave as a vampire, she is soon discovered attacking a small child. Van Helsing and the suitors work together to destroy the undead Lucy. When confronted, Lucy is eerily seductive, luring Arthur towards her with the promise of a kiss. He is nearly entranced but is pulled back just in time. Summoning his resolve, he drives a wooden stake through her heart; they proceed to decapitate her.

When *Dracula* was written and published, Victorian society was gripped by anxieties over the rise of the so-called "New Woman." Coined in the late 19th century, the term referred to an emerging archetype—an independent, self-sufficient woman eager to seize the expanding opportunities available to her gender. In contrast to the era's rigid expectations of women as pure, meek, and devoted to domestic life, the New Woman was intellectual, sexually liberated, and defiant of traditional roles. This radical shift ruffled many feathers, sparking widespread fears that such women were seditious and harmful.

Lucy Westenra's transformation into Dracula's victim has generated debates about her role in the story. Was she merely a helpless figure—too dependent on men, too easily swayed by Dracula's influence? Or did she embody the predicament of the New Woman, her burgeoning sexual desire deemed too modern, too unruly, leading her to willingly embrace a transgressive path—allegorised as vampirism? Lucy's longing exceeds what is socially permissible. In the novel, she laments having to choose between her three suitors, wishing she could marry them all. Stoker magnifies this insatiability to monstrous proportions in her undead form, describing her as a ravenous, wanton creature. As a vampire, Lucy is a perilous threat to male self-control—her seductive power rendering her too dangerous to exist. To neutralise this menace, she must be destroyed. Only in death is she restored to innocence, her corpse's placid expression reassuring the men who conquered her.

From a theoretical standpoint, Lucy's position in the story can be interpreted through the concept of the phallus. Jacques Lacan deliberately distinguishes the "phallus" from the biological penis, as psychoanalytic theory is concerned with its function in fantasy. While the phallus carries physical connotations, it primarily operates as a signifier of lack and sexual difference. In Lacan's framework, the phallus is a privileged signifier, foundational to the process of meaning-making itself. Within the Imaginary Order, the pre-Oedipal child perceives the phallus as the object of the mother's desire—something she longs for beyond the child. In an effort to secure the mother's love, the child identifies with this elusive object, seeking to embody what they believe will make them desirable.

In attempting to satisfy the mother's desire, the child identifies with the object it presumes she has lost, striving to become that object for her. The phallus is Imaginary in that the child associates it with a concrete and tangible object that has disappeared but might be recovered. However, as the child matures, they come to realise that they are neither identical to nor the sole focus of the mother's desire, as her longing is directed elsewhere. The Imaginary phallus, then, is what the child assumes one must possess in order to be desired. What Freud termed castration is not a literal loss, but a symbolic process—one in which the child recognises themselves as lacking something: the phallus.

My argument is that Lucy, at a rudimentary level, recognises that as a young woman in the Victorian era, she is excluded from the vast possibilities afforded to men. Confronting the deep frustration of this lack, she unconsciously seeks to embody the lost object of desire—the phallus—claiming a position of power in a society that denies her agency. She achieves this by co-opting the vampire's mode of being: not merely consuming, but voraciously devouring every pleasure that arouses her interest, asserting herself as a penetrating force in her own right.

Throughout Coppola's film, the motif of phallic penetration is repeatedly framed as a site of power and transformation. Mina's *Arabian Nights* book, with its explicit illustrations of penis-in-vagina sex, signals an undercurrent of suppressed erotic knowledge. Lucy, ever playful, teases Quincey Morris by handling his massive Bowie knife. Lingering shots of needles piercing Lucy's arms, Count Dracula's teeth sinking into her neck, and Arthur driving a stake through her heart—all reinforce this charged imagery. Lucy's embodiment of the New Woman is intrinsically tied to the theoretical function of penetration. Her curiosity about sex finds its ultimate expression in the encounter with Dracula, however fatal. Within the imagination of a repressed Victorian society, a young woman acting on carnal desires becomes a monstrous figure—her body marked for inevitable deterioration as punishment for breaching the boundaries of civilisation.

Lucy's entanglement with a demonic creature is merely a coded expression of her pre-existing lustful tendencies—desires for which she is destined to be castigated. Dracula serves as a convenient scapegoat, deflecting attention from the real offense: a woman's unrestrained desire for penetration. And not just in the literal sense of penis-in-vagina sex, but in a broader, more threatening way—penetrating society as an erotic force to be reckoned with. Her innocence is preserved only by framing Vlad the Impaler as the singular aggressor, a narrative designed to reassure us that phallic female desire does not, and cannot, exist. Yet, in doing so, it only confirms the very thing it seeks to deny.

Daughters of Darkness (1971)

In Harry Kümel's erotic horror film *Daughters of Darkness*, Stefan Chilton, an aristocratic Brit, travels through continental Europe with his newlywed wife, Valerie. The couple checks into a grand hotel on the Ostend seafront in Belgium, planning to catch a cross-channel ferry to England, where Stefan's mother supposedly resides. However, Valerie soon notices his reluctance to call her—revealing that she is unaware of their marriage.

At nightfall, a mysterious Hungarian countess, Elizabeth Báthory, arrives at the hotel with her secretary, Ilona. The middle-aged concierge, Pierre, recalls having seen the countess there when he was a child—yet she hasn't aged a day. In their suite, Valerie comes across a newspaper article detailing a series of child murders in Bruges, each victim a girl found with her throat slashed. Meanwhile, Countess Elizabeth becomes fixated on the young couple, revealing that she is a descendant of Erzsébet Báthory, the infamous serial killer who bathed in the blood of virgins to preserve her youth. Valerie is disturbed by the macabre conversation, but Stefan, oddly intrigued, listens intently—already seeming to understand the dark implications of her tale.

What is happening here? What underlying psychoanalytic significance is at play in this film? To paraphrase Countess Elizabeth, one must never be afraid to look deep into the shadows—into the darkest depths where light never reaches—to find the answers. So, let's examine this logically. Stefan and Valerie are intensely passionate with each other as they travel towards England, but when their journey is interrupted and they find themselves stranded on the Belgian seafront, a shift occurs. Valerie repeatedly urges Stefan to contact his mother, yet he continually delays, offering vague excuses. He insists that Lady Chilton's aristocratic heritage makes her believe their bloodline is different—God's gift, one that must never be sullied. Valerie begins to suspect the unspoken truth: her husband is ashamed of her lower-class origins.

As expected, Stefan's avoidance of his mother is strikingly conspicuous. He goes to great lengths to delay any contact with her, even bribing the hotel concierge, Pierre, to falsely report that there is no answer at Chilton Manor when he pretends to call. What was meant to be a brief overnight stay at the desolate seaside resort stretches into an indefinite pause, their journey mysteriously stalled. Despite Valerie's growing unease, Stefan appears intent on prolonging their joyless honeymoon in this barren, off-season limbo—as if he is avoiding something far more complicated than just his mother.

It is no coincidence that the newlyweds cross paths with the glamorous Countess Elizabeth precisely amid Stefan's evasions concerning his mother. Unlike Lady Chilton, who remains a distant, disavowed figure—an abstraction cloaked in avoidance—Elizabeth is up close and personal, intrusively so. She insinuates herself into their lives, inviting them for drinks and dinner, slipping into their private quarters, asking insolent questions, and encroaching on their most intimate moments. Her designs are clear: as a vampire, she seeks to seduce and corrupt. But her aristocratic status also mirrors that of Stefan's mother, suggesting that she may function allegorically—a projection of the maternal spectre he tries so desperately to suppress. In evading one, he conjures another. The mother he wishes to deny returns in a new form—overbearing, inquisitive, and inescapable.

It would be remiss not to acknowledge the significance of the repressed mother figure in *Daughters of Darkness*. There's a very interesting pattern emerging here. Psychoanalysis holds space for the complex emotional entanglements we develop towards parents and siblings, viewing childhood as a period of intense love, hatred, envy, and fear—all culminating in what

Sigmund Freud termed the Oedipus complex. This crucial developmental stage is often framed as a child's unconscious desire for the parent of the opposite sex, coupled with a sense of rivalry towards the same-sex parent. Freud considered this a universal and unavoidable phase, one that may be repressed but never entirely extinguished—it leaves an indelible imprint, shaping how we form relationships throughout life. Within this framework, the child experiences both love and hostility towards the mother, a dynamic that plays an important role in structuring personality and orienting human desire. Ideally, the child resolves the Oedipal crisis by identifying with the same-sex parent, integrating this identification into their sense of self. If this resolution fails, however, it can give rise to lasting neuroses in adulthood.

My argument is that the eroticisation of the mother is, at its core, a preoccupation with one's physical and emotional origins. In Stefan's case, something buried in his past—some secret aspect of his nature—unsettles him, and his whirlwind marriage to Valerie appears to be a desperate attempt to outrun this reality. A telling moment occurs early in the film, on the train, when Valerie asks Stefan if he loves her. He replies that he does not and adds that she must not love him either—insisting this is a good thing, as it proves they are suited for one another. Though presented as sarcastic banter, this exchange feels like a revelation of his true feelings. Countess Elizabeth's unavoidable presence at the hotel forces Stefan to confront his origins and reckon with the source of his buried feelings. Her secretary, Ilona, seducing Stefan can be understood as an Oedipal proxy war—an attempt to enmesh him back into the primordial maternal domain.

Stefan eventually calls Chilton Manor, and it is revealed that his so-called "mother" is, in fact, an older, feminine-presenting man wearing foppish makeup, who sounds disappointed upon hearing of Stefan's marriage to Valerie. The exact nature of their relationship is left deliberately ambiguous, adding to the film's intrigue. If we entertain the possibility that they are secret lovers, then Stefan's violent outbursts could be interpreted as expressions of repressed homosexuality—with Valerie as the recipient of his frustration. Sensing the underlying dysfunction in the marriage, Elizabeth and Ilona work to deepen the divide between the newlyweds. The countess, in particular, seizes upon Valerie's growing unease, exploiting her need to escape the oppressive dynamic she finds herself trapped in.

In *Daughters of Darkness*, time stands still—nothing moves forward. Stefan and Valerie remain trapped in a deadlock, their relationship stunted by dishonesty and reckless self-sabotage. Elizabeth and Ilona, as vampires draining the couple's life force, embody the inertia of a bond that cannot progress.

Director Harry Kümel has likened the countess to Marlene Dietrich and her secretary to Louise Brooks—glamorous spectres of classic cinema, immortalised in their allure. Their undead status mirrors the psychological impasse Stefan and Valerie are caught in, an endless cycle of entrapment. Elizabeth even warns Valerie that Stefan dreams of making her what every man dreams of making of every woman—a slave, an object of pleasure. The film's haunting conclusion suggests that this tragic pattern will inevitably repeat, the same doomed desires manifesting again and again.

Let's Scare Jessica to Death (1971)

In John Hancock's indie horror film *Let's Scare Jessica to Death*, a mentally fragile woman begins to suspect that the enigmatic drifter she has welcomed into her home may, in fact, be a vampire. Inspired by Henry James' *The Turn of the Screw* and Robert Wise's *The Haunting*, Hancock sought to craft a protagonist whose perception of reality could be questioned by both the characters around her and the audience itself. Some film scholars have drawn comparisons between *Let's Scare Jessica to Death* and Sheridan Le Fanu's 1871 novel *Carmilla*, further linking the film to gothic traditions of psychological ambiguity and vampiric seduction.

Jessica has just been released from an in-patient psychiatric facility. Her husband, Duncan, has sacrificed his career as a string bassist for the New York Philharmonic to care for her, and together they relocate to a remote, dilapidated farmhouse outside the city. Accompanying them is their free-spirited friend Woody. Upon arrival, they are startled to find a squatter—Emily—who assumed the house was abandoned. Emily offers to leave, but Jessica invites her to stay the night. It soon becomes clear that Jessica is struggling to distinguish reality from hallucination. She hears disembodied voices, senses a shadowy female presence following her, and sees a figure beneath the water while swimming in the cove. Yet she keeps these experiences to herself, afraid that Duncan and Woody will dismiss them as symptoms of relapse. Adding to her unease, she senses her husband's growing attraction to Emily, and notices a slightly off-kilter quality about the nearby townsmen. Every one of them is bandaged in some way, and their cold hostility towards the newcomers suggests that Jessica's paranoia may not be unfounded.

Needing extra money, Duncan and Jessica decide to sell old items they find in the house. Among them is a framed portrait of the former owners—the Bishop family: father, mother, and daughter Abigail. When they take it to a local antique dealer, they learn that Abigail drowned in the cove behind the house on the eve of her wedding in 1880. Her body was never recovered, and legend has it she still roams the countryside as a vampire. Later, Jessica studies the portrait more closely and is struck by a chilling realisation—Abigail bears an uncanny resemblance to Emily. The connection is sealed. Emily wasn't trespassing at the farmhouse; on the contrary, the New Yorkers are the intruders, dismantling and selling off fragments of her past. While Abigail is the supposed vampire, it is Duncan and Jessica who are scavenging through her possessions, repurposing them for profit, draining her home of its history. *Let's Scare Jessica to Death* cleverly flips the script, revealing vampirism not as a fixed state but as a shifting energy—an exchange of power in which both villains and victims take turns embodying its essence.

There are many subtle yet powerful details that shape the film's emotional texture. Take Jessica's unusual hobby of tombstone rubbing—seemingly a minor detail yet deeply revealing. She grazes charcoal across paper pressed against a headstone, reproducing its inscription. While this practice can serve as a personal memento or a tool for genealogical research, in Jessica's case, it taps into something more elusive—an unspoken yet profound preoccupation with the past. She is drawn to preserving fragments of a world that has ostensibly died yet still lingers in some spectral form. This paradox defines her existence. Perhaps, by studying these engravings, she is searching for reassurance—some tangible clue about the mystery of death. The tracing paper is fragile and fleeting, yet it captures a certain permanence carved in stone.

Touches of death pervade *Let's Scare Jessica to Death*. Instead of a regular car, Duncan drives a hearse to fit his enormous string bass in the back—the instrument's bulky case resembles a gothic coffin. This visual parallel speaks volumes. Being forced to abandon his prestigious music career has sucked the mojo out of Duncan; what once gave him purpose is now a lifeless relic of happier times. Symbolic imagery continues throughout. In one scene, Jessica reaches for an apple in the orchard, only for Duncan to warn her that it's poisoned—an unmistakable evocation of Eve in the Garden of Eden, reaching for the forbidden fruit of knowledge. This biblical reference is crucial. In the *Genesis* narrative, Eve's transgression leads to humanity's fall—her disobedience is met with divine punishment.

Here, Jessica's "sin" is different but equally damning: she dares to access prohibited supernatural knowledge, a dangerous pursuit that, within the logic of the film, is linked to her supposed psychosis. Duncan's resentment towards her is palpable. He sees her illness as the reason for his dwindling career, lowered social status, and financial insecurity, and as a result, he repeatedly dismisses and undermines her perceptions. This dynamic creates an oddly confusing effect, reminiscent of the ambiguity permeating *Rosemary's Baby* (1968). At times, it seems clear that Duncan is gaslighting and manipulating Jessica; at others, we question whether she is, in fact, delusional. The film thrives on this uncertainty, intensifying its horror. It is an exasperating feeling that lingers right until the final moment as Jessica is adrift in a boat, lost in thought: "I sit here, and I can't believe that it happened. And yet I have to believe it. Dreams or nightmares. Madness or sanity, I don't know which is which."

Let's assume, for the sake of argument, that Jessica is experiencing psychosis—a response to overwhelming stress and perceived danger in her environment. Her sense of self unravels, and the auditory hallucinations function as a desperate attempt to hold herself together. She is constantly invaded by a foreign entity—a relentless voice erupting from within, threatening the very construction of her identity. Jacques Lacan's concept of foreclosure offers a compelling lens through which to understand this. Lacan identified foreclosure as the key structural cause of psychosis, referring to the rejection of a crucial element of reality—a feature that is not merely repressed, but was never symbolised in the first place. This rejection often occurs when the paternal function fails. We know that Jessica's father has passed away; in psychoanalytic terms, this absence leaves a void where the Law should be. Without this stabilising force, there is a gaping hole in the Symbolic Order, one that cannot be filled retroactively, producing a psychotic structure in the subject. As a result, Jessica's reality begins to collapse, its fabric torn apart by fissures in meaning—gaps that can only be sutured by the voices that haunt her.

Incidentally, many critics have identified *Let's Scare Jessica to Death* as an allegory for the decline of 1960s counterculture. The hearse that Duncan and Jessica drive—graffitied with the word "love"—has been read as an ironic nod to the death of hippie ideals. Film critic and biographer Michael Doyle describes the film as a "haunting elegy" for the failures of the hippie movement, arguing that it "isolates and illuminates the death and corruption of counterculture values" and foreshadows the "festering paranoia" that would define the 1970s, culminating in events such as Watergate, the assassinations of Harvey Milk and George Moscone, and the Jonestown massacre. Director John Hancock has acknowledged this reading, even if it wasn't consciously integrated into the screenplay, commenting: "You could already feel that negativity brewing when we were making *Let's Scare Jessica to Death*—that things weren't working out the way some of us had hoped and dreamed they would."

A pervasive theme in *Let's Scare Jessica to Death* is the idea of the city slickers as "wandering spirits"—rootless, transient figures drifting aimlessly from one situation to the next. Something traumatic happened to Jessica before the events of the film, leading to her hospitalisation, yet the nature of her suffering remains unspoken. It is possible that unresolved grief over her father's death is at the heart of it, but this is never confirmed. She moves through life as if haunted—smiling through tears, carrying an invisible weight. Perhaps this is why she senses a spectral presence during Emily's séance. Jessica seems attuned to the spirit of the house's former occupants, as though their lingering trauma resonates with her own. We know that Abigail died young, but the exact circumstances of her tragedy remain a mystery. In the end, Jessica and the Bishops share an intangible sorrow—bound together by an unknowable heartbreak.

The Lost Boys (1987)

The title of Joel Schumacher's supernatural black comedy horror film *The Lost Boys* alludes to J.M. Barrie's *Peter Pan*—specifically, the group of boys who never grow up, much like vampires. The film follows teenage brothers Michael and Sam, who move with their mother to Santa Carla, a small town in northern California ominously dubbed the murder capital of the world. While Sam quickly finds camaraderie with geeky comic book aficionados Edgar and Alan, his older brother Michael is drawn into a dangerous crowd. He falls for the enigmatic Star—only to discover she is bound to David, the charismatic leader of a local gang of vampires.

At the gang's lair—an abandoned luxury hotel that sank beneath the cliffs after the 1906 earthquake—David initiates Michael into the group. Star warns him not to drink from the ornate bottle he's offered, insisting it contains blood, but Michael ignores her. The next morning, he wakes up at home with no memory of how he got there. His eyes are suddenly sensitive to sunlight, and an unfamiliar thirst for blood begins to take hold. When Sam notices that Michael's reflection has started to fade in the mirror, he realises the horrifying truth: his brother is turning into a vampire. Determined to save him, Sam enlists the help of his new comic book-obsessed friends to fight back against the undead.

One possible reading of *The Lost Boys* is that it functions as an anti-drug film, presenting vampirism as a grim allegory for substance abuse—particularly heroin addiction. The film leans into the nihilism of the vampire lifestyle: the characters wear dark clothing, stay out all night, sleep all day, and exist in a state of detachment from the "normies" of the world. Crucially, they develop a physical dependency on blood. Meanwhile, the adults running the local comic bookstore, presumably ex-hippies, appear perpetually zonked out of their gourds. The film doubles down on associations between severe yearning for a fix and a zombified state of being. The presence of habitual potheads as background characters reinforces the idea that substance abuse reduces once-vibrant individuals to lifeless, hollowed-out husks—cyphers who are basically dead to the world. In this context, Edgar and Alan use the comic bookstore as their headquarters, structuring their vampire-fighting mission through the lens of heroic mythology. Even their appropriation of Superman's motto, "Truth, justice, and the American way," signals a noble opposition to the corruption, deception, and decadence embodied by vampires coded as junkies.

The Lost Boys was released in 1987, at the dawn of the "Just Say No" campaign—an extension of the United States' "War on Drugs" that sought to dissuade children from engaging in illegal substance use by promoting assertive refusal strategies. The slogan was coined and championed by then-First Lady Nancy Reagan, who launched the campaign in a nationally televised address on 14 September 1986. This cultural backdrop of heightened anti-drug rhetoric offers a compelling lens through which to interpret the film's themes, reflecting the anxieties and moral preoccupations of the era.

Setting aside the anti-drug reading, another interpretation emerges when we return to the "lost boys" of J.M. Barrie's story—infants who fall out of their prams while their nurse isn't looking. If they remain unclaimed for seven days, they are sent away to Neverland, where Peter Pan becomes their surrogate leader. The premise is distinctly Freudian. At its core, the rupture occurs due to the absence of maternal anchoring in the child's life. In *The Lost Boys*, this idea is mirrored in the motivations of Max Lawrence, the seemingly affable video store owner who is later revealed to be the head vampire. Max's plan is simple: he instructs David to turn Sam and Michael, knowing that their transformation will compel Lucy to follow. His ultimate goal is to provide a mother for his lost boys. The film explicitly names maternal absence as the root cause of vampirism—without the nurturing and protection of the maternal agency, these children remain trapped in a static, suspended state, unable to confidently move forward in life.

The vampires in Schumacher's film are achingly cool. Their aesthetic is modern, urban, and cutting-edge—mysterious and alluring. It is easy to be glamorised by these creatures of the night! Even today, Kiefer Sutherland's peroxide-blond mullet and leather-clad swagger feel avant-garde. But therein lies the catch: while vampires promise agelessness and eternal beauty, they are ultimately stagnant. They do not evolve, they do not change—they remain in a state of developmental deadlock, trapped in time. In a world of constant upheaval, where everything is in flux, they become fixed freaks—the eternal outcasts, paradoxically predictable in their rebellion. Without a maternal figure to anchor them, to offer comfort and stability, they stop maturing altogether. The vampire myth with a Peter Pan twist eventually ceases to be cool and turns tragic. These fanged and intimidating style icons are merely children searching for a mother, doomed to a state of perpetual adolescence. In that light, I can't help but feel a pang of sympathy for these wayward guttersnipes.

The railroad bridge scene, where David and the gang coax Michael into hanging from the trestles above a fog-shrouded gorge, is thick with symbolism. It's a literal depiction of going off the rails—falling in with the wrong crowd, veering dangerously off course. *The Lost Boys* is, in so many ways, a cautionary tale. Michael is a promising young man, yet his choices threaten to derail his future. One by one, the vampires plummet into the abyss, vanishing into the mist, until only Michael remains—dangling, disoriented, untethered. It's a striking visual metaphor for his precarious state of mind, hovering between two worlds. This sequence calls to mind Nietzsche's warning: "Battle not with monsters, lest you become a monster, and if you gaze long into the abyss, the abyss gazes also into you." The abyss is not just an external void—it is the shadow self, the latent chaos within. To dwell too long in this aspect of one's psyche risks madness or self-harm. In this sense, *The Lost Boys* captures the raw turbulence of teenage years—the first brush with murkier instincts, the seductive thrill of transgression, and the looming danger of being swallowed whole by it. The film warns of what happens when one gets stuck in that descent, losing sight of a way back.

The film ends on a hopeful note. Just as Max prepares to transform Lucy into a vampire, the boys' Grandpa crashes his truck through the wall of the house, impaling Max on a wooden fence post and causing him to explode. I interpret this as a triumph of maturity—an older man, long dismissed as eccentric and irrelevant, is ultimately the one to break the vampire curse. When we first meet Grandpa, he plays a morbid prank on his family, pretending to be dead. But when it truly matters, he proves steadfast, saving his loved ones while never losing his dry, nonchalant humour. The film reassures us that with age comes not just wisdom but a necessary absurdist perspective—one that sustains the life force and prevents us from being swallowed by the torturous dark.

Interview with the Vampire (1994)

Neil Jordan's *Interview with the Vampire*, an American gothic horror film based on Anne Rice's novel of the same name, delves into the complex relationship between Lestat and Louis, chronicling their centuries-long entanglement. The story is framed by a present-day interview, in which Louis recounts his past to a San Francisco journalist. He describes his human life as a wealthy plantation owner in 1791 Spanish Louisiana, a life marred by grief after the death of his wife and unborn child. Despondent, he wanders the New Orleans waterfront in a drunken stupor, where he is attacked by the vampire Lestat. Sensing Louis's existential despair, Lestat offers him immortality. Louis accepts but soon comes to regret his decision. While Lestat revels in the hunt, taking pleasure in killing humans, Louis resists his predatory instincts, sustaining himself on animal blood in a desperate attempt to cling to his humanity.

Structurally, *Interview with the Vampire* mirrors the clinical setting of psychotherapy, with Louis opening up about his past in a confessional mode. The reporter assumes the role of analyst, prompting him with questions, while Louis responds with raw honesty, his words meticulously recorded. This soul-bearing process draws us into the forensic dissection of what is, essentially, a life of crime—macabre creatures crossing borders and centuries, never truly integrating, leaving a trail of bodies behind them. Louis's account is an attempt to unburden his conscience of a guilt he cannot escape. He loathes the instincts that have been forced upon him, ashamed of the cravings that define a vampire's existence: the unmistakable tingle of temptation at the sight of exposed veins, the intoxicating thrill of sinking fangs into tender flesh, the euphoria of warm blood surging into a cold body.

It would be remiss not to acknowledge the close link between vampiric ingestion and the oral stage of psychosexual development. In Sigmund Freud's theory, the oral stage spans from birth to roughly one year of age, during which the infant derives libidinal gratification from the mouth—primarily through feeding at the mother's breast, as well as from oral exploration of their environment (the instinctive tendency to place objects in the mouth). At this stage, the Id reigns supreme, as the Superego has not yet formed, and the infant has no established sense of self. Every action is dictated by the pleasure principle—the fundamental drive seeking immediate satisfaction of basic needs, wants, and urges.

Within the logic of the vampire world, Lestat's enthusiasm for human blood can be interpreted as a full-bodied acceptance of his condition. He embraces the breast, so to speak—surrendering joyfully to the oral dimension of vampirism. His indulgence in pleasure is what makes him such a compelling force in the film. Lestat is vibrant, animated, and electric—deliciously watchable as a one-man vampire festival. He is sexy, fun, and unapologetically himself. Louis, on the other hand, is tormented by ethical conflict—how can he allow himself to savour the taste of human blood when it comes at the cost of innocent lives? His refusal to meet the oral demands of vampirism leads to an obsessional neurotic disposition. His libidinal energy becomes dammed up, giving way to pathological self-repression. Unlike Lestat, whose Id flows freely, Louis's Superego is overpowering. He ruminates on his impulses, struggling to gain control over them. His moral refusal to kill, coupled with the relentless pressure to suppress violent urges, shapes him into a deeply closeted figure—hesitant, inhibited, fearful of his own nature, and delaying the inevitable. His constant effort to cope with sadness and anxiety makes him an enduring archetype of the vampire as a depressive figure.

My final and perhaps most significant interpretation of *Interview with the Vampire* is that the relationship between Lestat and Claudia resembles Munchausen syndrome by proxy—also known as Factitious Disorder Imposed on Another. This condition occurs when a caregiver fabricates, exaggerates, or induces illness in a dependent, often a child, to maintain control over them. This may include injuring the child or presenting the child as being sick or incapacitated. It is one of the most lethal forms of abuse, sometimes leading to permanent harm or even death. In the film, amid a plague outbreak in New Orleans, Louis—momentarily succumbing to temptation—feeds on a dying little girl whose mother has perished. Seizing the opportunity to keep Louis by his side, Lestat transforms the child, Claudia, into a vampire. Together, they raise her as their daughter. Louis harbours a paternal love for Claudia, while Lestat indulges her, treating her more as a protégé—shaping her into a ruthless killer. Decades pass, and while Claudia matures psychologically, her body remains frozen in time—trapped in an unchanging childhood. Lestat continues to treat her as a little girl, reinforcing her entrapment. When Claudia finally realises that she will never grow into a woman, fury consumes her. She persuades Louis that they must leave Lestat behind.

In Munchausen syndrome by proxy, a caregiver fabricates or induces sickness in a dependent, not only to gain attention but to maintain absolute control. To sustain the illusion, the caregiver actively harms the child—whether through poisoning, suffocation, infection, or physical injury. What distinguishes Munchausen by proxy from typical child abuse is the level of premeditation. While many forms of abuse involve reactive outbursts—striking a child for crying, for instance—Munchausen by proxy is calculated and deliberate. The abuse is not a response to behaviour but a systematic effort to keep the victim in a state of dependency. The caregiver's needs are fulfilled by the ongoing role of nurturer and protector, even as they are the source of harm. The only true cure for the victim is complete separation from the abuser. Key characteristics of Munchausen by proxy include: a highly attentive caregiver who refuses to leave the child's side; an emotionally distant relationship between the parents; a caregiver who exhibits symptoms mirroring the child's supposed illness; a child who is eerily articulate about medical conditions beyond their years; an abusive parent with an insatiable need for attention and validation; and, crucially, a caregiver who remains disturbingly calm—even pleased—by the child's suffering.

Considering Munchausen by proxy in this context, Lestat's actions appear disturbingly strategic—designed to ensure Louis remains bound to him. He knows Louis harbours guilt over his vampiric urges, taking advantage of his moment of weakness after feeding on the dying Claudia. By transforming the child, Lestat ensures Louis will never leave—Claudia becomes the substitute for the unborn human child he lost, a vessel for his unresolved grief, his hopes, and his lingering attachment to mortality. In this unnatural family structure, Claudia keeps Louis tethered, giving him a reason to stay. Crucially, her physical development is permanently arrested—she is a child with the mind of a woman, fully aware of her condition yet powerless to escape it. The "illness" of vampirism locks her into a permanent state of dependency, satisfying Lestat's need for control. Without a shred of remorse, he manufactures her affliction, ensuring she remains weak, fragile, and infantilised—just as a Munchausen caregiver ensures their victim remains sick. Inside the toxic parameters of the Munchausen system, he secures Louis's undivided devotion. And for a time, his twisted plan works…

Blade (1998)

In Stephen Norrington's superhero horror film *Blade*, Wesley Snipes stars as a half-vampire "day-walker" who, alongside his mentor Abraham Whistler and haematologist Karen Jenson, wages war against vampires—most notably the ruthless Deacon Frost. The film opens in 1967, with a pregnant woman attacked by a vampire, triggering premature labour. Doctors manage to save her baby, but she succumbs to an unknown infection. Thirty years later, that child has become Blade—a hybrid who possesses the supernatural abilities of vampires without their weaknesses, except for his insatiable need for human blood. Meanwhile, at a meeting of the pure-blood vampire council, Frost, the leader of a younger faction, is reprimanded for his reckless ambition to incite war between vampires and humans. As a turned vampire rather than one born into the lineage, he is regarded as socially inferior by the ruling class. Undeterred, Frost devises a ritual that requires the sacrifice of 12 pure-blood vampires to awaken the "blood god" La Magra—an ancient deity of vampiric supremacy. And for the ritual to succeed, he needs one final ingredient: Blade's blood.

The core structure of *Blade* is built upon the logic of Freud's Oedipus complex. My argument is that the film serves as a cinematic expression of the Family Romance taboo—specifically, the male child's unconscious desire for his mother. In psychoanalytic theory, the Oedipus complex emerges during the phallic stage of psychosexual development (ages 3 to 6), a critical period when both libido and Ego begin to take shape. Although the mother is the primary source of gratification, the child's evolving sexual identity reshapes family dynamics, casting the parents as objects of infantile libidinal energy. The boy fixates his desires on his mother, while directing jealousy and rivalry towards his father—the figure who possesses her. The boy's Id compels him to eliminate his father in order to claim the mother, yet his Ego (governed by the reality principle) recognises the father's superior strength, making direct confrontation impossible. This tension creates a deep ambivalence towards the father. Freud theorised that the boy unconsciously fears castration at the hands of his father—a symbolic anxiety rather than a literal threat, rooted in the subconscious turmoil of the Id.

If we apply these psychoanalytic ideas to *Blade*, it becomes evident that the film's narrative is structured along the principles of the Oedipus complex. Blade grows up without maternal attachment, believing his mother died on the night of his birth. Fuelled by grief and rage, he dedicates his life to hunting down the creature responsible—not only for her death, but for his own affliction as a human-vampire hybrid. The shocking revelation comes when Blade discovers that his mother is not dead—she was turned into a vampire the night she was attacked and now exists as Deacon Frost's lover, bound to the very monster who bit her. Blade is captured and brought to the Temple of Eternal Night, where Frost plans to perform the Magra summoning ritual. The realisation is devastating. His mother, whom he has spent his life avenging, has become the undead consort of his greatest enemy—the very being responsible for Blade's condition. In a twisted sense, Frost functions as a symbolic father, the figure who "created" Blade by orchestrating his unnatural birth. Though extreme, this scenario resonates on an emotional level. For a child who feels disconnected from his mother, the presence of the father figure becomes the barrier that excludes him, the reason he is cast aside. Blade's pain is existential and Oedipal, rooted in the agonising loss of maternal closeness, displaced onto a monstrous paternal rival.

In the film, Frost and Blade's mother, Vanessa, conspire against him, forcibly taking Blade's blood to activate a ritual that reawakens ancient vampire powers. This plot neatly aligns with the conspiratorial mindset of a child within the Oedipal structure—jealous of the bond between his parents, feeling abandoned and humiliated, perceiving himself as powerless against the overwhelming authority of the father. Another layer of the Oedipus complex is revealed through the child's crushing realisation that his mother desires a life beyond the confines of motherhood. Blade, incredulous, demands, "How could you be a part of this?" Vanessa responds, "These are my people now. I'm one of them. I've killed, I've hunted, and I've enjoyed it." She moves closer, caressing her son's face with a touch that carries a hint of sinister eroticism, a whisper of incest. Vanessa continues, "I wish you could see the world as I do. Deacon opened my eyes. There's no turning back from that. Sooner or later, the Thirst always wins." Within the Oedipal framework, a mother's admission that she has aligned herself with the father—an obscene figure in the child's eyes—and embraced his appalling desires, represents the ultimate betrayal. The film masterfully explores the fraught psychological dynamics of the Family Romance, positioning the mother's desire alongside violence and murder, rendering it taboo and unacceptable in the process.

The necessity of Blade's blood for the Magra ritual is particularly intriguing, as it underscores the child's pivotal role in the parental dynamic. Without Blade's blood, Frost cannot access the ancient power he so desperately craves—highlighting how the child's very existence stirs in the father a need to reconnect with and perpetuate ancestral bonds. However, the Oedipus complex, while central to Freudian theory, remains highly controversial in modern psychology. Critics argue that there is scant scientific evidence to support it, particularly as studies of children's attitudes towards their parents during the so-called Oedipal stage fail to demonstrate the predicted shifts in affection. Freud drew on myths and anthropological stories to illustrate his theory, which, while fascinating, do not provide empirical validation. Case studies like that of Little Hans, often cited by Freud, cannot be generalised or verified through broader research or experimentation. Furthermore, the type of evidence Freud and his followers relied on—clinical accounts from patients during psychoanalytic treatment—is inherently subjective and lacks the robustness needed to substantiate his core hypotheses.

That being said, from a post-modern perspective, Jacques Lacan argued against displacing the Oedipus complex from its central role in psychosexual development. He maintained that the Oedipus complex—insofar as we recognise it as encompassing the entirety of our understanding, with a signification that overlays the realm of culture onto the individual—marks a person's introduction to the Symbolic Order. Through this process, the child learns about power that exists independently of itself, encountering a symbolic system that operates beyond its own existence. Furthermore, Lacan's assertion that "the ternary relation of the Oedipus complex" liberates the "prisoner of the dual relationship" between mother and son has proven invaluable to later psychoanalysts. By introducing the third term—the father or the symbolic law—the Oedipus complex disrupts the dyadic bond, allowing the child to navigate a more complex social and cultural framework. In this way, Blade undergoes the Oedipal crisis upon discovering his mother's betrayal, confronting a Symbolic Order that exists independently of himself. Through this painful process, he ultimately transcends the trauma, freeing himself from the consuming fixation on his mother and reclaiming a sense of his own agency.

The Addiction (1995)

Abel Ferrara's *The Addiction* is a bold, black-and-white horror experiment that fuses urban vampire edginess with philosophical inquiry, offering an intelligent and unconventional take on the subgenre. Lili Taylor stars as Kathleen, an introverted NYU graduate student who, one night, is attacked by a mysterious woman who calls herself Casanova. Casanova pushes Kathleen into a stairwell, bites her neck, and drinks her blood—a moment that irrevocably alters Kathleen's existence. As she transforms into a vampire, her personality undergoes a drastic shift. Once a conscientious researcher guided by morality, she becomes a ruthless predator, killing without remorse to satisfy her insatiable hunger. Her descent into nihilism is swift and intense. One day, while studying in the library, she meets an anthropology student. Later, she bites her, observing the young woman's tearful disbelief with eerie detachment. "My indifference is not the issue here," Kathleen states coldly. "It's your astonishment that needs studying."

Director Abel Ferrara has described *The Addiction* as an explicit metaphor for drug dependence, conceptualising the film as a Catholic redemption tale in which Kathleen, consumed by her lust for blood, ultimately surrenders to her powerlessness and seeks salvation in God. Before we explore this redemptive arc, let us first consider the film's depiction of substance use disorder as a psychiatric category. Addiction is defined by compulsive craving, even when the user is fully aware of its destructive consequences. It manifests as a pattern of pathological substance abuse, leading to repeated harmful outcomes. Dependence is marked by withdrawal symptoms when the drug is suddenly removed—these include anxiety, depression, insomnia, and heightened sensitivity to pain. Essentially, addiction functions as a defense mechanism—an attempt to evade feelings of helplessness or powerlessness. Becoming a junkie is often a futile effort to compensate for an inner void. Drugs provide a chemically induced escape, masking real-life trauma and dulling distressing experiences. The addict constructs a buffer against reality, blocking external events in a desperate bid for oblivion. In *The Addiction*, vampirism operates along the same lines—Kathleen's insatiable thirst for blood mirrors the compulsions of an addict, a cycle of self-destruction that both sustains and annihilates her.

Ferrara's film presents Kathleen as someone profoundly affected by the disturbing historical events she studies at NYU—she cannot observe them with detachment. Her deep empathy for the oppressed leaves her raw and exposed to the world's brutality, making chronic avoidance—surrendering to the vampire lifestyle—an increasingly seductive prospect. Traditional vampire symptoms (aversion to daylight, distaste for food, hiding from mirrors) take on new meaning when framed through the Symbolic Order of heroin addiction. Kathleen turns nocturnal, permanently shaded behind dark sunglasses, looking pale and gaunt. Needle marks stand in for bite wounds, and her absent reflection indicates her growing inability to face herself. Despite her academic ambitions, her scholarly work rapidly declines—hunger eclipses everything.

Much of Kathleen's time is spent chasing the dragon, lost in the futile pursuit of a high equal to her first encounter with Casanova. But nothing comes close to the sublime, dizzying euphoria of that initial bite. It is worth considering the significance of "Casanova" as a signifier, designating the strange creature who turns Kathleen. The historical Casanova—Giacomo Casanova—was an Italian adventurer from the Republic of Venice, whose infamous memoirs provide an unfiltered record of 18th-century European social customs. His name has become synonymous with seduction, yet many of his exploits—affairs with emotionally vulnerable women and underage girls—would now be seen as predatory. For Casanova, love and sex were rarely endowed with the seriousness of 19th-century Romanticism; his world was one of flirtation, bedroom games, and short-lived trysts, shaped by the aristocratic tendency to marry for social advantage rather than love.

Though multifaceted, Casanova's self-narrative is dominated by his insatiable sensual appetites—a detail that takes on a sinister new resonance in *The Addiction*.

Casanova's pattern was always the same: he would discover an attractive woman in distress, offer his assistance, and earn her gratitude. From there, seduction followed, leading to a short-lived but exhilarating affair. As his passion waned, he would plead his own unworthiness, orchestrate her pairing with a more suitable man, and then vanish from her life. *The Addiction* echoes this dynamic—Casanova, the vampire, instantly senses Kathleen's existential crisis and, for a fleeting moment, alleviates her despair with an ecstatic rush. But just as in Casanova's real-life conquests, the seduction is transient. Kathleen is left to suffer alone in the aftermath, abandoned in the city's shadows.

Scholar David Carter interprets *The Addiction* as a radical reimagining of the vampire film, one in which victims don't just succumb to vampirism—they willingly embrace it, taking on bloodlust as their own. Carter explains:

> Historically within fiction, while vampires so often represent sexual desire, the baggage that came with that desire was being a slave to it. Vampires lust for blood at a primal level. Within *The Addiction* it's taken even further. Vampires are both the addicted and the addiction, foisting themselves alluringly upon people who want to dabble in something dangerous and all-consuming. The words Casanova speaks to Kathleen ("Look at me and tell me to go away. Don't ask—tell me") become a refrain in the film. The idea is that the prey want to become addicted, even when they know the risks.

This dynamic shifts the traditional power structure of vampirism. Here, it is not just about predators overpowering victims—the victims' own compulsion to surrender plays a crucial part in the narrative, courting destruction, craving the very thing that will consume them.

Building on the film's prevailing motif of drug dependence, *Slant Magazine*'s Ed Gonzalez calls *The Addiction* "perhaps the most fabulously serpentine political work of Ferrara's career, a quivering nexus of AIDS allegory, identity crisis, historical unease, and socio-economic panic." Film scholars Yoram Allon, Del Cullen, and Hannah Patterson highlight the film's preoccupation with religion, salvation, and self-destruction—recurring themes in Ferrara's work—adding that it "perfectly illustrates [his] obsession with the collapse of moral order." In this reading, *The Addiction* becomes a metaphor for the theological concept of sin, drawing on references to Nietzsche and Descartes. Notably, one vampire even quotes the theologian R.C. Sproul, a staunch critic of Roman Catholicism, further embedding the film in a discourse on faith and corruption. Meanwhile, film critic Stephen Hunter interprets *The Addiction* as a sharp critique of academia, pointing to Kathleen's gradual disillusionment with philosophy as a means of understanding morality. He argues: "She's got a grudge against philosophy, which, in the long run, with all its constructs and rationalisations and insights, has proved somewhat inefficient as salvation." In this light, Kathleen's descent reflects the limits of intellectual inquiry when confronted with raw, existential horror.

The Addiction delivers one of the most provocative academic takedowns ever committed to film. In the climactic scene, Kathleen defends her dissertation before a committee and is awarded her Doctor of Philosophy. But the joyful celebration is short-lived. At the department's graduation party, she, Casanova, and a cohort of vampire victims launch a full-scale massacre, descending upon the attendees in a blood-drenched orgy of violence. What are we to make of this? I read it as an intentional desecration of a ceremony that arrogantly claims mastery over the acquisition of knowledge—especially in a field as murky and paradoxical as philosophy. The devouring of the entire department—ripping flesh, draining blood—is an act of revenge. It is the ultimate indictment from those who dwell in the darker fringes of reality, tortured souls who see ivory tower academic activity as a woefully fake display of authority. "You're not a person, you're nothing... You are a slave to what you are, and you are nothing." These words, spoken to Kathleen earlier in the film by a more seasoned vampire, now take on new significance. She delivers this message to her professors in the most undeniable way possible. In the end, the ceremony of intellectual achievement is rendered meaningless—the hunger always wins.

The Twilight Saga (2008–2012)

Now, onto *The Twilight Saga*—the five vampire-themed romance fantasy films based on Stephanie Meyer's four bestselling novels. *Twilight* (2008) introduces the love story between teenager Bella Swan and vampire Edward Cullen, centring on their blossoming relationship and the Cullen family's efforts to protect Bella from a group of hostile vampires. Edward refuses Bella's request to turn her into a vampire, insisting that she deserves to live a normal human life. *New Moon* (2009) explores Bella's descent into depression after the Cullens abruptly leave town. Her despair lingers until she forms a close bond with Jacob Black, a shapeshifter from the Quileute tribe who transforms into a werewolf. As Jacob and his pack vow to protect Bella from the vengeful vampire Victoria, Edward offers Bella a deal—he will grant her wish to become a vampire, but only if she agrees to marry him.

In *Eclipse* (2010), Bella grapples with the complexities of marrying a vampire. Meanwhile, to ensure her safety, Jacob and his fellow shapeshifters form an uneasy alliance with the Cullens to battle Victoria and her army of newborn vampires. Jacob confesses his love for Bella and tries—unsuccessfully—to persuade her to choose him over Edward. Ultimately, Bella accepts Edward's marriage proposal. *Breaking Dawn—Part 1* (2011) follows their wedding and honeymoon in Brazil, where Bella unexpectedly conceives a half-human, half-vampire child. As the pregnancy takes a devastating toll on her body, she teeters on the brink of destruction. In *Breaking Dawn—Part 2* (2012), Bella, now a newly transformed vampire, must master her powerful shielding abilities while protecting her daughter, Renesmee. The film culminates in a climactic confrontation between the Cullens—joined by their wolf allies and an international network of vampire friends—and the authoritarian Volturi.

Critical reception of *The Twilight Saga* has been decidedly mixed. Some have hailed it as "a genuine pop classic," with Stephenie Meyer's vision described as "Brontë-esque." Writing for *The Washington Post*, Michael O'Sullivan noted, "Despite melodrama that, at times, is enough to induce diabetes, there's enough wolf whistle in these sexy, scary romps to please anyone." The films were undeniably box office juggernauts but also drew extensive derision. Mick LaSalle of *The San Francisco Chronicle* warned, "Get ready for a bizarre soap opera pageant, consisting of a succession of static scenes with characters loping into the frame to announce exactly what they're thinking." Meanwhile, Roger Ebert of *The Chicago Sun-Times* lamented the franchise's endless, unremarkable dialogue between the central trio, particularly taking issue with the protracted, brooding stares exchanged between Edward, Jacob, and Bella.

Breaking Dawn—Part 1 was particularly eviscerated by critics, with *Rotten Tomatoes* summing it up as: "Slow, joyless, and loaded with unintentionally humorous moments, strictly for fans of the franchise." The saga's grand finale fared slightly better, deemed passably entertaining—but the *Twilight* phenomenon continues to evoke wildly divergent opinions. Some dismiss it as objectively risible, a cringe-fest of melodrama and vacant stares; others hold deep sentimental attachment to it, crediting the series with modernising the vampire trope for a new generation. Yet, love it or loathe it, one fact remains indisputable: *The Twilight Saga* has raked in over

$3.4 billion worldwide. It is inconceivably popular. And I need to know—why? What precisely does *Twilight* tap into that makes it so utterly bankable? What raw nerve does it repeatedly smash, making audiences return for more, despite its aesthetic and narrative being, let's be real—bland, basic, and teetering on banal? Won't somebody tell me, what is this voodoo that *Twilight* do so well?

Before I attempt to answer these questions—inevitably through a psychoanalytic lens—I first need to take a moment to consider the psyche of *Twilight*'s creator, the legendary Stephenie Meyer. This American novelist, with no prior writing experience, crafted a vampire romance saga that sold over 100 million copies and was translated into 37 languages, spawning one of the most lucrative film franchises in history. Meyer was an avid reader but not an author when the idea for *Twilight* came to her in a dream on 2 June 2003—a vision of a vampire falling in love with a human girl while struggling with his thirst for her blood. Inspired by Jane Austen and William Shakespeare, she wrote the novel soon after. Though initially met with multiple rejections, Meyer eventually secured a book deal, setting in motion an empire of *Twilight* adaptations that would dominate pop culture and the box office.

Meyer's membership in The Church of Jesus Christ of Latter-day Saints strongly shaped her novels. Her books contain no drinking, smoking, or explicit sex, and in *Twilight*, Edward and Bella remain abstinent until marriage. Themes central to Meyer's Mormon values—agency, mortality, temptation, and eternal life—are woven throughout her work. Her personal life reflects a similarly traditional ethos. She met her future husband as a child in Arizona, married him at 21 in 1994, and together they have three sons. I highlight this biographical detail to underscore what a conventional gal Meyer is. She comes from a world where certain experiences are off-limits—a reality that fosters longing, a state of perpetual desire, and a tendency to fantasise about scenarios that exist far beyond her reach. And, naturally, the more outlandish, the better.

This is the divine nectar Ms. Meyer bottled—the essence of *l'objet petit a*, the unattainable object of desire in Lacanian psychoanalysis. Sometimes referred to as the object-cause of desire, it is the force that compels us towards a particular object, not because of its inherent value but because it fills a gap within us. The "object a" expresses the fundamental lack at the heart of human existence—a void that fuels our endless search for fulfilment beyond mere biological needs. It is the object we seek in the Other, the ever-elusive answer to our longing. Slavoj Žižek likens the "object a" to Alfred Hitchcock's MacGuffin, explaining, "The MacGuffin is *l'objet petit a* pure and simple: the lack, the remainder of the Real that sets in motion the symbolic movement of interpretation, a hole at the centre of the symbolic order, the mere appearance of some secret to be explained and interpreted." Meyer taps directly into this void, constructing a fantasy so intoxicating that it becomes an obsession—precisely because it offers everything and nothing at once.

In *Twilight*, Bella is uprooted from Arizona and sent to live with her father, Charlie, the police chief of a small town on Washington State's Olympic Peninsula. Her mother, Renée, has remarried Phil, a minor league baseball player whose career keeps them constantly on the move. As a Freudian, I interpret this abrupt geographical shift as a psychic wound. Renée's laissez-faire attitude might seem benign, but on an unsymbolised level, Bella will have experienced it as a painful maternal rejection. It will have hurt. And where there is hurt, there is a void—a chasm that demands to be filled.

Lo and behold, at her new high school, Bella becomes instantly fascinated by the mysterious, aloof Cullen siblings. She is seated next to Edward Cullen in biology class on her first day, but his reaction is nothing short of bizarre—he appears repulsed by her. Edward's cold indifference makes him the perfect object onto which Bella can project all her unmet desires—wishes that dissolved into the ether when aimed at her impulsive harebrained mother, who quite literally chose the streets over her daughter. Edward Cullen—a century-old vampire, preserved in the form of a teenage dreamboat, brimming with experience—slowly becomes obsessed with Bella. The guy no other high school girl could score wants her—this is a top-tier teenage daydream. Ironically, despite Bella's lack of enthusiasm for sports, her journey with the Cullens will eventually lead her back to baseball in one of the most iconic scenes of the film paired with Muse's song *Supermassive Black Hole*—this time with a supernatural twist, far removed from her stepdad Phil's minor league games that kept her mother on the move.

Critics have long decried Edward's behaviour as troubling—his obsessive tendencies, controlling nature, sneaking into Bella's room at night to watch her sleep. But from the perspective of a girl whose mother shipped her off thousands of miles away, the inordinately vigilant, even stalkerish, Edward fantasy is probably intoxicating. Bella craves attention, and Edward provides it in inexhaustible supply. What a coup! Her boyfriend tells her he can't get enough of her—that she's like his own personal brand of heroin. And heroin, of course, is the ultimate "object a," the emblem of bottomless longing, ceaseless desire. He wants her *that* much.

Edward's world soon begins to revolve entirely around Bella, and his devotion manifests in ever more elaborate—and increasingly weird—attempts to protect her. For a girl who spent most of her childhood parenting her chaotic mother, this is a radical reversal. Now, Bella is the one being shielded—not just by Edward, but by his entire clan, a wealthy and powerful immortal family devoted to keeping her safe. Being loved up is Bella's primary focus—and I don't say this to mock girly preoccupations. On the contrary, I'm on her side, rooting for her to follow her desire, which in psychoanalysis is the ultimate ethical act. At Cullen HQ, the vampires are perpetually arranged in pristine hetero couple formations—a visual motif that remains constant throughout the series. The unwavering (borderline waxwork) display of eternal love in the Cullen household functions as a kind of compensatory illusion, concealing the torn fabric of Bella's broken family. At this rate, who even cares that the Cullens are undead?

In this fantasy, Bella gets what she *needs*—safety, love, community, and responsible elders—but what she *wants* remains tantalisingly out of reach: sex with her boyfriend. Edward, being "old school," insists on waiting until their wedding night. As if this weren't enough to heighten the allure of the unattainable "object a," *Twilight* adds a delectable love triangle: Bella is ardently pursued not only by a vampire but also by a wolf. Werewolf Jacob later imprints on Renesmee, Bella and Edward's half-human, half-vampire child. This storyline has understandably sparked outrage, with many finding Jacob's fixation on a literal baby unforgivably creepy—and rightly so. But if we view this through the lens of Bella's sordid fantasy, Jacob's actions can be seen as a projection of an ex-boyfriend who continues to pine for her, clinging to some semblance of closeness through her daughter. This aligns with the concept of the "object a," the elusive object of desire that drives the narrative, always orbiting Bella. The extended honeymoon scenes in *Breaking Dawn—Part 1* are equally fascinating. Edward and Bella's passion is so intense that they break the bed and trash the room. While nothing explicit is shown, everything is implied, and the film makes it clear that Bella is no pillow princess; she fully embraces the fervour of her wedding night, leaning into its romantic, passionate energy.

A central concern of the *Twilight* series is the unrelenting protection of Bella Swan. To shield her from harm, sworn enemies—vampires and werewolves—set aside their animosity and unite. Later, this safeguarding extends to Renesmee, an extension of Bella herself, who becomes the top priority. An international coalition of elite, glamorous vampires drops everything to rally in defence of Bella's family. At first glance, it's easy to dismiss Bella as a megalomaniac, delusional about her own importance. But this isn't about Ego—it's about desire. I would argue that the intensity of desire exhibited by a teenage girl is the most unsettling horror element in the *Twilight* films. The fact that a young woman, written by a female author, is portrayed as capable of such frankly deranged levels of longing is unthinkable. That she dares to believe she is worthy of this overwhelming love is the tacit fear object, perhaps only unconsciously hinted at by the writer and directors. In a society that routinely dismisses and suppresses the desires of women and girls, *Twilight* becomes a taboo-breaking act of defiance.

And this is why the franchise utterly killed at the box office. Women feel seen in these movies—our wants are front and centre. I'm happy to state, in no uncertain terms, that I'm a *Twilight* fan and, for the record, firmly Team Edward. No hate. Long live the teenage girl's imagination. May her daring spirit carry her beyond the permitted limits of the forest. May topless, sparkling torsos comfort her. May the thousands of hours spent obsessively daydreaming be worth it. May her crush protect her where her caregivers failed her. This is the snow-covered hill I'll die on, so pitch that tent and tell Jacob I'm gonna need some of that body heat action.

A Girl Walks Home Alone at Night (2014)

Ana Lily Amirpour's Persian-language American vampire western *A Girl Walks Home Alone at Night* unfolds in the fictional Iranian ghost town of Bad City, centring on its enigmatic titular figure—"a lonesome vampire," played by Sheila Vand. A striking blend of genres and influences, the film reimagines the vampire mythos through a moody, monochrome lens. In his review for *Variety*, Guy Lodge praised Amirpour's debut as a sly, slinky vampire romance, while Drew Taylor of *Indiewire* remarked that watching the film gave him the rare sense of witnessing something iconic and important unfold in real time.

The chador-clad girl drifts through Bad City's desolate streets, spending her time skateboarding, listening to music alone, or bedevilling unsuspecting pedestrians in the dead of night. One evening, she crosses paths with Saeed, a sleazy drug-dealer and pimp. He invites her back to his apartment, oblivious to the danger lurking beneath her silent, watchful exterior. As he does drugs and blasts dance music, she remains still. Unbeknownst to Saeed, she had been observing him earlier that night—witnessing his cruelty as he abused a sex worker, forcing fellatio on her. With this in mind, the Girl's intentions crystallise. Without warning her fangs emerge. She seductively lures Saeed into a false sense of control, gently sucking on his finger—before curtly biting it off. What follows is swift and brutal. The misogynist aggressor gets his comeuppance.

Director Ana Lily Amirpour has described vampires as multifaceted beings—serial killers, romantics, historians, drug addicts—all bound together in one entity. *A Girl Walks Home Alone at Night* explores these dimensions in various ways, presenting its protagonist as an antihero vigilante who targets corrupt men. As a vampire, she moves through the streets at night without fear, inverting the implications of the film's title. She is not the victim—she is the predator, wielding a power rarely afforded to women in a place like Bad City. A feminist reading emerges naturally. One moment, in particular, stands out: the Girl stops a child on the street, giving him the heebie-jeebies. "Are you a good boy?" she asks. He acquiesces, desperate to convince her. She warns him not to lie. He insists on his innocence, but she leans in closer: "I can take your eyes out of your skull and give them to the dogs to eat. Till the end of your life, I'll be watching you. Understand?" The scene takes on a deeply subversive charge, evoking Iran's religious morality police—who patrol the streets, keeping guard over women's behaviour and clothing. In *A Girl Walks Home Alone At Night*, the power dynamic is reversed.

In Amirpour's film, the vampire functions symbolically as the Superego, enacting a revenge fantasy that redirects inherited guilt from the Iranian state. There is a fascinating paradox at play—the female figure co-opts the authoritarian tactics of the state, wielding them not to suppress women, but to shield them from harm. Much like Iran's religious ruling class that prowls the streets, sucking the life from cities, the Girl adopts a similarly authoritarian posture. But here, the relational hierarchy is inverted. The veiled woman—typically a symbol of chastity and submission—is reimagined as a predator in the urban underworld of Bad City.

When I describe the veiled girl in Amirpour's film as embodying the Superego, I refer to the part of the psyche that acts as a self-critical conscience, internalising social standards of acceptable behaviour. The Superego forms through identification with parental authority, operating as an unconscious regulator of morality. It strives for perfection, shaping ideals, goals, and prohibitions—often clashing with the Id's primal urges. The Ego, caught between these opposing forces, struggles to mediate their divergent demands. In Amirpour's film, the chador-clad Girl functions as the internal voice that punishes perceived misconduct with guilt and retribution. She takes on the role of Iranian culture's inner critic, but rather than working to manifest the repression of women, she sets her sights on male criminals and potential abusers—subverting the state's moral authority into a force of vigilante justice.

Freudian theory suggests that the greater the repression, the more rigidly the Superego asserts control over individuals and society. In Iran, the morality police administer religious law through surveillance and arrests primarily against women deemed to be in violation of the Islamic dress code. Since the 1979 Islamic Revolution, Iranian law has required all women to wear a hijab or headscarf covering their hair and neck. The morality police, often operating from vans, patrol public spaces alongside chador-clad female enforcers, detaining those who fail to meet state-imposed dress standards. According to Amnesty International, even girls as young as seven are subjected to this mandate.

On 16 September 2022, the arrest and subsequent death of 22-year-old Mahsa Amini for allegedly wearing her hijab improperly sparked mass protests and global condemnation. Director Ana Lily Amirpour has used her platform to highlight these issues and express solidarity with the protestors. *A Girl Walks Home Alone at Night* serves as a cinematic counterpoint to this reality. It reclaims the mechanisms of control—surveillance and retribution—but instead of targeting women, it redirects them towards predatory men. The veiled vampire in Bad City is an avenger, turning the gaze back on those who exploit and oppress. Amirpour's film upends the Superego's role, reconfiguring its restrictive forces into a means of resistance. Where Iran's morality police suppress agency, the film's protagonist asserts it. What we find is a provocative cultural critique—interrogating the ways in which institutional authority regulates behaviour and imposes compliance, reimagining longstanding power dynamics.

Doctor Sleep (2019)

Mike Flanagan's supernatural horror film *Doctor Sleep*, based on Stephen King's novel of the same name, serves as a sequel to *The Shining*, continuing the story of Dan Torrance. Decades after surviving the horrors of the Overlook Hotel, Dan remains deeply scarred by his childhood trauma. Guided by the ghost of Dick Hallorann, he learns to contain the sinister hotel entities within psychic "lockboxes." By 2011, however, he has turned to alcoholism as a way to suppress his Shine. Seeking a fresh start, Dan moves to a small town in New Hampshire, where he begins attending Alcoholics Anonymous meetings and finds work as a hospice orderly. There, he uses his Shine to ease the passing of dying patients, earning the nickname "Doctor Sleep."

Meanwhile, a secretive cult known as the True Knot, led by the enigmatic and ruthless Rose the Hat, hunts down children with supernatural abilities. The cult extends its members' lifespans by feeding on "steam"—a powerful psychic essence released through the torture and murder of those who possess the Shine. Stephen King has said that he wrote *Doctor Sleep* because he wondered what Danny Torrance would be like as an adult. Having endured unspeakable terror as a child, Dan deliberately suppresses his Shine, seeking to bury his past. But even in adulthood, the ghosts of the Overlook continue to haunt him, pushing him towards self-destruction.

Director Mike Flanagan described *The Shining* as "very much about addiction, which is doom. It's about annihilation and the destruction of a family," whereas *Doctor Sleep* is about recovery—a journey of rebirth and salvation. In the context of this chapter, the film's most relevant figures are the True Knot, a cult of quasi-immortal "vampires" who sustain themselves by torturing and feeding on the psychic life force, or steam, of children gifted with the Shine. The True Knot is ancient, its origins shrouded in mystery. At their peak, their numbers were so vast that splinter factions emerged—hence the name "True" Knot, denoting the original group. To mask their activities, they own businesses, campgrounds, and remote properties, where they conduct their rituals of turning and feeding. One such location is the desolate landscape surrounding the Overlook Hotel.

Only select members of the True Knot possess the ability to detect children with the Shine, but all share a degree of psychic awareness. Their foresight is so powerful that they anticipated 9/11 months in advance, sensing an impending catastrophe. While they prefer consuming the steam of children, if an adult with the Shine possesses a particularly rare or desirable ability, they may attempt to recruit and turn them. However, adult Shine is likened to eating bad meat from an old cow—far less satisfying. The True Knot operate as psychic vampires—folkloric entities believed to feed on the vitality of others. The term also extends to real-world encounters—those people who seem to drain energy from others, leaving them feeling exhausted or depleted. While there is no scientific basis for the existence of psychic vampirism, the concept is universally understood. We've all experienced it—some people simply suck the life out of us.

The notion of psychic vampirism has taken on various interpretations. In *What We Do in the Shadows*, Colin Robinson is portrayed as a literal "energy vampire" who drains people's life force by being insufferably boring or frustrating. American author Albert Bernstein coined the term "emotional vampire" to describe individuals with personality disorders who leave others feeling depleted. More broadly, energy vampire is often used metaphorically to describe people whose presence leaves others exhausted, unfocused, or depressed—without invoking supernatural explanations. Dion Fortune explored "psychic parasitism" in her 1930 book *Psychic Self-Defense*, distinguishing between true psychic vampirism and psychological conditions like folie à deux. In the 1960s, Anton LaVey and the Church of Satan popularised the term "psychic vampire," describing individuals who sap others' emotional and spiritual energy. Meanwhile, in the 1970s, English musician Peter Hammill credited violinist Graham Smith with coining "energy vampires" to describe overzealous, intrusive fans.

What sets the True Knot apart from traditional vampires is their specific fixation on humans with the Shine—a psychic ability that enables telepathic communication, mind-reading, retrospective visions, and glimpses into the future. Unlike conventional vampires, the True Knot are not immune to disease; their extreme age makes them vulnerable to modern viruses. In this framework, the Shine functions as an advanced mental capacity—highly prized because it offers a more sustaining life force.

Dan becomes aware of the True Knot's threat and sets out to destroy them, ultimately returning to the Overlook as a last resort (in every sense of the term), believing its malevolent power will be just as dangerous for Rose, their leader. During their battle, Rose attempts to overpower him, but Dan turns the tables by unlocking the mental lockboxes that contain the Overlook's terrifying entities. Drawn to Rose's power, the hotel's spectral figures swarm and devour her, consuming her psychic steam as she perishes. This pivotal scene reveals a lot about the Overlook: beyond its history of suicides, gangland hits, and mysterious ownership changes, its dread-inducing inhabitants may not simply be ghosts but psychic vampires—feeding on the life force of those who survive its horrors.

Danny is not just a survivor of his father's alcoholic rage and domestic abuse at the Overlook; his Shine also grants him the ability to perceive the hotel as a liminal psychic space, one that records and endlessly replays past violence through the Shine. The Grady sisters, the decaying woman in Room 237, the bloodied former hotel owner cheerfully asking, "Great party, isn't it?" and the axe-wielding Jack Torrance—these figures live rent-free in Danny's mind, just as trauma does. They intrude on the present, stoke fear and anxiety, dim his Shine, and sap his cognitive potential. Like the True Knot, Danny's demons are psychic vampires of a different kind, feeding on his suffering, exploiting his perpetual mental distress.

Danny grows up learning to compartmentalise his trauma, storing away the horrors of his childhood in psychic lockboxes—silent, inexpressible, too overwhelming to confront. As an adult, he turns to alcohol, numbing himself to escape the tyranny of his demons. But it is only in the final act of *Doctor Sleep*, when Dan releases the Overlook's spectral figures from their mental prisons and faces them head-on, that he truly begins to break free. In doing so, he enacts the ultimate act of healing—driving an allegorical stake through the heart of his trauma, no longer its captive, but its conqueror.

Glossary of Psychoanalytic Terms

- **Castration Anxiety**—A Freudian concept referring to the unconscious fear of losing power or authority, often tied to masculinity.
- **Foreclosure**—A Lacanian term describing a psychotic structure where a key element of reality is rejected rather than repressed.
- **Imaginary Order**—The register of images, identification, and illusion through which the Ego is formed, grounded in misrecognition and the Mirror Stage.
- **Liminal Space**—A transitional or in-between state, often evoking feelings of unease and transformation.
- **Munchausen Syndrome by Proxy**—A psychiatric disorder where a caregiver, often a parent, fabricates or induces illness in a dependent to gain attention or maintain control.
- **L'Objet Petit A**—In Lacanian theory, the "object a" is the unattainable object of desire that fuels human longing. It represents the void that can never be fully satisfied, often projected onto external figures or fantasies.
- **Oedipus Complex**—A Freudian theory describing a child's unconscious desire for the opposite-sex parent and rivalry with the same-sex parent.
- **Oral Fixation**—A term from Freud's psychosexual development theory describing an unresolved dependency on oral pleasures (e.g., sucking, biting, or consuming). In adulthood, it can manifest as addictions, excessive talking, or attachment issues.
- **The Phallus**—In Lacanian theory, the phallus is not simply the male organ but a signifier of desire and symbolic power. It represents what is perceived as "lacking" in the subject and plays a role in structuring identity and sexual difference.
- **Psychic Vampirism**—A concept describing individuals who drain the emotional or psychological energy of others. This idea is often linked to dependency, manipulation, and the parasitic nature of certain relationships.
- **Superego**—One of Freud's three psychic structures (alongside the Id and Ego), the Superego represents the internalised voice of authority, societal norms, and moral conscience. It criticises and regulates desires, often inducing guilt.
- **Symbolic Order**—A key Lacanian concept referring to the structured realm of language, law, and social rules that govern human identity and relationships. Entry into the Symbolic order marks the individual's integration into society.

Home Invasion 6

Paranoia, domestic space, and psychosexual threat

Vampires channel fear of an outside force breaching the boundaries of the self. Home invasion horror dispenses with the supernatural buffer and confronts us with the most intimate terror of all—violence erupting within the supposed safety of the domestic sphere. In these films, the home, traditionally a place of refuge and security, is transformed into a site of violation. The terror does not come from mythical creatures or extraterrestrial entities but from human perpetrators, whose presence shatters the illusion of control over one's private space.

The horror of home invasion stems from its stark plausibility. Unlike monsters and ghosts, intruders require no unique supernatural abilities—they can simply walk in. Whether the invasion is meticulously planned or disturbingly random, it exposes the fragility of personal boundaries and the scary reality that the structures we build to protect ourselves are, ultimately, permeable. These films confront our deepest anxieties about vulnerability, surveillance, and the collapse of order, revealing that sometimes the most disturbing horror is not some unknown creature lurking in the shadows, but the uninvited guest who is already inside.

Gaslight (1944)

Let's start this final chapter of the book with an examination of George Cukor's American psychological thriller *Gaslight*, adapted from Patrick Hamilton's 1938 play. The film follows a young woman whose husband slowly manipulates her into believing she is losing her sanity. The story begins with the murder of world-famous opera singer Alice Alquist in her

London home. Her niece, Paula, is sent to Italy to follow in Alice's footsteps as a singer. However, during a lesson, her teacher, Maestro Guardi, expresses frustration with her performance:

> There's no use, Paula. You are not concentrating. Your mind's not on your singing. All these years you've worked so hard. Now what's come over you? This opera is tragedy, signorina. You seem incapable of understanding. Did you never hear your aunt sing *Lucia*? [...] The trouble is not in your voice alone. Your heart is not in your singing anymore. Each time you come here now, you look happier and you sing worse. Tell me, Paula, you're in love?

Let's put a pin in this—I'll return to it later.

Paula's secret lover is her accompanist, Gregory Anton. After a whirlwind two-week romance, they marry, and at his suggestion, return to London to live in Alice Alquist's long-vacant townhouse. Haunted by memories of her aunt's murder, Paula struggles to settle in. Gregory encourages her to store away the old furnishings in the attic, subtly erasing traces of the past. When Paula discovers a letter addressed to Alice from a man named Sergis Bauer, Gregory reacts with sudden aggression, before swiftly apologising. Soon, strange occurrences escalate. Gregory insists that Paula is forgetful, that she misplaces things, and is losing touch with reality. At night, she hears noises coming from the attic, and the gaslights mysteriously dim when Gregory is out—yet he dismisses her fears, insisting it's all in her mind. Isolated from the outside world, Paula is made to believe she is a kleptomaniac, unfit to be in public. Gregory claims that her mother died in an asylum and that the letter from Sergis Bauer never existed. Doubting her own sanity, Paula begins to unravel. The truth, however, is chilling: the attic noises and flickering gaslights are real. Gregory has orchestrated everything. His marriage to Paula was a calculated ploy to access Alice's home. His true goal? To drive Paula mad, have her institutionalised, and claim Alice's estate—allowing him to finally seize the hidden jewels he has been searching for all along.

The term "gaslight" has transcended its cinematic origins, becoming widely recognised in self-help and popular psychology. It describes a form of psychological manipulation in which a person's perception of reality is systematically undermined, much like Paula's experience with Gregory. The first recorded use of "gaslighting" in its gerund form appeared in a 1995 *New York Times* column by Maureen Dowd. Though initially obscure, the term gained widespread traction in the mid-2010s and is now embedded in everyday language. Merriam-Webster defines gaslighting as "psychological manipulation that makes someone question their perception of reality, leading to dependence on the perpetrator." While occasionally referenced in clinical literature, the American Psychological Association still considers it a colloquialism rather than a formal psychological diagnosis.

A surface-level reading of *Gaslight* might frame it as a straightforward case study of domestic emotional abuse—an account of a man scheming against his wife, exploiting her vulnerability to enrich himself while eroding her grip on reality. However, I see this as merely the film's manifest content, with a deeper meaning lurking beneath its surface. Paula's journey to Italy to study opera under Maestro Guardi—the same teacher who trained Alice Alquist—suggests that singing is more than a profession; it is a vital link to her late aunt. Opera, in this context, symbolises vitality and artistic passion. But Paula's lessons are stagnating. Maestro Guardi senses that her mind is elsewhere—distracted, unfocused. He deduces that only one force could have disrupted her devotion to her craft: love. Encouraging Paula to follow her heart, he tells her:

> Free yourself from the past... and forget your singing, too, for a while. Happiness is better than art. Will you let me meet the man who is taking my pupil away from me? Yes, of course. You have a rendez-vous with him. The moment your lesson is over, you fly to him. Is he jealous of your music, these hours you spend away from him?

Paula's romance with her piano accompanist, Gregory, abruptly disrupts her trajectory in the opera world. He overwhelms her with affection, a tactic known as "love bombing"—a manipulative strategy often employed by narcissists and abusers in tandem with gaslighting. Love bombing involves grand romantic gestures, excessive flattery, placing the target on a pedestal, demanding premature commitment, resisting boundaries, and making sweeping promises about the future. The goal is to secure devotion quickly before methodically breaking the victim down. Gregory initially appears charming and exhilarating, but this façade rapidly disintegrates, giving way to emotional abuse and sinister exploitation.

Unbeknownst to Paula, Gregory is, in fact, Sergis Bauer—her aunt's murderer. He deliberately sought her out in Italy, married her, and lured her back to London with the sole intent of gaining access to Alice's home, where he obsessively searches for her hidden jewels. Alice Alquist, a world-famous opera singer adored for her voice, was strangled to death in her own home. How bitterly ironic that her defining gift—her throat—became the very site of her demise. My reading is that Sergis Bauer enacts this stranglehold again, this time on Paula's future. He squeezes the life out of her singing career by luring her away from her lessons under the guise of love, effectively silencing her. What begins as an over-elaborate display of affection transforms into suffocating control—soon Paula is completely isolated from the outside world.

The house—a freakish mausoleum and a site of psychological torment—preserves past achievements in amber, stifling the possibility of anything new. Paula resists returning to the London home, still haunted by the unprocessed trauma of her aunt's murder. "She had been strangled. Her lovely face was all… No, I can't stay here," she recalls, visibly distressed. Gregory, ever the manipulator, seizes the moment:

> Then how would it be if we took away all these things that remind you so of her? The painting, all this furniture. Shut it away so you can't even see it? Suppose we make it a new house with new things, beautiful things, for a new, beautiful life for us. We'll put everything away and board it up, so you'll never have to see it again, never even think of it. While you are afraid of anything, there cannot be any happiness for us. You must forget her.

Gregory's strategy operates according to the logic of repression—a key psychoanalytic defence mechanism that keeps unacceptable or anxiety-inducing thoughts from entering conscious awareness. In this way, the act of strangulation serves a dual purpose: it both extinguishes vitality and erases all trace of the event. My reading of *Gaslight* positions it as an allegory, tracing the artist's turbulent journey—from inexperience, through emotional chaos and self-doubt, to ultimately mastering the ability to transmute tragedy into art.

The opera Paula performs in her lesson is *Lucia di Lammermoor*, renowned for its famous scene in which the title character descends into madness. Recall Maestro Guardi's words: "This opera is tragedy, signorina. You seem incapable of understanding. Did you never hear your aunt sing *Lucia*? The trouble is not in your voice alone. Your heart is not in your singing anymore. Each time you come here now, you look happier, and you sing worse." In this sense, Gregory Anton—later revealed as the murderer Sergis Bauer—fulfils his role as the ever-present accompanist to a rising opera star. He leads her to the site of trauma, an unavoidable space for an artist, where she is forced to confront torment, insecurity, and the darkest recesses of her own mind. The accompanist's role is to push the artist towards tragedy, compelling her to process it in its rawest form. In this warped way, Gregory becomes a paradoxical guide—compelling Paula to unflinchingly endure suffering so that she may ultimately transcend it, reclaim her voice, and assert herself.

Rear Window (1954)

Alfred Hitchcock's mystery thriller *Rear Window* is often hailed as the godfather of surveillance films—a study of Hitchcock's fixation on voyeurism and the neurotic impulse to watch. The film follows Jeff, a professional photographer confined to a wheelchair while recovering from a broken leg in his New York City apartment. His rear window overlooks a courtyard, offering a direct view into the lives of his neighbours. During a relentless heatwave, they leave their windows open to stay cool, allowing Jeff to indulge in silent observation. Among them are: a lonely woman he dubs "Miss Lonelyhearts," a newlywed couple, a struggling pianist, an attractive dancer he nicknames "Miss Torso," a middle-aged couple with a small dog that enjoys digging in the flower garden, and Lars Thorwald, a traveling costume jewellery salesman with a bedridden wife.

Jeff receives frequent visits from his girlfriend, Lisa—a stylish Park Avenue fashion designer and model—who urges him to take an assignment that would keep him in New York rather than chasing perilous stories abroad. But Jeff enjoys adrenaline, he is drawn to the exotic and the extreme. His reputation is built on capturing images no one else dares to get, including the precise moment an out-of-control race car crashed—smashing his camera and breaking his leg in an instant. Now, grounded by a heavy cast that runs up to his hip, the daredevil photographer is reduced to the role of passive spectator. The irony is inescapable: the man who thrives on dynamic movement is now completely immobilised. Later, I will argue that his fixed, impotent position exposes the true nature of his pathology—that of a sexless obsessional neurotic, drawn to self-sabotage and retreating from the life-force in favour of absence.

In *Rear Window*'s opening scene, Hitchcock's camera lingers on the residential building Jeff fanatically watches—each open window outlining a private drama, like an enormous gallery exhibition, a multiplex of unfolding films, or even an Instagram grid. Hitch's camera then pans inside, revealing Jeff's apartment walls, densely covered with framed photographs from his assignments. The interior squares mirror the exterior ones, reinforcing Jeff's preference for compartmentalised, neatly arranged windows of activity. We also glimpse the cover of a fashion magazine featuring a beautiful blonde woman, whom we are invited to associate with Lisa. Curiously, a photo-negative of the same image is framed and displayed. Why would Jeff preserve a reversed, inside-out version of femininity? Perhaps Lisa—and the stability she represents—poses the greatest threat to him, scarier than crashing cars and war zones. The act of framing an image carries a sense of finality, like a full stop at the end of a photographic sentence. Yet Jeff's choice to showcase a negative suggests a deep ambivalence, a subconscious resistance to the conventional life Lisa offers.

One night, Jeff is jolted by the sound of a woman screaming and glass shattering across the courtyard. The next morning, he notices that Thorwald's wife has vanished, and watches as Thorwald meticulously cleans a large knife and handsaw. Convinced that Thorwald has murdered her, Jeff shares his suspicions with Lisa and his nurse, Stella. Soon after, the neighbour's dog is found dead—strangled. Its distraught owner cries out, prompting everyone to rush to their windows—except for Thorwald, who remains seated in the dark, silently smoking a cigar. This unnerving detail cements Jeff's theory: Thorwald must have buried something in the flower bed and killed the dog to stop it from digging. When Thorwald leaves, Lisa and Stella seize the moment to investigate. They dig through the flowers but find nothing. Then, to Jeff's astonishment, Lisa takes a bold risk—climbing the fire escape and slipping into Thorwald's apartment through an open window. When Thorwald unexpectedly returns, she is trapped. If he discovers her, he could kill her on the spot. Jeff frantically calls the police, reporting an assault in progress. But before help arrives, Thorwald notices Lisa signalling across the courtyard—and then, in a chilling moment of realisation, his gaze shifts. He sees Jeff.

So, what's really going on here? *Rear Window* is a masterful exploration of scopophilia, the psychoanalytic concept referring to the pleasure of looking, which Hitch understood as fundamental to the cinematic experience. Jeff likes to watch. As a photographer, he's trained to see, to capture the world through his lens. But in my reading, he hides behind the camera in a dysfunctional way. The demands of his profession—rushing off at a moment's notice, risking life and limb for the perfect shot—allow him to avoid deeper emotional and intimate engagement. He is, in every sense, developmentally stuck, diverting all his libidinal energy into far-off scenarios that have nothing to do with him. Of course, the irony of *Rear Window* is that Jeff, one of the best eyes in the biz, completely fails to see the woman right in front of him. Lisa catwalks chicly through his apartment like something out of a dream—a vision—but she barely gets a look-in! Seriously, what's the matter with this Jeff guy? Lisa is the full package: elegant, thoughtful, and whip-smart. She's even willing to abandon her New York lifestyle and travel the world with him, but he dodges every opportunity for meaningful connection, offering excuse after excuse to keep things in a holding pattern. She tries to sleep with him, and he cockblocks himself. As Hitchcock scholar Rebecca McCallum once remarked, "Jeff is a man who likes to watch porn but doesn't have sex." *Touché.*

Jeff's relentless evasion of the erotic brings to mind Freud's *Rat Man* case study—a 1907 analysis of a 29-year-old Austrian lawyer, Ernst Lanzer, who sought therapy for obsessive fears and crippling compulsions (Freud 1909). Freud gave him the moniker "Rat Man" due to his recurring nightmarish fantasies about rats. Lanzer had been in love with his girlfriend, Gisela, for nine years, yet he endlessly postponed marriage—kicking the relationship can down the road—trapped in a cycle of inhibition, rumination, and compulsive rituals. His neurosis caused him to obsessively repeat bizarre time-consuming activities, and he seemed to associate sexual gratification with injury, threat, and harm—a pattern that feels eerily reminiscent of Jeff in *Rear Window*. Jeff is utterly engrossed in the drama of his neighbours, a voyeuristic tableau that presents sexuality (Miss Torso and the newlyweds), heartbreak (Miss Lonelyhearts), and outright murder (Thorwald and his wife) as facets of the same spectacle. Eroticism here is linked with destruction; pleasure is laced with punishment. In this building, if you get off, you get offed!

Like the Rat Man, Jeff is paralysed by ambivalence and procrastination, unable to act. His cast bears the inscription, "Here lie the broken bones of Jeffries," evoking both humiliation and a kind of living death—he exists as a mortified man in every sense, embarrassed and undead. Obsessional neurosis conveniently spares the subject from making difficult life decisions, sidestepping the burden of managing erotic and hostile impulses directly. In Jeff's case, his intrusive thoughts and sordid spy fetish serve as compulsive rituals—prolonging his avoidance, staving off the existential discomfort of confronting his life with any real depth or intention.

What astonishes me about *Rear Window* is the sheer extent to which Lisa goes to prove her love—not only indulging Jeff's convoluted true-crime theories but literally breaking and entering the very space that transfixes him. In a last-ditch attempt to command his attention, she physically climbs into his fantasy world. She scales the wall and inserts herself inside the object of his fascination—Thorwald's flat—because, apparently, this is the only way he'll see her. It's utterly shocking when she does this! It might seem like Lisa is revealing a daring, adventurous side of herself in this stunt, but perhaps she's merely overcompensating for Jeff's powerlessness to affect the scenes he obsessively watches. She wholly aligns herself with his lack, transposing her body onto the building itself. Lisa is backed into a corner—fusing her material self with the site of her boyfriend's desire—because, more than anything, Jeff is aroused by *this*.

Earlier, when Lisa still doubted Jeff's theory about Thorwald, she remarked, "If someone came in here, they wouldn't believe what they'd see. You and me with long faces plunged into despair because we find out a man didn't kill his wife. We're two of the most frightening ghouls I've ever known." My argument is that they're ghouls regardless of Thorwald's guilt, because they have projected their eroticism onto a situation that doesn't concern them. They are libidinally divested and irredeemably dissociated—a condition that strikes a deep-seated fear in me and one that Hitchcock notably replicates in *Vertigo* and *The Birds*.

In the final scene of *Rear Window*, Jeff rests in his wheelchair, now with casts on both legs after his climactic confrontation with Thorwald. Beside him, Lisa lounges with a book titled *Beyond the High Himalayas*—an ostensible nod to Jeff's idealised thrill-seeking life. But once she sees that he's asleep, she quietly swaps it for the fashion magazine *Harper's Bazaar*, indulging in the world she truly enjoys. This subtle gesture tells us everything: Lisa is indefinitely maintaining the tiresome adventure-woman façade to appease her excuse-prone, non-committal boyfriend. In centring his desires, she diminishes her own. She'll have to pursue what pleases her in secret, living authentically on the periphery of his awareness. The final images of *Rear Window* leave Lisa and Jeff experientially twinned with Miss Lonelyhearts—the neighbour who once performed a dinner date with an invisible suitor, desperately enacting the fantasy of companionship while entirely alone. In the same way, Lisa and Jeff are role-playing and kidding themselves. Terrifyingly, they are in a relationship with phantoms, imaginary versions of each other that do not exist in a substantial way. They're together, but upon closer inspection, they are simply not there.

The Slumber Party Massacre (1982)

Amy Holden Jones's *The Slumber Party Massacre* follows a high school student who invites her friends over for a sleepover, unaware that an escaped killer—armed with a power drill—is lurking in the neighbourhood. Originally written as a parody of the slasher genre, the film was ultimately shot as a straightforward horror, retaining a satirical edge that sets it apart from its contemporaries. Though it received mixed reviews upon release, it has since gained a dedicated cult following. At the slumber party, the girls smoke marijuana and drink alcohol, while two boys from school spy on them through the window as they undress. Diane steps outside to meet her boyfriend, only to find him decapitated before she, too, is murdered. Later, the pizza delivery man arrives—his eyes gruesomely drilled out. The terrified teens arm themselves with knives, but the driller killer soon forces his way into the house.

The opening scene of *The Slumber Party Massacre* sets the tone for the film's underlying themes. Eighteen-year-old high school senior Trish wakes up and begins clearing her room of childhood toys and objects. As she changes out of her sleepwear and into a day dress, the camera lingers on her body, marking a visual transition from girlhood to womanhood. In my reading, this moment encapsulates the film's essence—a liminal phase bursting with transformation and possibility. This threshold of change propels the narrative forward, evoking a voyeuristic response—not in a harmful, objectifying sense, but as an expression of pure cinematic pleasure derived from looking.

Sure enough, the scenes that follow take place at the high school, where the camera leisurely roams through the girls' shower room, flooding the screen with images of naked, dripping-wet young women. This is no accident—the abundance of female nudity serves an intentional, alluring function. The sequence brings to mind *Hylas and the Nymphs*, John William Waterhouse's 1896 painting depicting a moment from Greek and Roman mythology in which the young Hylas, on a heroic quest, is lured into a pond by Naiads—water nymphs who seduce and ultimately consume him. In both the painting and the film, the emergence of female eroticism is framed as an overwhelming, devouring entity—one capable of erasing male subjectivity. In *The Slumber Party Massacre*, this perceived threat demands an extreme response. Enter the Driller Killer, less a man than an abstraction—a primal force locked in perpetual combat against the supposed danger of feminine power.

The film's topography is deliberately constructed to shrink the world from families, school, and community into the claustrophobic interiors of Trish's house. This inward movement suggests that the true horror unfolding is, predominantly, a psychological event. Early in the film, the killer attacks a telephone repair woman outside the high school, fatally wounding her in the back of her van. This establishes his initial motive: the systematic shutdown of communication within the feminine register. Killing the telephone repair woman serves as a symbolic act—the silencing of female voices and the severing of their access to the outside world.

The film presents the slumber party as an exhilarating, carefree adventure—a sweet slice of Americana, never meant to be taken too seriously. The guests are doing everything except sleeping. Lingering shots of the young women disrobing while chatting casually contribute to an atmosphere that is easy-going, sensual, and playful. A few high school boys eagerly peer through the window, but this is ultimately a psychologically female space—the men are mere tourists, fleeting intrusions into the scene. Except for one man. Russ Thorn, the escaped mass murderer known as the Driller Killer, looms like an unwelcome spectre, looking a hell of a lot like Bob from *Twin Peaks*, similarly a double denim clad creepy home invader with a frozen maniacal glare. Like Bob, Thorn is a nightmarish allegory—an aesthetic energy that skulks on the periphery, waiting to rupture the illusion of safety.

Forgive me, but it's impossible to ignore the phallic symbolism of Thorn's weapon of choice: the power drill. This is simply how a Freudian mind operates. Even his name, Thorn, evokes a stiff, sharp-pointed projection—an image of penetration that extends into his relentless use of the drill, closing in on his targets and impaling them. But why should it matter that a drill-wielding lunatic fixates on a girls' slumber party, picking off the guests one by one? What's really at stake here? My take is that the teenagers in the film are curious about sex and open to exploring it, but there is a deep tension in this zone of interest. The drill's violent penetration externalises a larger cultural anxiety—an exaggerated fantasy standing in for the real taboo: female sexual desire and enjoyment. The Driller Killer embodies the unresolved terror surrounding female sexuality, an unprocessed force that punctures society.

This brings us to the second implication of Russ Thorn's name—sex being a thorny issue, a source of discomfort, irritation, or complication for these girls. Whether it's the fear of heterosexual intercourse being painful or the frustration of navigating sexist double standards, women are often conditioned to feel ashamed for desiring sex. Many cultural forces contribute to the persistent belief that sex is dangerous and can harm women, and must therefore be policed or controlled. The Driller Killer, ever-present and prowling, represents this tension. He is never far from the girls—just as sex is never far from their thoughts. But crucially, it is not pleasure that preoccupies them; it is the looming spectre of sex as a threat, the fear-laden dimension that overshadows desire.

Jacques Lacan's notion of the Imaginary Phallus is also worth considering here. In the pre-Oedipal phase, the child perceives the Imaginary Phallus as the object of the mother's desire—something she wants beyond the child itself. In response, the child unconsciously seeks to identify with this object, striving to be what the mother desires. The Oedipus complex marks the moment when this illusion is shattered. The child gradually realises that they are not the sole object of the mother's desire, as her attention is directed elsewhere. In an attempt to regain the initial state of blissful union, the child endeavours to reclaim this lost status. The Imaginary Phallus, then, is what the child assumes one must possess in order to be desired by the mother. Since her desire is often directed towards the father, the child presumes that he is the one who possesses it.

In striving to satisfy the mother's desire, the child identifies with the object it believes she has lost, attempting to become that object for her. The Phallus is Imaginary in the sense that the child associates it with a lost, recoverable entity. For Lacan, the Oedipus complex marks the process of relinquishing this identification—realising that the phallus is not a tangible thing but a signifier that was never truly there. The logic of the Imaginary Phallus is subtly established early in *The Slumber Party Massacre*, in the driveway scene just before Trish's parents leave for their holiday. Her mother, Annette, issues a string of maternal reassurances: "The chips are under the sink, and there's soda in the fridge, and our number at the hotel is right by the phone. [...] Mr. Contant will be home all weekend and he'll look in on you. [...] You lock all the doors and windows." Trish, visibly irritated, pushes back: "Mom, I'm 18 years old, remember?" But Annette insists, "You'll always be my baby."

My claim is that Annette's statement, "You'll always be my baby," promises a rekindling of the initial maternal bond, presenting it as eternal and unbreakable. This declaration casts a kind of spell, reactivating the Imaginary Phallus and inviting Trish to identify with her mother's desire—in this case, the hope that Trish's eroticism remains tightly controlled all weekend, closely monitored by their killjoy neighbour, Mr. Contant. He eagerly embraces his role as deputy dad, glibly assuring, "Don't worry, I won't let the girls get into any trouble." Trish internalises her mother's desire and, in doing so, unconsciously stages the shame associated with sex. She casts Russ Thorn as a malevolent, penetrative force obsessed with invading the wholesome family home and defiling innocent girls, the subtext being that when women engage in and enjoy sexual intercourse, they risk a kind of social death.

Misery (1990)

Rob Reiner's psychological thriller *Misery*, adapted from Stephen King's 1987 novel, unfolds as a chilling tale of obsession and artistic captivity. The story follows a world-famous author held hostage by his most fervent admirer, who forces him to rewrite her favourite book. Novelist Paul Sheldon, the creator of the bestselling *Misery* series—Victorian romance novels centred on the beloved heroine Misery Chastain—has grown weary of his franchise. Longing for creative liberation, he reaches a turning point in his career, completing a manuscript that he hopes will mark the dawn of his post-*Misery* era.

While travelling from Silver Creek, Colorado to New York City, Paul is caught in a blizzard and skids off the road. He regains consciousness in a remote home, bedridden with shattered legs and a dislocated shoulder, under the care of Annie Wilkes—a nurse who claims to be his "number one fan." Annie gushes about his novels, but her admiration quickly sours. After reading his latest manuscript, she furiously condemns the profanity, and when she purchases his newest book and discovers that her beloved Misery dies at the end, she flies into a rage. What follows is a special brand of cruelty: Annie forces Paul to burn the only copy of his unpublished manuscript and demands that he write a new book, *Misery's Return*, resurrecting the character. She pompously frames this as a divine calling, smugly instructing him to "rid the world of this filth. Light the match. Can't you see it's what God wants? You were put on this earth to help people, Paul. Please, help me help you." The patronising way she delivers this line is maddening—where the hell does she get the nerve?

But thinking about it more deeply, perhaps all of this is unfolding on an interior front—meaning, the entire premise of the film could be situated within the psyche of the artist. The monster, Annie Wilkes, may not be a separate entity at all but rather an externalisation of Paul's own creative anxiety, a nightmarish embodiment of his worst fears. She represents the extreme rejection he imagines from his devoted fans as they confront the radical shift in his work—from frivolous romance novels to gritty urban tales. I once saw someone on Twitter argue that Annie Wilkes is emblematic of the modern cultural landscape, where morally indignant, self-appointed arbiters of righteousness demand that creators conform to their specific set of values.

Annie, as a so-called "superfan," feels entitled to the labour of the writer she claims to hold in high regard, compelled to encroach upon the artist's sovereignty. Paul's very survival—his physical well-being—is contingent on Annie's arbitrary verdict on his work, a judgement she believes supersedes his own creative prerogative. The film rightly presents this as evil. We see Paul trapped, utterly isolated, his whereabouts unknown to the outside world. Drugged and confined, he is provided only the bare essentials required to write—his freedom reduced to the condition that he resurrect the very franchise he had deliberately laid to rest. The pressure is relentless, his artistic will held hostage.

"Misery" is an aptly chosen title—both for the film and as an existential descriptor of Paul's emotional ordeal. Being coerced into rehashing a creative chapter he had long since outgrown, simply to appease this insufferable figure, is an exasperating form of torment. During the dinner scene, in which Paul attempts to spike Annie's wine with crushed painkillers, he makes a pointed toast: "To Misery, and to Annie Wilkes, who brought her back to life." This line exposes the paradox of an obsessive fanbase. These devoted readers, so enamoured with the fictional Misery, demand her eternal life. Yet their refusal to let her go inflicts immense suffering on Paul, rendering him literally miserable. His livelihood—his very life force—is now inextricably bound to resurrecting a character he had already relinquished. It is grotesque, and downright obscene, to browbeat a creator to participate in the zombification of their own work.

Annie insists that Paul use her as his muse while he writes in captivity, but in reality, she is strong-arming him into crafting precisely the story she desires—policing his every word, reacting with tyrannical control at the slightest deviation. How ghoulish that the final product should reflect the consumer's will rather than the artist's vision. Earlier in the film, she issues an ominous warning: "You better hope nothing happens to me, because if I die, you die." This thinly veiled threat speaks to a deeper fear in the writer's psyche—the anxiety that disappointing one's readership means losing everything. Paul is forced to navigate the crushing weight of expectation, the implicit demand that he must keep his audience happy or risk professional and personal ruin. *Misery* masterfully captures the harrowing, sacrificial nature of the artistic process, which demands suffering, discipline, and near-masochistic endurance. Paul's imprisonment in Annie's house—strapped to a bed, tortured, physically broken, verbally berated—mirrors the psychological torment of the creative journey. Writing is portrayed here as an act of violence, an isolating event, a descent into madness. When he is deep in the throes of composition, he is unreachable, swallowed whole by scarier features of the flow state.

The film opens with Lauren Bacall as Paul's literary agent—an elegant, high-powered figure who, beneath her polished exterior, exerts quiet pressure on him to keep churning out chart-topping romance novels. She is the polite, glamorous, public face of Annie Wilkes. The agent's refined expectations gnaw at Paul's artistic integrity, but when the high gloss of metropolitan sophistication falls away, what remains? A dreadful mutation—his stylish New York agent with film-star looks dissolves into the murderous village weirdo. Annie Wilkes is the lurid embodiment of this same pressure, stripped of its civility and laid bare in its rawest form. It's fascinating to consider the psychological topography of a person cooped up alone in a room, grappling with the creative act and its suffocating implications. *Misery* takes this internal struggle and externalises it into a terrifying, tangible threat. The film also masterfully weaves Hitchcockian suspense into its premise—Paul, trapped in his personal Hell, sets small, meticulous tasks for himself in an attempt to escape, always under the shadow of being caught. The tension simmers, his agency reduced to fleeting acts of defiance, each one carrying the risk of catastrophic punishment.

When Annie shoots the police officer dead, it can be read as a manifestation of the psychotic state—a literal disavowal of the law, a rejection of the very structure that binds the Symbolic Order together, here represented by the local sheriff. At this point, Annie has completely lost the plot; she is fully submerged in delusion. This moment underscores the perilous nature of the creative process—the artist must engage with a psychotic condition of sorts, fully inhabiting the world they are conjuring in service of their work. It parallels the suspension of disbelief; the artist must surrender to their imagined reality, occupying it as long as necessary, forsaking conventional logic and external constraints. In this sense, Annie's psychosis taps into a state of imagination and creation that exists beyond the bounds of law and order, where reality itself is malleable.

A sense of resolution is affirmed in the film's closing moments, as Paul is shown back in New York, safe and sound, having survived his ordeal in Silver Creek, Colorado. He feels invigorated by the publication of his new book, marking the dawn of a fresh creative chapter. Reflecting on his experience, he tells his agent, "In some way, Annie Wilkes, the whole experience, helped me." As such, *Misery* serves as a striking case study on the necessity of confronting trauma head-on and engaging with difficult emotions rather than retreating from them. Today, there is immense pressure to sanitise art—to strip away discomfort and censor anything deemed "problematic." But this film reminds us of what is truly at stake: the raw, unfiltered exploration of the human experience. It argues, persuasively, for the immense value of wrestling with the hard stuff—pushing through darkness to create something artistically meaningful, and, in its own way, profoundly beautiful.

Single White Female (1992)

Moving swiftly on to *Single White Female*, Barbet Schroeder's psychological erotic thriller with a horror twist. After breaking up with her fiancé, Sam, software designer Allie takes in a new flatmate, Hedy, in her gorgeous New

York apartment. The two women quickly form a bond, but when Allie reconciles with Sam, worrying patterns start to emerge. Hedy's behaviour grows increasingly possessive, her jealousy escalating into outright hostility—and eventually, violence—in a desperate attempt to eliminate Sam from the picture. As tensions rise, Allie uncovers disturbing truths about Hedy's past and the identity she has so carefully constructed.

Let's consider the striking Ansonia apartment building, where much of the film's action unfolds—a space teeming with uncanny doubling, where Alison Jones's ontological security is repeatedly destabilised. The drama begins when Allie discovers that her fiancé, Sam, had an intimate encounter with his ex-wife, Lisa, earlier that day. Lisa is never seen, only heard—her tense voice crackling through the answering machine. She becomes a spectral presence, a painful replication, an unwelcome second option drawing Sam's erotic interest. Understandably, Allie resents this—Lisa is an image external to herself, a disruptive force she cannot control.

Another instance of doubling emerges during Allie's business lunch with Mitchell Myerson, a fashion house owner interested in acquiring her revolutionary new software. When Mitchell alludes to her disgruntled former business partner, Allie is quick to clarify: she did all the work, while her ex-colleague attempted to take credit. The anguish of one's labour being co-opted—claimed by another as their own—is a triggering form of doubling, a violation that recurs across horror cinema. Darren Aronofsky's *Black Swan* and Daniel Goldhaber's *Cam* similarly explore the terror of stolen identity and artistic erasure, tapping into the existential fear of being copied, replaced, or rendered obsolete.

Unwilling to live alone, Allie advertises for a new flatmate to share her Upper West Side apartment. She settles on Hedra Carlson, whom she nicknames "Hedy," and the two quickly form a close bond. One day, Hedy reveals that her twin sister was stillborn, leaving her with a profound sense of loneliness throughout her childhood. This disclosure introduces a compelling psychological thread linked to phantom pain—the sensation of perceiving a missing limb or organ, either because it was removed or, in Hedy's case, never existed in the first place. Her absent sibling represents a deep loss, an unfillable void that haunts her. The shadow of this missing twin lingers in Hedy's psyche, shaping her compulsive need for mirroring.

Hedy grows increasingly possessive of Allie, secretly deleting Sam's voicemail and intercepting the letter in which he asks for reconciliation. When Sam wins Allie back and they proceed to search for their own apartment, Hedy perceives it as an unforgivable betrayal. Her frustration escalates to intensely irrational levels. During a trip to the salon, Hedy emerges with the same haircut and red colouring as Allie, a chilling act of imitation. The slow-motion shot of her walking down the salon stairs, smiling serenely, is so iconic in its weirdness—she looks like Allie's long-lost identical twin. That night, Allie follows Hedy to a sex club and is horrified to see her masquerading as her, stepping further into the bizarre realm of identity theft and psychological fixation.

Hedy's obsession is erotically charged. What truly excites her is cosplaying as Allie, slipping seamlessly into her like a second skin. When Allie discovers a shoebox filled with letters addressed to Ellen Besch (Hedy's real name) and a newspaper clipping about the accidental drowning of Hedy's twin sister, Judy, it becomes clear that her *idée fixe* is rooted in unresolved grief. Hedy's behaviour aligns with what Freud termed secondary identification, which occurs following the loss of a cherished object. A common expression of this is wearing a deceased loved one's clothes or unconsciously embodying aspects of a lost figure. In these cases, the subject recreates circumstances that evoke feelings of inferiority associated with the original bereavement—an unconscious attempt to fuse the self with what was taken away. Hedy, in losing her twin, seeks to dissolve into another, to mend the absence by becoming the presence.

Hedy has often been cited as a cinematic example of borderline personality disorder (BPD). She exhibits a fractured sense of self, attempting to compensate by trying to absorb the wholesome and well-defined qualities of her flatmate Allie. BPD is characterised by a long-term pattern of unstable relationships, an uncertain self-identity, and extreme emotional dysregulation. Those with BPD often report a fear of abandonment, reckless or self-destructive behaviours, a pervasive sense of emptiness, and episodes of self-harm. Even seemingly minor events can trigger overwhelming emotional responses. The disorder is frequently associated with substance abuse, depression, and eating disorders, all of which reflect the struggle to regulate internal turmoil.

The borderline structure is tied to difficulties in defining a stable sense of self. It is a personality shaped by identity fragmentation—as if the self is hollowed out or gradually dissipating. In this context, personal relationships become a means of self-construction, with the individual unconsciously absorbing the traits of those they admire. In BPD, fear of abandonment is acute—the sufferer invests so wholly in their chosen attachment that, if the loved one leaves, their own identity collapses. The externalised ideal becomes pathologically enmeshed with their sense of self, often leading to an unrelenting preoccupation with the object of attachment. In *Single White Female*, Allie and Hedy's bond is initially forged through time spent together, slipping into each other's rooms, borrowing clothes, perfume, and jewellery. Shared objects and spaces serve as a bridge between them—an intimate exchange through which they sense each other's realities, temporarily blurring the boundaries of selfhood.

The dramatic shift occurs when Allie and her ex-boyfriend Sam reconcile and reinstate their engagement. This romantic reunion triggers Hedy's worst fear—she casts herself as the expendable third wheel, doomed to be cast out of the dynamic. This is a quintessential illustration of the borderline experience: the person forming the attachment has a fragile or splintered sense of self, relying entirely on their chosen loved one to define the parameters of their identity. The prospect of being discarded is existentially catastrophic, as it severs their emotional lifeline, leaving them to flounder in an unbearable void.

Hedy lacks a clear sense of personal style—she is a blank slate with no discernible individual fashion tastes openly admitting she has no idea what looks good. This absence of self-awareness leaves her feeling unmoored, adrift in a state of depersonalisation. She fixates on Allie's sartorial choices, absorbing them like a sponge—buying identical outfits, mimicking her haircut, configuring herself into a reflection of the woman she idolises. Hedy's compulsion to adopt the traits of others offers temporary relief from her split sense of self, but it is an unsustainable strategy—one that ultimately leads to an even greater psychic collapse.

In extreme cases, BPD sufferers intrude on the boundaries of people they love—stalking, manipulation, and violent outbursts. Such reactions stem from sheer terror; if they lose the person they venerate, they also lose themselves. Allie's software application, which allows users to overlay and superimpose different fashion items onto electronic models, mirrors the logic of the borderline structure. It reflects a frantic search for identity—trying on different versions of the self at a rapid pace, desperately seeking a perfect fit. And once something feels right, it is clung to with a strong sense of urgency.

The scene in which Hedy sneaks into Sam's hotel room is fascinating for its Live Action Role Play dimension. She fully inhabits Allie's identity—wearing her clothes and perfume, styling her hair to match, layering a heady mix of similarities as she slips into Sam's bed. For a fleeting moment, she convinces him that she is his fiancée, luring him into repeating his earlier infidelity. Hedy then proceeds to perform oral sex, an act that aligns eerily with the borderline condition—she is, quite literally, drinking him in, absorbing the desired other into herself. Sam, caught in a fog of confusion, appears unsure of who is pleasuring him—a darkly humorous callback to the flatmate application scene, where Hedy joked about her unusual name and the teasing it invited. In the hotel room, she begs Sam to leave Allie, but when he refuses and threatens to expose her, she flies into a rage. She kills him by gouging his eye out with her stiletto heel—another borrowed item from Allie's wardrobe. I read this as the unconscious fantasy of a betrayed lover "walking in the shoes" of a temptress—catching their partner in the act through a proxy. Here, the shoe as a fetish object transforms into a murder weapon, delivering a symbolic act of vengeance.

The stiletto heel, usually seen as an object of feminine allure, is actually the perfect weapon of reprisal. By stabbing Sam in the eye, Hedy reclaims the shoe as a phallic symbol of power rather than submission, subverting its association with desirability and turning it into an instrument of control. The act invokes castration anxiety, as the eye—symbolising perception and dominance—is violently ruptured, blinding Sam and punishing his toxic wandering gaze. The gendered object is requisitioned—Hedy's attack is horrifying yet undeniably cathartic, an eruption of repressed female rage against objectification and betrayal. While her actions are criminal, they reveal a certain logic tied to power and identity, turning seduction into destruction.

Midway through *Single White Female*, in a quietly revealing moment, Allie snoops through Hedy's belongings, browsing her journals and jewellery. She dabs on Hedy's perfume—*Moi-Même*—which translates from French as "Myself." She remarks that it's a fragrance she's always wanted to try. This subtle detail suggests that Hedy's aura, and the borderline structure itself, resonates with Allie's own identity crisis. As a newcomer in the city, reluctant to live alone, and reeling from Sam's betrayal, Allie is in a state of flux. She had poured so much of herself into her relationship, allowing Sam to shape her choices and worldview. The film hints that, in moments of vulnerability, it is terribly easy to absorb the values of another—to take on their essence, just as Hedy does with Allie. The act of applying the perfume functions as an unconscious transference of energy, marking a fleeting but evocative realisation: something about Hedy, strange as it is, reflects Allie back to herself.

Creep (2014)

Patrick Brice's found-footage psychological horror film *Creep* originates from a story by Brice and Mark Duplass, who also star in the film. Brice plays a struggling videographer hired to document an eccentric client, portrayed by Duplass. The film draws inspiration from character-driven thrillers like *Misery* and *Fatal Attraction*, as well as a series of bizarre Craigslist encounters experienced by the creative team over the years.

Aaron accepts a job that takes him to a remote mountain cabin in Crestline, where he meets his client who explains that he has an inoperable brain tumour and is expected to die before his pregnant wife, Angela, gives birth. Wanting to leave behind a video diary for his unborn child, Buddy—much like the protagonist of *My Life*—Josef hires Aaron to document his final days. However, as the day unfolds, his behaviour grows increasingly volatile, making Aaron uneasy. In a particularly upsetting moment, Josef confesses to raping his wife. As Aaron's discomfort escalates, he realises he cannot find his car keys, preventing him from leaving. Soon after, he intercepts a phone call from Angela—who shockingly reveals that she is not Josef's wife, but his sister. She urges Aaron to escape immediately.

Reflecting on his approach to playing Josef, Duplass explained:

> We were interested in the psychological profile of this very strange person. We were interested in how you meet people and don't quite understand what's up, but you start to get signs. For us, that was intense eye contact, lack of personal space, oversharing, maybe a little bit too much love here and there. But there's something wrong with both of these guys. Deeply. It's like, "Who is the creep in this scenario?"

Duplass's insight exposes the misdirection at the heart of *Creep*. On the surface, the film positions Aaron as the ordinary everyman and Josef as the unhinged weirdo. But on closer inspection, the two characters can be seen as complementary facets of a single psyche—the conscious personality and its lurking primordial instincts—locked in an uneasy interaction.

Freud's seminal work *The Ego and the Id* (1923) offers a valuable framework for understanding *Creep*. In this study of the psyche, Freud explores the internal tensions that shape both normal and pathological states. He argues that the Ego—positioned between the Id and the Superego—is caught in a perpetual struggle: it must contend with the unruly, repressed desires of the Id while simultaneously being subordinated by the moral authority of the Superego. Furthermore, the conflict between the love instinct (Eros) and the death drive (Thanatos) can manifest at any level of the psyche, creating a turbulent interplay that defines human behaviour.

All concepts in *The Ego and the Id* rest on the division between conscious and unconscious thought—a premise at the heart of psychoanalysis. However, Freud does not suggest a simple one-to-one mapping of the Id onto the unconscious and the Ego onto the conscious. Instead, he argues that the supposedly conscious Ego can itself harbour unconscious thoughts, particularly when it unknowingly resists parts of itself. This introduces a third category of unconscious thought—neither fully repressed nor latent, yet still integral to the Ego's function, the act of repression. Freud conceptualises the Ego as merging into the Id, likening their dynamic to that of a rider and a horse. The Ego, like the rider, must control the Id's impulses—but at times, it is forced to follow where the Id leads. In this way, the Ego does not simply restrain the Id; it must also negotiate with its desires.

Let's explore how these ideas manifest in *Creep*—a film that ingeniously stages the interplay between the Ego and the Id on multiple levels. The opening shot shows Aaron driving his car, "leaving the flatlands and heading towards the mountain top"—an ascent that evokes the Freudian iceberg model of the mind. In this framework, the Ego—the so-called conscious personality—appears to be all that exists, much like the visible tip of an iceberg. Yet beneath the surface lies the vast, unknowable expanse of the unconscious, the true force governing our thoughts and behaviours. Aaron's upward trajectory, then, suggests an aspiration to reach the peak of self-awareness, yet he is unwittingly on a more primal path.

Aaron even remarks that he's "not sure who he's meeting" in this "cute little town with the cute little lake"—a telling reflection of the Ego's tendency to present a polished, harmonious image. The Ego strives for order, curating a version of reality that appears conflict-free, yet beneath this carefully arranged surface lurks an unsettling mystery, a concealed instability that betrays its picture-perfect aspirations. Upon arriving, Aaron must ascend a steep driveway, then climb a long flight of stairs to reach the yellow front door perched atop a towering porch. Soon after, Josef remarks, "I never get used to those stairs." The cabin's altitude is no accident—it visually reinforces the Ego's lofty ambitions, the tenacious pursuit of control, striving to rise above the tumultuous impulses bubbling beneath.

One of the most striking features of *Creep* is its frequent use of jump scares—a popular horror technique designed to startle the audience through an abrupt shift in image or action, often punctuated by a loud, jarring sound. Typically, these moments disrupt an otherwise quiet scene, catching the viewer off guard. Josef's habit of suddenly leaping into the frame and screaming—repeatedly—suggests more than just an attempt to frighten Aaron; it hints at hidden underlying activity, a volatile energy on the verge of eruption. Josef attributes his bonkers behaviour to dizziness and cognitive misfirings, a vague explanation that seems to mask a nuanced reality. Yet this disruption in mental functioning doesn't belong to Josef alone—it acts as a mirror, subtly reflecting Aaron's own emotional crisis, revealing cuts in the Ego's veil.

Josef tells Aaron that his job is simply to keep the camera rolling—to walk alongside him and document him as he truly is. He insists that he doesn't need Aaron to glorify him or make him look cool, but rather to capture an unfiltered, honest portrayal so that his son, Buddy, can see him for the man he was. The implication here is that, through operating the camera, Aaron gains access to raw, unvarnished truth—piercing through the Ego's relentless attempts to smooth over unflattering complexities buried in the unconscious. Josef hands Aaron $1,000 and solemnly states, "This is no longer a business transaction, okay? This is a partnership, a journey into the heart. I'm really glad it's you coming with me." This moment reads like a symbolic pact—one in which the Ego finally agrees to confront inner workings, ceasing active denial of the unconscious, and instead dares to face its most troubling depths directly.

Aaron appears visibly uncomfortable as he watches Josef undress and step into the bathtub, but Josef reassures him, "It's okay. We're gonna go to a lot deeper places than this." The film unfolds like Aaron's internal dialogue with a disavowed part of himself—an aspect he has long refused to admit into consciousness. Josef, with his absurd and hair-raising behaviour, externalises elements from a murky, uncharted space, dragging them into the light. Disrobing here functions like an unmasking, a willingness to confront facets of the self that have been long buried beneath layers of repression. Not long after, Aaron stumbles upon the enormous Peachfuzz wolf mask. Josef explains that his father created it along with a children's song: "Hello my name is Peachfuzz, I might look like I'll eat you up, but I'm as friendly as a rabbit, and I make a very good friend. I am here and there's nothing to fear." The wolf mask ties directly into the zany ambiguity that has characterised Josef so far. We seem to be nudged in the direction that he is not actually dying, but rather a serial killer. But this is a red herring; there is something more complex at play.

The name Aaron means "mountain of strength" in Hebrew, and I see *Creep* as a Freudian hero's journey—one that descends from the Ego's lofty mountaintop of self-assured power into the spiralling depths of the psyche, where true understanding can be attained. The lyrics of the Peachfuzz song—"I make a very good friend"—ring true in a psychoanalytic sense: Josef, like the mask serves as a destabilising force, pushing Aaron off his Ego's high perch and cracking open his carefully ordered mindset. Before they leave the cabin, Josef picks up two identical fur-trimmed hats for them to wear, grinning as he declares, "Twinsies!" This moment foreshadows the deeper truth of the film—Josef repeatedly hints at a shared likeness with Aaron because, in a structural sense, they are already entwined.

The men set off in search of the miracle waters of the heart along the Crestline trail—a legendary healing spring said to flow beneath a heart-shaped rock formation. According to folklore, only those pure of heart can be restored by bathing in its waters. As they trek the path, Josef startles Aaron, triggering a big response. He laughs, exhilarated, and says:

> You need to see your face! All right, you're a little mad. I'm sorry. My God, that was incredible. You had a near-death experience. That's what it feels like when you feel like you're gonna die. It's incredible and powerful, isn't it? There was about two seconds after you were done being scared where it looked like you wanted to kill me. I don't take it personally. I think it was a visceral reaction, it's a defence thing, but there's an animal in you. There's a little Peachfuzz inside you yet.

Josef's relentless prodding of Aaron feels like an unacknowledged part of the psyche forcing its way to the surface—provocations designed to expose the Ego's hypocrisy as it stubbornly denies its animal instincts. After a prolonged search for the miracle waters, Aaron begins to worry: Does Josef even remember the way back? He voices his concern, noting the many forks and switchbacks they've taken without keeping track. But Josef, unfazed, responds: "That's back there, man. We've got to go forward. We can't find the miracle if we've got a rope attached to us." I love this line—it captures the essence of psychoanalysis in a single stroke. Josef embodies the animating force that propels the subject through uncertainty, compelling them to keep moving despite the discomfort. When Aaron, the so-called rational part of the mind, hesitates—anxiously clinging to a sense of direction—Josef reminds him that true transformation requires risk. Security is the enemy of revelation; by loosening the Ego's stiff grip, really important psychic material can be unearthed.

This scene carries the weight of a fortifying ritual—one that strengthens the heart rather than the Ego, preparing for the inevitable psychological battle ahead. When the men finally reach the heart-shaped rock, the supposed cure for Josef's illness feels like a misdirection. After all, Aaron immerses himself in the water too, as if instinctively drawn into the same radical process. They leisurely rub the water on each other, an intimate and sacred ceremonial act, and Josef carves their initials—A+J—inside a heart on a nearby rock. This moment brings to mind the classic hero's journey, marking the threshold before the most arduous stage. The goal is not to reinforce the Ego's dominance, but to fortify the heart—to embrace vulnerability and withstand whatever is coming next.

Later, over whiskey, Josef insists on sharing something "off camera" before he dies. The screen cuts to black, yet the audio continues—a clever formal choice that heightens the eeriness of his confession. Josef describes discovering animal pornography in his home browser history and confronting his wife, Angela, who denied any involvement. Her refusal to admit the truth, he claims, drove an irreparable wedge between them. What follows is a disturbing revelation: Josef recounts how, sometime later, he donned a mask, tied Angela up, and had what he calls "ravenous animalistic sex" with her—leaving her bound and escaping through the window. He claims that after the rape, Angela had "never looked happier." Then, as abruptly as the confession begins, the camera flicks back on. The visual return to normalcy is jarring—Josef behaves as if nothing happened.

This scene exemplifies the savage bluntness that emerges when confronting primordial desire—precisely when the perception is that nothing is being documented. Off record, Josef confesses to longings that carry the weight of societal taboo, admitting to having acted on his most extreme animalistic urges. Moreover, the obscenity of these desires appears, in his telling, to have awakened something in the woman in his life. It reminds me of a line I once read on social media: "The unconscious reveals itself through dreams, jokes, slips of the tongue, symptoms, and browser history." Josef's depraved confession is relayed from the glacial void of a black screen. The moment the camera is back on, he switches seamlessly into civilised small talk, as if the previous admission never occurred.

Horrified, Aaron tries to leave the house, but Josef blocks the door while wearing the Peachfuzz mask. Desperate, Aaron pleads, "Are you gonna let me go? Why are you doing this to me? Are you just trying to scare me? Well, I'm terrified, okay? You won. Now, will you just please step aside and let me go?" This moment is terrifying precisely because Josef's intentions remain unclear. The dread stems from the awful sensation of the "rational" conscious personality—the Ego—being cornered in a surreal dream state, taunted by the fitful impulses of the Id. Josef is not overtly violent in this moment; rather, his sheer unpredictability alarms Aaron in an overwhelming state of panic. His ominous presence alone is enough to dissolve any illusion of control. The confrontation escalates into a scuffle, ultimately leading to Aaron's escape. Yet crucially, his actual departure is never shown onscreen, reinforcing the film's disorienting quality.

Back at home, Aaron receives disturbing packages in the mail, including a video recording of Josef digging a grave. Despite clear signs of stalking and harassment, the police are unable to intervene due to the lack of identifiable information about Josef. Aaron dreams about the encounter at Heart Rock in which he's a baby wearing a tiny wolf mask in a hot tub. Josef, donning the Peachfuzz mask, pours wine over Aaron's head. The water is tinged with blood. The imagery is like a morbid baptism—Josef initiating Aaron into the pulsating depths of the unconscious, uniting them in a single beating heart beyond Ego control. The supposed "miracle" of Heart Rock is reaching a universal understanding: that the psyche is not governed solely by the rational conscious mind, but by something primordial and instinctual. Upon waking, Aaron records his reaction to the unnerving dream, stating, "I've got to stop thinking about this guy." But once the Ego has glimpsed the truth—that it is not the master of its own house—it becomes nearly impossible to maintain the illusion of conventional order. The great terror of the Ego is to feel itself dissolving into the Id, swallowed by the very impulses it sought to repress.

Aaron is urged to "dig a little deeper" when another odd package arrives. In the accompanying video, Josef shares his philosophy on wolves, claiming they struggle to express love and often destroy the very things they cherish. He says that inside the wolf is a beautiful, misguided heart. Josef then recalls the moment he startled Aaron in the woods, insisting that, for a brief instant, he saw a certain flash in his eyes—baby murder. He tells Aaron, "You're not ready to accept that yet. But I want to encourage you to embrace your inner wolf." His words take on an instructional tone, leading up to a final provocation: "Take the knife and don't be afraid to murder it; when you stick a knife in something and you gut it and you really dig inside, there's all this beautiful stuff. See you soon, buddy."

Digging deeper functions as a psychoanalytic mantra, with Freud likening therapy to archaeology—clearing away pathogenic psychical material layer by layer, much like excavating a buried city. The deeper the dig, the richer the narrative. Josef calling Aaron "Buddy" marks a full-circle moment, as this was the name Aaron originally gave to Josef's supposed unborn son. This detail aligns with Aaron's anxiety dream of being a baby bathed by Josef, symbolising his initiation into an unconscious system.

That *Creep* ends with Josef striking Aaron in the head with an axe signifies an Ego death—a total loss of self-identity and a radical transformation of the psyche. It recalls the Tower card in tarot, often linked to danger, crisis, and destruction, yet also to sudden change, higher learning, and, ultimately, liberation. The conscious personality is forcibly humbled, made to reckon with deeper dimensions of itself. That this moment is captured on video suggests a meta-commentary on filmmaking, with Aaron and Josef embodying opposing yet equally essential forces in the creative process—the material that must be confronted, picked apart, and endured to complete an artistic endeavour like cinema.

The Strangers 1 and 2 (2008 and 2018)

The psychological horror films *The Strangers* and *The Strangers: Prey at Night* are based on an original story by Bryan Bertino. Both movies follow three masked sociopathic home invaders who terrorise innocent victims in the dead of night. Bertino has cited the inspiration for these films as a blend of true crime influences, including the Manson family murders and a series of break-ins that occurred in his childhood neighbourhood.

In the original *Strangers* film (dir. Bryan Bertino), James and Kristen arrive at his secluded childhood summer house after attending a friend's wedding. Tensions simmer between them—earlier that evening, Kristen rejected James's marriage proposal. At around 4:00 am, there is a loud knock at the door. A young blonde woman, her face obscured by darkness, asks, "Is Tamara here?" James tells her she has the wrong house. She leaves, but returns soon after, repeating the same question. Kristen reminds her that she already knocked only moments ago and promptly locks the door. A third knock follows, sending a ripple of dread through the house. Apprehensive, Kristen moves to the kitchen—unaware that a masked man is already inside, watching in eerie silence.

The situation escalates. James arms himself with a shotgun. His friend Mike arrives at the house and, noticing James's vandalised car in the driveway, senses something is wrong. Entering cautiously, he is mistaken for one of the intruders—James shoots him dead. Devastated, James recalls a radio transmitter in a barn on the property, his last hope for rescue. After a long, harrowing struggle with the three masked home invaders (Pin-Up Girl, the Man in the Mask, and Dollface), the couple is subdued and tied to chairs in the living room. Kristen, trembling, asks the prowlers why they are doing this. In a chilling deadpan, Dollface replies, "Because you were home." Scholar Tony Williams suggests that the film's setting—a 1970s-era home—points to an "American tradition of violence that is random and without any coherent explanation." He interprets the three masked intruders as manifestations of the "repressed and unresolved tensions affecting the couple inside the house." Unsurprisingly, I share this view entirely.

The plot of *The Strangers* hinges on the pain of a rejected marriage proposal. James is left wondering where his relationship can go from here. His childhood home—decorated in quiet anticipation of Kristen saying *yes*—instead becomes a site of embarrassment and sadness. From this moment on, Kristen feels like a stranger in his house. Unwilling to discuss his unease, James seeks refuge in physical intimacy, initiating sex as a way to smooth over the awkwardness. He whispers that she's "his girl," attempting to reassert their bond. Just then, at the precise moment before intercourse, the first knock at the door shatters the moment. This intrusion feels too deliberate to be incidental. The obscured figure at the threshold—an externalised symbol of a faceless barrier—mirrors an unresolved element within the couple's dynamic. It marks the presence of an impenetrable core at the heart of their relationship, something unspeakable that blocks desire and leaves their romantic connection at an impasse.

The interloper, Dollface, calls out through the darkness: "Is Tamara here?" The enigma surrounding her presence is not confined to the doorstep—it seeps into the house. The masked figures, their faces veiled in obscurity, cast a gloom over the home, their unknowability amplifying a sense of disorientation. The space, once familiar, is now thick with an opaque, creeping unease. As James locates bullets for his father's shotgun, he hesitates. "How do you use this thing? I'm not sure I even know how to load it." Kristen, surprised, reminds him, "But you said you used to hunt with your dad." James admits, "No, I never did. It was just something that I said." Again and again, the script shows that these two individuals barely know each other, they might as well be strangers. What should be a place of familiarity becomes virtually unrecognisable—both the house and in the people in it.

Of course, it is not uncommon for people to wear masks in society, projecting a polished façade to shape how they are perceived. *The Strangers* serves as a vehicle for illustrating Carl Jung's concept of the persona—the social mask an individual presents to the world. Jung defines it as "a kind of mask designed on the one hand to make a definite impression upon others, and on the other to conceal the true nature of the self." The development of a stable persona is a necessary part of adapting to adult life. However, Jung warns of the danger of over-identification: "The professor with his textbook, the tenor with his voice." When a person becomes indistinguishable from their persona, they risk developing a shallow, brittle, and conformist identity—one excessively preoccupied with external perception. In such cases, individuals remain unconscious of any distinction between themselves and the social roles they perform. Jung describes what follows as enantiodromia—the emergence of the repressed individuality from beneath the persona later in life: "The individual will either be completely smothered under an empty persona or an enantiodromia into the buried opposites will occur."

In *The Strangers*, the masked intruders systematically cut off James and Kristen's ability to make outside calls. All communication devices, from old radio transmitters to modern mobile phones, are deactivated or wrecked. I interpret this as the mask functioning paradoxically—not as a means of connection, but as an insurmountable barrier to survival. While the persona exists to facilitate social interaction, in the extreme horror scenario, it obstructs even the most fundamental human needs. Here, the mask does not serve as a tool for engagement but as an instrument of isolation, condemning the characters to the suffocating weight of their public façade.

The intruders break in simply because James and Kristen "were home." Rather than reading this as a nihilistic act of random violence, I see it as an intrusion that mirrors the cracks already forming in the couple's masks. The attack occurs because James and Kristen are *home* to a destructive aura— something they have unwittingly invited in. The film carries an apocalyptic quality in the sense of revelation, an exposure of hard truths. The scales fall from their eyes, and the unresolved fractures in their relationship can no longer be ignored. They are past the point of denying the writing on the wall; their avoidance has finally caught up with them.

In *The Strangers: Prey at Night* (dir. Johannes Roberts), the sequel released a decade later, a family vacations at a relative's secluded trailer park in Ohio—only to be hunted by the same three masked intruders: Dollface, Pin-Up Girl, and the Man in the Mask. Mike and Cindy, along with their children, Kinsey and Luke, plan a quiet weekend together before sending their daughter off to boarding school. The film's tension is largely mapped onto Kinsey; her parents view her as a troubled teen, though the specifics of her misbehaviour are never disclosed. All we know is that Cindy experienced a similar rebellious phase in her own youth. Kinsey resents being sent away, feeling abandoned, while her brother remains the golden child—seemingly untouched by the weight of parental disappointment.

After arriving, an unmasked Dollface knocks on their trailer door, asking for Tamara. Cindy turns her away, but discomfort lingers. Meanwhile, Kinsey and Luke take a walk and stumble upon a nearby trailer with its door ajar. Inside, they make a gruesome discovery—their aunt and uncle's lifeless bodies. Back at the family trailer, Dollface knocks a second time, only to be turned away again. Sensing a problem, Mike and Cindy set out to find their children, who return in a panic. Chaos erupts—every cell phone has been smashed, Dollface kills Cindy, and the Man in the Mask murders Mike. The violence escalates relentlessly, plunging the family into a night of sheer terror.

Applying the theoretical framework of the first *Strangers* film to its sequel, it becomes evident that a sense of unfamiliarity pervades this family, particularly revolving around Kinsey. As a troubled teen, she has become an enigma to her parents, who, despite financial strain, are willing to send her away to boarding school out of concern for her future. The changes in their daughter make her feel like a stranger to them—and vice versa. Kinsey, feeling abandoned, struggles to recognise the parents she once trusted. The schism in their bond leaves them all unmoored, making the family ripe for the intrusion of the masked figures who embody this estrangement.

This brings me to individuation, a key Jungian concept describing the process by which a person's sense of self emerges from an undifferentiated unconscious. This complex developmental journey involves integrating innate personality traits, aspects of the immature psyche, and life experiences into a cohesive whole. For Jung, individuation requires shedding the false wrappings of the persona and disentangling oneself from the seductive pull of primordial images. It unfolds through successive stages of growing awareness, confronting and integrating unconscious elements until the Self is fully realised. Viewed through this lens, *The Strangers: Prey at Night* can be interpreted as an allegory for the growing pains within a family when a child transforms drastically, seemingly overnight, beyond recognition. While this is a natural process, it can feel disorienting—like a disruption of order, a veering off the expected path, or even a violation of unspoken boundaries. Kinsey, in particular, seems to be moving through a stage of individuation in which she must break away from group attachment and narcissistic self-absorption—a process that, while necessary, can feel terrifying and traumatic.

In both films, the breakdown of the persona constitutes the typically Jungian moment when that excessive commitment to collective ideals (the persona), masking deeper individuality, disintegrates. Jung asserts that "the persona is a semblance; the dissolution of the persona is therefore absolutely necessary for individuation." However, this collapse can lead to a destabilising period in which one feels like a stranger to others—and even to oneself. One consequence of the persona's dissolution is the relinquishing of fantasy, giving way to befuddlement. As individuation unfolds, "the situation has thrown off the conventional husk and developed into a stark encounter with reality, with no false masks, veils, or adornments of any kind." Though painful, this process must be embraced—it is the only way to foster true psychological growth.

The Invitation (2015)

Karyn Kusama's masterful horror film *The Invitation* unspools jarring tensions and shocking events when a man attends a dinner party hosted by his ex-wife. Kusama described the film's central theme as "a metaphor for what the nightmare of anxiety really is—this irrational sense that people are trying to hurt you somehow."

Will and his girlfriend Kira arrive at his former house in the Hollywood Hills. Will and Eden divorced following the accidental death of their young son, Ty, in their home. In the aftermath, Eden met her new husband, David, at a grief support group in Mexico, where they also befriended Sadie, who is present at the dinner party. It is the first time their old friend group has reunited in over two years. As the evening unfolds, Will drifts through his erstwhile home, haunted by dark memories—including Eden's suicide attempt. A strange atmosphere coalesces with the arrival of David's friend Pruitt, a large, physically imposing man. When David locks the front door, citing a recent home invasion in the neighbourhood, an undercurrent of tension intensifies. Will later stumbles upon Eden hiding a bottle of barbiturates, further fuelling his growing unease.

David and Eden introduce their guests to their support group, which claims to help people process grief. To illustrate its philosophy, David plays a video of the group's leader, Dr. Joseph, gently comforting a dying woman as she takes her final breaths. Will senses an unsafe atmosphere at the party, but his concerns are dismissed—he's told it's natural to feel awkward revisiting the site of personal tragedy and that showing up at all is an act of bravery. Later that evening, David and Eden pour drinks for a toast. But before anyone can sip, Will, overcome with suspicion, shatters the glasses, fearing they are poisoned. In the madness, Sadie lunges at Will, and in the ensuing struggle, he accidentally knocks her unconscious. Moments later, Gina, who had already taken a sip, collapses and dies. The night erupts into violence—David, Pruitt, and a recovered Sadie launch a brutal attack, killing Miguel, Choi, and Ben. Will, Kira, and Tommy scramble to escape, hiding inside the house. Will overhears David whisper to Eden that they have been "chosen" and that completing their plan is the only way to leave the Earth and finally be free of their pain.

At the core of this community is a bleak doctrine: life on Earth is nothing but suffering, defined by loss and sorrow, and the only true solace lies in death—a gateway to reunification with lost loved ones. It is essentially a suicide cult, urging its followers to reject the life force and surrender to self-annihilation. The film subtly foreshadows this ideology in its opening scene.

On his way to the dinner party, Will accidentally hits a coyote with his car. Seeing the animal gravely wounded, he delivers a mercy killing, putting it out of its misery. This moment sets the tone for what follows, aligning with the cult's morbid belief system: that ritualistic murder is an act of compassion, a means of sparing others from the inevitable misery of existence. To do nothing—to let life continue—is, in their view, to be complicit in the perpetuation of pain.

When Will enters Eden's house, she immediately notices the coyote's blood on his face and wipes it away, remarking, "You're a mess." This isn't just a literal statement—she is commenting on Will's unresolved grief, his inability to move on from their son's death. In contrast, Eden believes she has transcended earthly suffering through her faith, viewing Will's pain as a personal failing. The first time Sadie appears, she stands at the end of a hallway—Will is the only one who notices her at first. She is naked from the waist down, reinforcing her role as the cult's erotic lure, the seductive force that draws people in. Meanwhile, Will is engulfed by devastating mental images upon re-entering his former home. Flashbacks flood his mind—his recall is vivid and intrusive. His numb, zoned-out demeanour signals psychological dissociation punctuated by hypervigilance—scanning his surroundings, bracing for danger. His state of mind is reflected in David's unnerving remarks:

> You've been acting very suspicious of our hospitality. And frankly, it upsets me a little. I lock the door so we can have some peace of mind, and you have a fit about it. My friend needs to move a car, and you stand at the window like you're going to catch him stealing something. You seem very distant. Very off somehow. You must feel like you have to be on the lookout. That the world is unsafe, and chaotic. What happened before can always happen again.

These words cut to the heart of Will's trauma—his fear that catastrophe can strike at any moment, that grief is never truly in the past. He doesn't feel safe and can't shake the overwhelming hunch that something is wrong at the dinner party. His persistent flashbacks, dissociation, and hypervigilance align with key diagnostic criteria for post-traumatic stress disorder (PTSD). This condition develops after experiencing events such as sexual assault, warfare, natural disasters, traffic collisions, the unexpected death of a loved one, life-threatening illness, child abuse, or domestic violence—any occurrence that threatens a person's life or well-being. PTSD symptoms can also include nightmares, avoidance of triggering cues, and an exaggerated fight-or-flight response. Those suffering from PTSD face a heightened risk of suicide and self-harm, as the mind struggles to process and contain overwhelming trauma.

The dinner party's premise—the cult's belief that ending human suffering through murder-suicide is an act of mercy—serves as an externalised manifestation of Will's internal conflict. He struggles to comprehend how his ex-wife appears so at peace with their son's death. Eden tells her guests, "Pain is optional. It's really pretty simple. All of the negative emotions—grief, anger, depression—it's all just chemical reactions. It's entirely physical and changeable. You can actually learn to expel those emotions from your body so you can live life the way you want to." But what exactly is being expelled? The answer becomes clear: the cult seeks to erase the will to live. For them, earthly existence is synonymous with suffering, and the only way to truly move on is to die. Their leader preaches that death is not an end but a peaceful passage to the afterlife. David affirms this belief: "I was a slave to my own grief. Doctor Joseph freed me from that." By reframing death as liberation, the cult dubiously sells suicide as a sacred communal ritual—a final, transcendent act of togetherness.

What I find most fascinating about Will's experience is its reflection in the character of Pruitt. During the dinner, Pruitt shares a chilling confession about his late wife, Margaret, a talented and charismatic artist whom he describes as being "all light." They were married for eight years when, one night, after drinking, they argued over a minor problem—and something inside him snapped. He turned and struck her with full force. Her knees buckled, she hit her head and collapsed. She died instantly. Pruitt explains that it was a terrible mistake, one for which he served time in prison. Yet despite the horror of his actions, he insists that he is still the same person. It was only through the cult, he claims, that he was able to destroy the part of himself capable of such violence. By abandoning his grief, he believes he has been cured. He admits he misses Margaret and thinks of her every day—but he no longer mourns, nor does he feel guilty. To Pruitt, emotions like remorse and sorrow are useless. He has chosen to let them go, secure in the belief that he will see her again soon in a better place, and he eagerly awaits his own passage, telling the group, "Forgiveness doesn't have to wait. I'm free to forgive myself. And so are you. It's a beautiful thing."

Will is visibly unsettled by Pruitt's story—it strikes a nerve, as he carries his own unbearable guilt over Ty's death. Later, he confesses to Kira:

> I'm not okay. My son is dead. Where do I put that? It's like a scream trapped inside me. And nothing changes the fact that I should have been watching more closely that day. It was another kid, and Ty loved

him, and they were just playing. They were just messing around. I shouldn't have let them have the bat. I've been waiting to die since the moment it happened.

As the violence erupts towards the film's climax, Pruitt urges Will to "let go," reassuring him, "There's a plan for us. We'll be there soon. I promise." This moment conveys the weight of Will's unresolved guilt over Ty's death—a guilt so overwhelming that it tempts him towards the abyss of suicidal ideation, the longing to simply disappear. This, more than anything, is what Will is truly fighting against.

Pruitt embodies how Will sees himself—a ruthless, irredeemable killer. This parallel intensifies when, later in the film, Sadie attacks Will in a violent outburst. Acting in self-defence, he strikes back, causing her to lose her balance. Her head slams against the sharp edge of a piece of furniture, and she collapses. The moment eerily mirrors Pruitt's account of Margaret's death, reinforcing Will's internal fear that he is no different from Eden's thuggish, ex-convict friend. Adding to the unease, Sadie had previously made an unwanted sexual advance towards Will—one he instinctively rebuffed. She said:

> You can fuck me right here. Why should we deny that ever? That's the way we were in Mexico. Everyone was just going for it, it was awesome. I can make you like me so much. I can make you beg me. I can do it without even touching you. Just with my voice, with my breath. You can hurt me if you want.

Even in this failed seduction attempt, there is a certain implication—that Will might derive some unconscious excitement from harming another person. This, I believe, is linked to his guilty conscience, where violence is repressed yet remains a driving force beneath the surface.

One of the most striking scenes in *The Invitation* unfolds as the guests ascend the stairs to the dining room, where a beautifully set table awaits. We observe from above, faintly catching snippets of their conversation as they settle into the warm pool of candlelight. A low, insistent droning sound begins to hum beneath the chatter. The camera washes in and out of fragmented dialogue—laughter, the clinking of plates, hands passing food back and forth. The focus narrows on Will's face—he is struggling, disconnected from the group, deeply locked in his own perspective. The dinner conversation feels artificial, its seams exposed. There is something disturbingly primal in the way the guests tear at their meat, something grotesque in the atmosphere. Echoes of a child's cries distort the soundscape, ghosting over Gina's face—her mouth open in laughter, it's like she's screaming. Will watches uneasily as Pruitt devours his meal. Red wine spills onto the white tablecloth, staining it like fresh blood. Eden smiles through her tears. The droning sound amplifies. Time warps—everyone seems to be moving too fast and too slow, all at once. Across the table, Kira's face blurs, her features dissolving into an indistinct haze. Will calls out to her, his voice buried in the busy air. Panic sets in.

Will is inside a flashback—no longer at the dinner table but trapped in the past. It's daytime at a child's birthday party. Adults chatter in the background. Ty, his son, and another boy are playing, roughhousing with baseball bats. Sunlight splinters across the sky. Suddenly, Will is running—pushing through people—panic setting in. Eden is on her knees in front of them. She screams. This scene meticulously captures the mechanics of a flashback—the way trauma violently splices time, forcing the past to hijack the present. It illustrates how PTSD fractures consciousness, ensnaring the sufferer in an unbearable loop of reliving. The jagged, intrusive nature of these memories leaves Will utterly disconnected from his surroundings, reinforcing the deep alienation of post-traumatic distress.

As harrowing as Kusama's film is, I believe the torment displayed onscreen is not without purpose—an essential issue is being confronted and processed. Will has spent too long in avoidance mode, numbing himself to grief. But returning to the house forces him to face the full spectrum of his buried emotions—sadness, anger, and guilt—dragging him out of autopilot and into painful but necessary reckoning. He can no longer pretend that everything is okay, and sharply demands to know:

> Why is everyone is being so fucking polite? This isn't right. Something very strange is going on and no one is saying anything. We don't see you for two years, Edie. And then suddenly you invite us to this lavish dinner, all smiles, spewing all of this jargon. Don't tell me this is normal. The Invitation? It's a cult. Look at the video. It isn't about communion or family. It's about denial. It's a fucking brainwash. Our son died, and you're ignoring it! It meant something when he died. You're trying to erase him. Ty was real. It was real. It is real. Tell me why the doors are locked. Tell me why there are bars on the windows. Tell me why there's a big fucking bottle of barbiturates stashed in your bedroom. Something is going on here. Something dangerous, and we're all just ignoring it because David brought out some good wine!

This powerful moment cuts through the illusion of civility. Will refuses to play along—he expresses his grief openly, even if it disrupts the party ambiance, even if he is seen as unreasonable. He insists on carrying the weight of his bereavement, refusing to mask it for the sake of social decorum. In speaking up, he honours Ty's life and keeps his son's memory alive. Eden's locked doors, barred windows, and reliance on sedatives function as repression tactics—desperate attempts to block out the horror of losing a child. In the film's final moments, when Eden shoots herself in the abdomen, it serves as an allegorical admission—finally designating the place on her body where it hurts. For both parents, the film becomes a process of dismantling defences and achieving emotional liberation through reprocessing.

Gerald's Game (2017)

Mike Flanagan's psychological horror thriller *Gerald's Game* is based on Stephen King's long-considered unfilmable novel of the same name. The story begins with a married couple arriving at an isolated house for a romantic getaway. Jessie slips into new lingerie, and Gerald, after taking Viagra, handcuffs her to the bedposts with police-grade restraints. He begins to enact a stranger rape fantasy; Jessie initially humours him but quickly becomes distressed and asks him to stop and unfasten her. A heated argument follows, during which Gerald accuses her of not making any effort to revive their sex life. Mid-rant, he suddenly collapses and dies of a heart attack.

A few hours pass. Jessie begins to hallucinate: Gerald appears to speak to her, though his lifeless body remains on the floor. She also conjures a more self-aware, assertive version of herself—a projection that articulates truths Jessie has never had the clarity to confront. Exhausted, she falls asleep, only to wake in the darkness and see a deformed figure lurking in the corner of the room. The figure reveals a bag of bones and trinkets, but Jessie refuses to believe it's real. Gerald's spectre insists that the shadowy form is Death, waiting to claim her. In her delirium, Gerald calls Jessie "Mouse," a nickname that triggers a harrowing memory of her father, Tom. When she was 12, during a solar eclipse, Tom had her sit on his lap while he masturbated to her. Afterward, he gaslit her, manipulating her into silence and ensuring she would never speak of the horrific abuse.

Alone in the room, Jessie smashes a water glass, cuts her wrist, and peels back the skin, freeing her blood-soaked hand from the cuff. With her hand now loose, she retrieves the key and unlocks the other restraint. At the end of the hall, the so-called Moonlight Man waits. In a symbolic gesture, she removes her wedding ring and hands it to him, as if paying a toll to cross a border into freedom. Six months later, Jessie writes a letter to her 12-year-old self. Sleep has eluded her since the traumatic ordeal. From the news, she learns that Raymond Andrew Joubert, a necrophiliac serial killer and grave robber, has been apprehended and is standing trial. It turns out Joubert was the real-life home invader Jessie had mistaken for the hallucinated Moonlight Man. Jessie attends his arraignment. In the courtroom, she approaches him and, in a moment of clarity, sees the features of Gerald and her father, Tom, superimposed over Joubert's face. Triumphantly, she declares, "You're so much smaller than I remember," before walking away.

I've already discussed the psychological structure of obsessional neurosis in the *Rear Window* section, referencing Freud's "Rat Man" case study, in which the subject is trapped in an incapacitating state of ambivalence and procrastination, unable to take decisive action. In *Gerald's Game*, however, I want to focus on the mortified aspect of the neurotic individual—mortified both in terms of being deeply humiliated and in the sense of being undead, like an "animated corpse." My reading of Jessie is that her subjectivity is markedly depleted; she is detached, putting up a façade and going through the motions of what is expected of her like a programmed automaton. Being chained to the bed evokes a hostage metaphor, where Jessie's autonomy is utterly suppressed, and her survival hinges on appeasing her captor. As long as she remains in this lifeless state, she denies herself the possibility of liberation.

In psychoanalytic terms, Jessie is libidinally divested. Her childhood trauma has confined her to a mindset that stifles the life instinct. Freud argued that the libido fixates on different erogenous zones during psychosexual development, and failure to navigate these stages successfully results in pent-up energy, leading to pathological character traits in adulthood. Psychotherapy aims to identify where repression occurs, allowing these drives to be confronted directly and freeing up energy for conscious use in sublimation. Ultimately, for the subject to reconnect with their libidinal energy, they must consciously confront and work through these repressed experiences.

Gerald's ghost taunts Jessie, saying:

> You were chained to that bed for so many hours. You did what you always do when it gets too much, you ran. In here (he gestures at her head). You just laid here, calling my name again and again, and let critical time tick by. You should have been thinking about life support. You're a life support system. You've been unplugged. There's still juice in there, but the charge is running down. And if you don't get out of the cuffs, it will go all the way to zero.

Jessie's lifelong pattern of avoidant behaviour is laid bare: when faced with overwhelming stress, she shuts down, retreating into her mind and disconnecting from reality. This aligns with the Lacanian concept of mortification, as her impulse to withdraw causes her to leak away the vitality of conscious life. She strikes me as an escape artist, but only in the sense of mentally zoning out—her life feels haphazardly cobbled together. Yet, there's still a part of her that clings to survival and fights back by confronting hard truths. Her projected self tells her:

> This is you all over. Problem, panic, denial. Hoping if you look away, it'll magically vanish. If you don't wake up, you're gonna die in those handcuffs. And we both know you've been sleepwalking since you were 12 years old. [...] You married an older man. Your father was a lawyer. Gerald was a lawyer. Your father minimized you, objectified you. Jessie, you married into the only dynamic you've ever known. You were a girl, he was a man, and you never walked away from that. That afternoon never ended.

Jessie's ideological collusion with her abuser is so profound that she unconsciously accepts the terms of Gerald's sex game, trading her father's chains for Gerald's handcuffs. Both men derive arousal from exploiting her vulnerability, turning her suffering into a perverse ritual—a form of mortification that eroticises the corpse. In this dynamic, sexual excitement emerges from abjection, where Jessie is violently excluded from the interpersonal exchange, reduced to neither subject nor object but something far more dehumanised. The concept of mortification as a signifier of death is strikingly relevant to Joubert, the grave robber who desecrates crypts, mausoleums, and cemeteries, stripping corpses of their jewellery. He gouges out eyes, cuts throats, and removes noses, hands, and ears—each act targeting the sites of the five senses: vision, taste, smell, touch, and hearing. Symbolically, Jessie's tendency to avoid difficult situations by shutting down her senses mirrors Joubert's desecration, linking her self-nullifying impulse to his necrophile violence. Joubert pursues Jessie precisely because she exists in a near-death state, lulled into a grave state of dormancy.

Jessie's father giving her the nickname "Mouse" commands her to stay "as quiet as a mouse"—a directive that manipulates her into never telling anyone about his heinous exploitation. Her silence figuratively chains her to her captor. The trauma confines Jessie to a deep, unrelenting space of shame, where she remains in a prolonged state of mortification. The solar eclipse scene is a harrowing depiction of child sexual abuse: Jessie's father masturbates behind her while she sits on his lap, her body *covers* his vile act just as the moon *covers* the sun during an eclipse. She is later asked by her dad to *cover up* for him, a literal concealment of the truth. Astrologically, a solar eclipse—when the moon casts its shadow over the sun—serves as a cosmic call to pause, reflect, and face what has been hidden. Solar eclipses have the power to reveal truths we've been avoiding, illuminating what has long been obstructed. It is through resolving these buried conflicts that we find the strength to move forward.

The monstrous Moonlight Man steals precious objects from the dead, engages in necrophilia, and consumes dead flesh—actions that metaphorically parallel how the moon (and her father) flung young Jessie into a sunless world, forcibly removing her precious life force and innocence. This pattern repeats when her husband, Gerald, imposes his sexual will on her, perpetuating the cycle of violation. The recurring motif of the "hand" in the film signifies the illicit masturbation of her father, as well as the collusion between him and Gerald, who work hand in glove to keep Jessie bound in emotional chains. Jessie's escape from the handcuffs—by cutting her own hand—becomes a visceral act of liberation. Blood lubricates her extraction, and the skin of her hand peels away from the muscle tissue in the process. What remains hidden stays shrouded in darkness, but confronting and processing these buried truths strips away deceit and reintroduces light. As gruesome as it is, the exposed hand symbolises action and freedom. The gloves are off: Jessie finally takes decisive, uncompromising steps forward.

It's worth noting that young Jessie got her period just one month before her father sexually abused her. When she escapes from Gerald's handcuffs, she wraps the wound on her hand with maxi pads to stop the bleeding—a striking symbol of healing and reclamation. By reconnecting with this divested part of herself, Jessie comes to understand that her father's shackles were silence, and Gerald's chains were comfort. The very people who were supposed to protect her from monsters turned out to be the monsters. This realisation compels Jessie to come out from the shadows of her inner eclipse. In this moment of personal growth, the nefarious influence of her abusers shrinks: they are, as she declares, "so much smaller than I remember."

Mother! (2017)

I conclude this chapter—and book—with an analysis of Darren Aronofsky's controversial psychological horror film *Mother!* In the charred remains of a large, decimated house, a renowned poet, plagued by writer's block, places a mysterious crystal object on a pedestal in his study. The structure then transforms into a beautiful home nestled within a pristine landscape. The film unfolds as a symbolic study of biblical mythology: Javier Bardem embodies the Abrahamic God as a tortured artist, while Jennifer Lawrence plays his wife and muse. She not only renovates their home but also becomes the very ground upon which divine contemplation and human madness unfold. Her being serves as the material substrate for the Lord's creative process—the stage on which all the drama of existence is enacted.

Clay appears in the film as the elemental foundation of creation. Earth itself is made of clay and mud—the very substance of life. "We spend all our time here," the woman says. "I want to make it paradise." The home she lovingly remodels is shaped in the image of Eden. She mixes clay as plaster for the interior walls—walls that encase the beating heart of the house, which she can perceive through a kind of inner vision. Into the plaster, she blends a yellow powder—a touch of alchemical magic to heal the scars. This same powder, which she also ingests when anxious, appears to soothe her mind, as if it restores not only the house but her psyche as well.

One night, the couple's idyllic tranquillity is interrupted by a knock at the door: an orthopaedic surgeon appears, claiming to be looking for a bed and breakfast. The doctor and the poet become fast friends, but the visitor seems uneasy around the woman; he insists he doesn't want to be a bother. The poet warmly welcomes him to stay, and his wife reluctantly complies. Later that night, the guest suffers from dry heaves. Orthopaedic surgeons treat diseases and injuries of the musculoskeletal system—tellingly, a wound appears on his ribcage, as if a bone has been removed. The next morning, his wife arrives at the house—like Eve sprung from Adam's rib. These events follow the biblical timeline: in the beginning, God created the heavens and the earth, and on the sixth day, God created man. *Mother!* unfolds as a fever dream structured like a creation myth, attempting to order the cosmos from the depths of chaos.

The visitor appears like a figment of the artist's imagination, a catalyst that stirs his dormant creative drive—a radical element that suddenly manifests in his home, invading the immaculate environment staged by his female muse. This first transgression is absorbed as trauma, then repeated and amplified as more and more people begin to encroach on the sacred space of a loving home, this miraculous terrain where life has been carefully nurtured. The uninvited humans are entitled, messy, and disrespectful. They fail to appreciate the Earth's nourishing power and instead exploit her. Adam drinks and smokes; he suffers from lung cancer—humanity brings disease and decay to the holy site of creation.

The woman of the house grows increasingly frustrated by the ever-multiplying guests. When the interloping couple accidentally shatters the precious crystal object they had been forbidden to touch, the poet flies into a rage and boards up his study. The smashed crystal stands as a clear analogue to the biblical tale of Adam and Eve eating the forbidden fruit from the tree of knowledge—a catastrophic transgression that led to their banishment from the Garden of Eden. Soon after, the guests' two sons arrive unexpectedly and begin to argue over their dying father's will. The older son fatally wounds his younger brother, then flees the scene. This re-enactment of Cain and Abel evokes Genesis once again: God punishes Cain by condemning him to a life of wandering for murdering his brother. The ancient story serves as both warning and lamentation—a meditation on the primal rupture of kinship and the sanctity of human life.

After the incident, a bloodstain appears on the floorboards—impossible to scrub clean. The mark resembles a vulva, the ominous site of a cursed birth. This is the place where a man killed his brother, and it soon becomes a magnet for further violence and bloodshed. It's as though the poet's wife—whose generative powers once promised new life—has had her womb hijacked, repurposed to birth only tragedy. Following the murder, the heart of the house, perceived by the woman through the walls, grows darker and weaker. More rude, presumptuous visitors turn up uninvited. They break the kitchen sink, causing a partial flood—another nod to biblical catastrophe. The woman feels increasingly neglected, yet her husband insists, "I want to bring life into this house, open the door to new people, new ideas." Their argument erupts into passionate lovemaking, and she conceives. Elated by the pregnancy, the poet finds his creative voice once more.

Time passes. The woman prepares for the arrival of her child and is moved to tears upon reading her husband's beautiful new poem. When it is published, the work is met with acclaim and sells exceptionally well—we are now transitioning from the Old to the New Testament. In celebration, she prepares a special dinner, hoping for an intimate evening, but a group of admirers interrupts. She asks her husband to send them away, yet he insists on being gracious and showing his appreciation. The same pattern repeats. In frustration, she pleads, "Look at me! I'm about to have our baby! Why is that not enough for you? I want to be alone with you." But the house is soon overrun with adoring fans. Their behaviour devolves into chaos—stealing items as souvenirs, vandalising the property. The phone is ripped from the wall, severing any connection to outside help. Delirious crowds worship the poet, weeping as he marks their faces with ink. Blinded by adulation, he fails to see the ruin around him.

A cult forms around the writer, his devotees dance in a frenzied circle. The house's heart withers further, becoming fainter with every passing moment. Outside, thousands more queue to gain entry—fighting erupts, and the scene mutates into a frenetic nightclub. The delicate, painstaking touches once used to refurbish the house are trampled and desecrated. Screaming fans continue to surge inside. Riot police storm in and pepper spray the poet and his wife. The turmoil escalates: bodies crush together in the overcrowded house, women are caged like victims of sex trafficking, and military forces arrive to suppress the madness. Pandemonium rips through the space, executions unfold en masse—what was once a sanctuary spirals into a full-blown war zone with soldiers, bombings, and refugees.

The film moves into apocalyptic overdrive. The Book of Revelation—the final book of the New Testament—takes its name from the Greek word apokalypsis, meaning "unveiling" or "revelation." In this climactic section, the woman goes into labour, and her husband reopens his study—previously boarded up—so she can give birth inside. It's telling that the poet never produces anything within this space himself; the study is a site of creative stagnation for him. By contrast, it is his wife who generates two miraculous offerings there: the birth of their child, and, in the final scene, the giving of her heart. These two acts—of creation and sacrifice—become the true sources of inspiration and nourishment, allowing a new cycle of life to begin.

Against his wife's wishes, the writer presents their newborn to the ravenous crowd, who kill and cannibalise the infant—a grotesque rendering of communion with the body and blood of the Lord. Enraged, the mother lashes out at them, but they retaliate, beating her mercilessly until her husband intervenes. She refuses to forgive them, escapes to the basement, and ignites a tank of oil—causing an explosion that incinerates everyone and obliterates the house. The flame that sparks the destruction comes from Adam's zippo lighter, implicating the very first human in this final act of annihilation.

Javier Bardem's character is portrayed as a narcissistic artist. For him, being admired by others—playing the gracious host—is more important than tending to the partner he claims to love. What truly animates him is the adoration of ecstatic fans, the formation of a cult around his persona, complete with rituals and worship. The film poses provocative questions: "What if the world is like a house, and humans invade and destroy it in the name of love for someone? In the name of God—a narcissistic artist?"

Central to my interpretation of *Mother!* is Freud's theory of narcissism, which he divided into two categories: primary and secondary narcissism. We all have innate impulses to nourish ourselves and protect against danger; these impulses are intertwined with our desires. Importantly, Freud argued that we cannot neatly separate our sexual desires—those directed towards others—from the inward need to care for and preserve the self. He introduced the concept of narcissism as a form of self-love, a kind of libidinal investment in the self, and viewed it as a developmental necessity that, when intensified, could become neurotic. In Freud's view, all humans experience a degree of narcissism during their psychological development.

Primary narcissism, according to Freud, exists in all human beings from birth. It is evident in young children who see themselves as powerful beings capable of remarkable feats. In healthy development, we are meant to outgrow this early stage, rebalancing our auto-eroticism by directing love outward towards external objects. Hoarding all that self-adoration internally generates too much inner conflict. Secondary narcissism, by contrast, emerges when the subject withdraws their libidinal investment from external objects and redirects it inward. The result is a psychic severing from the social world—a disinterest in others, and a withdrawal into the self. This retreat of libido from the outer world gives rise to megalomania. It is this pathological form of narcissism that becomes clinically diagnosable, and which I believe is embodied in Javier Bardem's character in Aronofsky's film.

Freud observed that the narcissist often suffers from low self-esteem, stemming from an inability to genuinely express love towards others or meaningfully absorb love from them. Burdened by shame and guilt, the narcissist becomes highly defensive, seeking constant validation from a devoted, worshipful audience. Sound familiar? Freud argued that both the individual and the species depend on maintaining a delicate balance between primary and secondary narcissism. When too much libidinal energy is directed inward—towards the self—this balance collapses, resulting in irrational behaviour and a compulsive need to remain at the centre of the social world.

Writing for the *Chicago Tribune*, Michael Phillips (2017) observed that "Aronofsky delivers a damning critique of the artist/muse arrangement." At a pivotal moment in the film, the writer says to his wife, "I love you." She replies, "You never loved me. You just loved how much I loved you. I gave you everything. You gave it all away. [...] What hurts me the most is that I wasn't enough." He responds, "It's not your fault. Nothing is ever enough. I couldn't create if it was. And I have to. That's what I do. That's what I am. Now I must try it all again." This exchange lays bare the destructive loop of narcissistic artistic obsession—the muse becomes a vessel to be emptied, rather than cherished.

The relationship between a megalomaniacal artist and a loyal muse escalates to a fever pitch—until there is nothing left to give. Aronofsky frames this as a dynamic between the Abrahamic God and the finite ground that sustains life. Eventually, resources are depleted, because narcissistic humans—made in God's image—crave too much attention, become greedy, consume everything, and leave only devastation in their wake. The invasive nature of humanity wounds the Earth, reminding us that muses get bruises. It's a fitting conclusion to Aronofsky's apocalyptic vision and a reflection of his environmental activism: a stark warning against our species' ravenous excess.

Glossary of Psychoanalytic Terms

- **Borderline Personality Disorder (BPD)**—A psychiatric condition characterised by unstable moods, relationships, and self-image, often accompanied by intense emotions and fear of abandonment.
- **Castration Anxiety**—A Freudian concept referring to a male child's unconscious fear of losing the penis, often symbolising a broader fear of loss or punishment.
- **Death Drive (Thanatos)**—Freud's notion of an unconscious drive towards destruction, aggression, and a return to an inanimate state.
- **Dissociation**—A psychological process where thoughts, memories, or awareness become disconnected from conscious experience, often as a defence against trauma.
- **Ego**—In Freudian theory, the part of the psyche that mediates between the Id, Superego, and external reality.
- **Ego Death**—The experience of a complete loss of subjective self-identity, often associated with transformation or psychic renewal.
- **Enantiodromia**—A Jungian term for the emergence of an opposite tendency when one pole is over-dominant, leading to a necessary psychic correction.
- **Flashback**—The involuntary reliving of a past traumatic event, as though it is happening in the present.
- **Freudian Slip**—An accidental error in speech, memory, or action that is believed to reveal unconscious thoughts or desires.
- **Gaslighting**—A form of psychological manipulation in which a person or group covertly sows seeds of doubt in a targeted individual, making them question their own memory, perception, sanity, or judgment. This tactic is often used to gain control over another by distorting reality.
- **Hypervigilance**—A heightened state of sensory sensitivity, often as a trauma response, where one is constantly on the lookout for danger.
- **Iceberg model of the mind**—Freud's metaphor depicting the mind as an iceberg, with the small visible tip representing conscious thought and the vast submerged mass symbolising the unconscious.

- **Id**—The unconscious reservoir of instinctual drives and desires, according to Freud.
- **Identification**—A psychological process by which a person assimilates aspects of another person, often as a defence or developmental function.
- **Individuation**—A term from Carl Jung referring to the process of integrating unconscious elements of the psyche into conscious awareness. Individuation allows a person to develop a cohesive sense of self, distinct from societal expectations and external influences.
- **Libido**—Psychic energy derived from instinctual drives, particularly sexual desire in Freudian theory.
- **Mirroring**—A developmental process where a caregiver reflects the child's emotional state back to them, helping to build a stable sense of self.
- **Narcissism (Primary)**—A developmental phase in which a person's libidinal energy is focused inward, often seen in infancy.
- **Narcissism (Secondary)**—A pathological return of libido to the self, leading to self-absorption, detachment from others, and potential megalomania.
- **Obsessional Neurosis**—A condition characterised by intrusive, repetitive thoughts and compulsive behaviours that serve to ward off anxiety. Individuals with obsessional neurosis often struggle with overthinking, rigidity, and an avoidance of emotional and sexual intimacy.
- **Oedipal Complex**—A Freudian theory describing a child's unconscious desire for the opposite-sex parent and rivalry with the same-sex parent.
- **Persona**—In Jungian psychology, the social mask or façade that an individual presents to the outside world, often covering the true self. The persona is shaped by cultural expectations and personal adaptation but may obscure deeper, more authentic aspects of the self.
- **Phallic Symbol**—An object that symbolically represents power, dominance, or masculinity, often unconsciously associated with the penis.
- **The Phallus**—In Lacanian psychoanalysis, the phallus is a privileged symbolic signifier of authority, power, and desire, rather than a literal anatomical reference to the penis. It plays a key role in structuring identity and social relationships.
- **Post-Traumatic Stress Disorder (PTSD)**—A psychiatric condition triggered by exposure to a traumatic event, leading to symptoms such as flashbacks, nightmares, emotional numbness, and hypervigilance. PTSD often involves an ongoing sense of threat and difficulty regulating fear responses.
- **Projection**—A defence mechanism in which unwanted feelings or thoughts are attributed to another person.

- **Psychosis**—A severe mental state marked by a loss of contact with reality, often involving delusions, hallucinations, or disorganised thinking.
- **Repression**—A key psychoanalytic defence mechanism where distressing thoughts, feelings, memories, or desires are unconsciously pushed out of awareness to avoid anxiety. Repressed content can still influence behaviour and surface in disguised forms.
- **Scopophilia**—A term from psychoanalytic theory referring to the pleasure derived from looking. This concept is closely linked with voyeurism and the cinematic experience, where the act of watching becomes a source of fascination, desire, or control.
- **Seduction Theory**—A Freudian hypothesis suggesting that neurosis results from childhood sexual abuse or trauma (later revised in Freud's metapsychology).
- **Superego**—The internalised moral standards and ideals acquired from parents and society, functioning as the conscience.
- **Symbolic Order**—In Lacanian theory, the domain of language, law, and social structures that mediate desire and identity.
- **Transference**—The redirection of unconscious feelings from one person to another, especially onto a therapist in psychoanalytic settings.
- **Uncanny**—A feeling of eerie familiarity, often arising from something once familiar that has become strange or repressed.
- **Unconscious**—The part of the mind outside of conscious awareness, containing thoughts, memories, and desires that influence behaviour.

Bibliography

Benjamin, Walter. 1999. *The Arcades Project*. Translated by Howard Eiland and Kevin McLaughlin. Harvard University Press.
Bernstein, Albert. 2001. *Emotional Vampires: Dealing with People Who Drain You Dry*. McGraw-Hill.
Bordo, Susan. 1993. *Unbearable Weight: Feminism, Western Culture, and the Body*. University of California Press.
Burke, Edmund. 1757. *A Philosophical Enquiry into the Origin of Our Ideas of the Sublime and Beautiful*. R. and J. Dodsley.
Charcot, Jean-Martin. 1887. *Clinical Lectures on Diseases of the Nervous System*. New Sydenham Society.
Creed, Barbara. 1993. *The Monstrous-Feminine: Film, Feminism, Psychoanalysis*. Routledge.
Ebert, Roger. 2009. *Roger Ebert's Movie Yearbook 2010*. Andrews McMeel Publishing.
Fortune, Dion. 2001. *Psychic Self-Defense: The Classic Instruction Manual for Protecting Yourself Against Paranormal Attack*. Weiser Books.
Freud, Sigmund. 1900. *The Interpretation of Dreams*. Translated by James Strachey. Basic Books.
Freud, Sigmund. 1905. *Three Essays on the Theory of Sexuality*. Translated by James Strachey. Basic Books.
Freud, S. 1909. *Notes Upon a Case of Obsessional Neurosis*. Standard Edition, vol. 10, edited by James Strachey. Hogarth Press.
Freud, S. 1913. *Totem and Taboo*. Standard Edition, vol. 13, edited by James Strachey. Hogarth Press.
Freud, Sigmund. 1920. *Beyond the Pleasure Principle*. Translated by C.J.M. Hubback, Standard Edition, vol. 18. W.W. Norton & Company.

Freud, Sigmund. 1923. *The Ego and the Id*. Translated by Joan Riviere, edited by James Strachey. W.W. Norton & Company.

Freud, Sigmund. 1924. *The Dissolution of the Oedipus Complex*. Standard Edition, vol. 19, edited by James Strachey. Hogarth Press.

Freud, Sigmund. 1930. *Civilization and Its Discontents*. Translated by James Strachey. W.W. Norton & Company.

Freud, Sigmund. 1991. *On Narcissism: An Introduction*. Translated by James Strachey. Liveright Publishing Corporation.

Gabler, Neal. 1988. *An Empire of Their Own: How the Jews Invented Hollywood*. Crown.

Giger, H.R. 1993. *Necronomicon*. Morpheus International.

Heim, Leah. 2017. Telekinesis as the Female Abject in Stephen King's Carrie. *Digital Literature Review*. https://blogs.bsu.edu/dlr/2017/04/10/telekinesis-as-the-female-abject-in-stephen-kings-carrie.

Horvat, Srećko. 2011. The Future Is Here. *NeMe*. www.neme.org/texts/the-future-is-here

Jung, Carl G. 1954. *The Development of Personality*. Translated by R.F.C. Hull. Princeton University Press.

Jung, Carl G. 1973. *Synchronicity: An Acausal Connecting Principle*. Translated by R.F.C. Hull. Princeton University Press.

Jung, Carl G. 1981. *The Archetypes and the Collective Unconscious*. Translated by R.F.C. Hull. Princeton University Press.

Kristeva, Julia. 1982. *Powers of Horror: An Essay on Abjection*. Translated by Leon S. Roudiez. Columbia University Press.

Lacan, Jacques. 1977. *The Four Fundamental Concepts of Psychoanalysis*. Edited by Jacques-Alain Miller, translated by Alan Sheridan. W.W. Norton & Company.

Lacan, Jacques. 1992. *The Ethics of Psychoanalysis, 1959–1960*. Edited by Jacques-Alain Miller, translated by Dennis Porter. Routledge.

Lacan, Jacques. 2006. *Écrits: The First Complete Edition in English*. Translated by Bruce Fink. W.W. Norton & Company.

Laing, R.D. 1960. *The Divided Self: An Existential Study in Sanity and Madness*. Tavistock Publications.

Leach, Neil. 2006. *Camouflage*. MIT Press.

McIntee, David A. 2005. *Beautiful Monsters: The Unofficial and Unauthorised Guide to the Alien and Predator Films*. Telos Publishing.

McLuhan, Marshall. 1994. *Understanding Media: The Extensions of Man*. MIT Press.

Mulvey, Laura. 1975. Visual Pleasure and Narrative Cinema. *Screen*, 16 (3): 6–18.

Nietzsche, Friedrich. 1989. *Beyond Good and Evil: Prelude to a Philosophy of the Future*. Translated by Walter Kaufmann. Vintage.

O'Bannon, Dan. 2019. *Something Perfectly Disgusting: Dan O'Bannon on Alien*. Edited by Diane O'Bannon. Perfect Bound Press.

Phillips, Michael. 2017. 'MOTHER!' Trouble in Paradise. *Chicago Tribune*. www.chicagotribune.com/2017/09/13/mother-review-trouble-in-paradise-starring-jennifer-lawrence.

Profrol. 2020. Carrie: A Period Piece. *Long Live the King*. https://longlivetheking.family.blog/2020/02/10/carrie-a-period-piece/.

Wilde, Oscar. 1905. *De Profundis*. Methuen.

Williams, Linda. 1991. Film Bodies: Gender, Genre, and Excess. *Film Quarterly*, 44 (4): 2–13.

Williams, Tony. 1996. *Hearths of Darkness: The Family in the American Horror Film*. Fairleigh Dickinson University Press.

Žižek, Slavoj. 1989. *The Sublime Object of Ideology*. Verso.

Žižek, Slavoj. 2012. *The Pervert's Guide to Ideology. Directed by Sophie Fiennes, narrated by Slavoj Žižek*. P Guide Ltd.

Zuboff, Shoshana. 2019. *The Age of Surveillance Capitalism: The Fight for a Human Future at the New Frontier of Power*. PublicAffairs.

Index

abjection, 33–34, 39, 74, 190
Addiction, The, 141–144
   academia, 144
   Casanova, 141–142
   philosophy, 144
   religion, 143
   seduction, 142
   sin, 143
   substance abuse, 142
Alien, 101–105
   archaic mother, 104
   artificial intelligence, 104
   chestburster scene, 104
   dehumanisation, 103
   facehugger, 104
   Final Girl, 104
   Giger, H.R., 104
   sexual assault, 104–105
alien horror, 92–123
alienation, 13, 18, 33, 42, 96–98, 100, 107, 116–119, 121, 187
Allon, Yoram, 143
anal stage of development, 58, 74
Anderson, Paul W.S., 111–114
Annihilation, 119–121
   addiction, 120
   cancer, 121
   extramarital affair, 120
   molecular diffusion, 121
   mourning, 120
   self-destruction, 120
   self-harm, 120–121
   Shimmer, The, 118–120
   Thanatos, 120–121
Antichrist, 7–10
   clitoris, 8
   cognitive behavioural therapy, 9
   Eden, 9
   gynocide, 9
   nature, 8
Antigone, 101
anxiety, 183–188
archaic mother, 104, 122
Arendt, Hannah, 61
Aronofsky, Darren, 61–74, 169, 191–196

banality of evil, 61
Barrie, J.M., 133–134
Bates Jr., Richard, 34–43
beautiful, 81–82, 90
Benchley, Peter, 87
Benjamin, Walter, 18
Bernstein, Albert, 152
Bertino, Bryan, 179–182
Birds, The, 76–80
   gender reversal, 77–78
   female sexuality, 77–78
   obsessional neurosis, 79

Oedipus complex, 79
water motif, 78
Black Swan, 61–74, 169
   Dostoyevsky, Fyodor, 62
   ecstasy, 69–70
   fingernails, 67, 70–71
   hangnail, 66
   masturbation, 67
   Shadow, the, 74
   Tchaikovsky, Pyotr Ilyich, 62
Blade, 138–141
   Family Romance, 139
   Little Hans, 140
   Oedipus complex, 139
   phallic stage of development, 139
   Symbolic Order, 141
body horror, 31–75
borderline personality disorder, 170–172, 196
Bordo, Susan, 69
Bram Stoker's Dracula, 124–127
   Imaginary, the, 126
   New Woman, 125
   phallic penetration, 127
   phallus, the, 126
   Victorian society, 125
Breuer, Josef, 22
Brice, Patrick, 172–179
Burke, Edmund, 81–82

Cam, 169
Campbell, John W., 108–111
Capgras Syndrome, 96–97, 122
Carmilla, 130
Carpenter, John, 108–111, 114–116
Carrie, 31–34
   menstrual blood, 32
   religious trauma, 34
   split screen, 33
   telekinesis, 32–34
Carter, David, 143
Cartwright, Veronica, 104
Cassavetes, Alexandra, 27–29
castration, 19, 35, 42, 51, 53, 56, 71, 74, 107–108, 122, 126, 139, 154, 172, 196
catharsis, 112
cathexis, 84–86, 90

censorship, 88
Chan-wook, Park, 10–12
Chaplin, Charlie, 103
Charcot, Jean-Martin, 26
civilisation, 54, 60, 80, 88, 97
Climax, 12–14
   electrical room, 13
   Eros, 13–14
   LSD, 12–14
   mirror stage, 12–13
   Psyche, 12–13
   sangria, 12–14
clinical psychology, 15, 20
Coppola, Francis Ford, 124–127
Coscarelli, Don, 98–101
Creed, Barbara, 21, 32, 53, 104
Creep, 172–179
   archaeology, 178
   Ego, 173–178
   Eros, 173
   Iceberg Model of the Mind, 174
   Id, 173–178
   jump scares, 174
   Superego, 173
   unconscious, 173–174
Cronenberg, Brandon, 16–18
Cullen, Del, 143
Cujo, 84–86
   cathexis, 84–86
   denial, 84–86
   extramarital affair, 84–86
Cukor, George, 155–159

dark night of the soul, 90
Daughters of Darkness, 127–130
   maternal projection, 128
   Oedipus complex, 128–129
   repressed homosexuality, 128–129
   serial killer, 127–128
De Palma, Brian, 31–34
death drive (Thanatos), 45, 74, 79, 100, 120–122, 173, 196
defence mechanism, 9, 85, 89, 159
delusion, 3, 6, 35–43, 96, 132, 168
Demme, Jonathan, 14–16
denial, 84–86, 88–90, 121, 175, 187, 190
depression, 8, 142, 144
desire, 21–22, 77–78, 100, 122, 146–149

dissociation, 39, 74, 184, 196
Doctor Sleep, 151–153
   alcoholism, 151
   liminal space, 154
   psychic vampirism, 152
   Shine, the, 151–152
   recovery, 152
Donnie Darko, 5–7
   conspiracy theories, 6–7
   delusion, 6
   Greene, Graham, 5
   hallucination, 5–6
   paranoia, 6
   presidential election, 5–7
double, 61–74, 96–98, 169–171
Dowd, Maureen, 156
Doyle, Michael, 132
Duplass, Mark, 172–179

Ebert, Roger, 145
Ego, 88–91, 100, 113, 119, 122, 139, 148, 173–179, 196
Ego death, 178, 196
enantiodromia, 180–181, 196
ennui, 18
Eros (life instinct), 14–15, 67, 90, 100, 103, 106, 121–122, 135, 167, 173
Event Horizon, 111–114
   black hole, 112
   general relativity, 112
   Oedipus, 113
   unconscious, 112–113
Excision, 34–43
   casting choices, 36–38
   cystic fibrosis, 34, 39–40
   magical thinking, 40
   necrophilia, 39
   phallus, the, 41–42
   sex education, 37–39
   surgery, 34–43

female sexuality, 19, 23, 25, 49–56, 78–79, 83–84, 127, 164
feminine jouissance, 19–29, 77–80, 90
femme fatale, 19
Ferrara, Abel, 141–144
Fiennes, Sophie, 79, 114
Finney, Jack, 95

Flanagan, Mike, 151–153, 188–191
flashback, 16, 44, 184, 187, 196
foreclosure, 95, 119, 122, 132, 154
Fortune, Dion, 152
Freud, Sigmund, 11, 18, 35, 53–54, 85–88, 94, 97, 99, 104, 106–107, 112–113, 120, 129, 134, 136, 139–140, 147, 150, 161, 170, 173–178, 194–195
Freudian slip, 112, 122, 177, 196

Gabler, Neal, 89
Garland, Alex, 119–121
Gaslight, 155–159
   coercive control, 158
   love bombing, 158
   Lucia di Lammermoor, 158
   narcissist, 157
   psychological manipulation, 156
   repression, 158
gaslighting, 155–159, 188, 191, 196
gaze, 4, 7, 13, 24–26, 28, 63–64, 83, 94, 108, 122
Gerald's Game, 188–191
   abjection, 190
   avoidance, 190
   child sexual abuse, 188, 190
   hand motif, 190–191
   gaslighting, 188, 191
   libidinal divestment, 189
   mortification, 189–190
   solar eclipse scene, 188, 190
Girl Walks Home Alone at Night, A, 149–151
   feminism, 150
   morality police, 150–151
   Superego, 150–151
   surveillance, 150–151
   vigilante justice, 149–150
Goldhaber, Daniel, 169
Goldwater Rule, the, 2
Gonzalez, Ed, 143
Greek mythology, 14, 52, 101, 163

hallucination, 5–6, 46, 70–71, 111–112, 130, 132, 188
Hamilton, Patrick, 155
Hammill, Peter, 153

Hancock, John, 130–133
Hitchcock, Alfred, 76–80, 146, 159–162
hive mind, 59, 74
home invasion, 155–198
Hopkins, Stephen, 106–108
Horvat, Srećko, 110
Human Centipede Trilogy, The, 56–61
   anal fixation, 58
   bureaucracy, 61
   copycat crimes, 58
   digestion, 59
   free speech, 59
   hive mind, 59
   prison system, 61
Hunter, Stephen, 144
Hydraulic Model of the Mind, 87–88, 90
hypervigilance, 184, 196
hysteria, 19–20, 22–23, 26, 29

Iceberg Model of the Mind, 174, 196
Id, 87–90, 139, 150, 174–179, 197
identity, 16–19, 170–171, 198
ideology, 114–116, 122
Imaginary, the, 126, 154, 164
imposter syndrome, 42
incest taboo, 11–12, 29, 79, 140
individuation, 71, 73, 182, 197
Interview with the Vampire, 136–139
   Id, 136
   dependency, 138
   depression, 137
   Munchausen syndrome by proxy, 138
   obsessional neurosis, 137
   oral stage of development, 136
   pleasure principle, 136
   psychotherapy, 136
   Superego, 136
Invasion of the Body Snatchers, 95–98
   alien duplicates, 95–98
   Capgras Syndrome, 96–97
   Cold War, 97
   dehumanisation, 97
   groupthink, 97
   paranoia, 97
   political messaging, 96
Invitation, The, 183–188
   anxiety, 183–188

denial, 187
dissociation, 184
domestic violence, 186
flashback, 187
grief, 183
mercy killing, 184
post-traumatic stress disorder, 184, 187
suicide cult, 183–188

James, Henry, 130
Jaws, 87–90
   economic growth, 89
   Ego, 87–90
   Hydraulic Model of the Mind, 87
   Id, 87–90, 136
   Superego, 87–90
   suspense music, 87
   topography, 88
Jones, Amy Holden, 162–165
Jordan, Neil, 136–138
jouissance, 19, 29
Jung, Carl, 71, 73, 117–118, 180–182

Kaufman, Philip, 95–98
King, Stephen, 84, 151, 165, 188
Kiss of the Damned, 27–29
Kristeva, Julia, 33–34
Kümel, Harry, 127–130
Kusama, Karyn, 183–188
Kelly, Richard, 5–7

Lacan, Jacques, 12, 15, 19–29, 48, 101, 109–111, 119, 126, 132, 140–141, 146, 165
lack, 19, 107, 119, 122, 126, 146, 162
lamella, 109–111, 122
language, 20, 22
Laing, R.D., 6, 13
Lanzer, Ernst, 161
LaSalle, Mick, 145
Laugier, Pascal, 43–49
LaVey, Anton, 152
Le Fanu, Sheridan, 130
Leach, Neil, 111
Lem, Stanisław, 113
Let's Scare Jessica to Death, 130–133
   1960s counterculture, 132
   biblical narrative, 131

death, 131
drowning, 130–131
foreclosure, 132
psychosis, 131–133
tombstone rubbing, 131
trespassing, 131
libido, 4, 39, 65, 85, 88, 90, 136, 139, 160, 189, 195–196, 197
Lichtenstein, Mitchell, 49–56
life instinct (Eros), 13–14, 67, 88, 99, 103, 107, 122, 135, 167, 173
liminal space, 36, 154, 163
Lindsay, Joan, 80
Little Hans, 140
Lodge, Guy, 149
Lost Boys, The, 133–135
    absurdism, 135
    abyss, 135
    aesthetics, 134–135
    developmental deadlock, 135
    maternal anchoring, 134
    Peter Pan, 133–135
    railroad bridge scene, 135
    substance abuse, 134
    teenage years, 135
    war on drugs, 134
Lynch, David, 1–5, 38

MacGuffin, The, 146
male gaze, 24
Martyrs, 43–49
    Real, The, 49
    transfiguration, 43, 46–47
McCallum, Rebecca, 161
McIntee, David, 104–105
McLuhan, Marshall, 103
McTiernan, John, 105–106
Meyer, Stephanie, 144–149
mirror stage, 12–13, 29
Misery, 165–168
    creative process, 168
    cultural landscape, 166
    psychosis, 168–169
    superfandom, 166–167
    Symbolic Order, 168
    trauma, 168
Monstrous-Feminine, the, 21, 32, 75, 104, 122

mother, 7–10, 13, 21, 34, 44, 63–65, 79, 104, 126–128, 134, 139–141, 147, 165, 194–195
Mother!, 191–196
    artist/muse arrangement, 195
    biblical stories, 191–196
    creation myth, 191–194
    environmental activism, 196
    home renovation, 194–195
    human chaos, 194–196
    narcissism, 194–195
    pregnancy, 193
    writer's block, 194
Mulholland Drive, 1–4
    amnesia, 3
    coffee, 4
    delusion, 3
    Goldwater Rule, the, 2
    jitterbug, 1–4
Mulvey, Laura, 24
Munchausen syndrome by proxy, 137–138, 154

narcissism, 157, 194–196, 197
nature-as-horror, 76–91
Nelson, Ray, 114
Nietzsche, Friedrich Wilhelm, 135, 144
Noé, Gaspar, 12–14
Norrington, Stephen, 138–141

O'Bannon, Dan, 104
objet petit a, 100, 122, 146–148, 154
obsessional neurosis, 18, 79, 161–162, 189, 197
Oedipus complex, 10–11, 29, 79, 90, 129, 139–141, 154, 165, 197
Oldboy, 10–12
    incest taboo, 10–12
    Oedipus Rex, 10
ontological insecurity, 6, 13, 29, 169
oral stage of development, 136, 154
O'Sullivan, Michael, 145

paranoia, 6, 28–29, 42, 70–71, 97, 108, 123, 130
Paranormal Activity, 23–26
    female sexuality, 25
    scopophilia, 24–26
    strategy of containment, 25–26
    surveillance, 24–26

Patterson, Hannah, 143
Peli, Oren, 23–26
penis envy, 42, 75
persona, 16, 36, 180–182, 197
Pervert's Guide to Cinema, The, 79
Pervert's Guide to Ideology, The, 114–116
phallic, 22–23, 30, 52, 59, 91, 104, 164, 172, 198
phallocentric order, 19, 24, 51, 53, 77–80
phallus, the, 41–42, 75, 107, 126, 154, 165, 197
Phantasm franchise, 98–101
   death motif, 98–101
   ethical conduct, 101
   fear of abandonment, 99
   primal scene, 99
   sexual non-rapport, 101
   silver sphere, 98
Phillips, Michael, 195
Picnic at Hanging Rock, 80–84
   defining horror, 81
   female sexuality, 83–84
   sublime, the, 81–82
pleasure principle, 88, 91, 136
pornography, 11, 50, 177
Possession, 20–23
   Berlin, 20
   Dahmer, Jeffrey, 21
   doppelgänger, 21
   hysteria, 20, 22–23
Possessor, 16–18
   data collection, 16–17
   ennui, 18
   identity, 16–18
   scopophilia, 18
   surveillance capitalism, 16–17
post-traumatic stress disorder, 39, 43, 184, 187, 197
Predator franchise, 105–108
   castration anxiety, 107
   fetishisation, 108
   overcompensation, 107
   scopophilia, 107
   surveillance, 107
   voyeurism, 106–108
   weapons, 107
primal scene, 99, 123
projection, 116, 128, 148, 188, 197
psychic vampirism, 152, 154
psychological horror, 1–30
psychosexual development, 58, 136, 139, 189
psychosis, 4–6, 13, 35–42, 61–74, 118, 131–133, 168–169, 198

Reagan, Nancy, 134
Real, the, 48–49, 75, 146
reality principle, 88, 91
Rear Window, 159–162
   lack, 162
   mortification, 161
   obsessional neurosis, 161–162
   Rat Man, 161
   scopophilia, 160
   surveillance, 159–162
   true crime investigation, 161
Reiner, Rob, 165–168
repetition compulsion, 120, 123, 130
repression, 11, 19, 23, 30, 32, 56, 75, 84, 88, 91, 95, 97, 113–114, 119, 137, 150, 158–159, 174, 189, 198
return of the repressed, 85, 91, 95
Rice, Anne, 136
Roberts, Johannes, 181–182
Rosemary's Baby, 132

Schroeder, Barbet, 168–172
Schumacher, Joel, 133–135
scopophilia, 18, 24, 30, 106–107, 123, 160, 198
Scott, Ridley, 101–105
sex education, 39, 51
Shadow, the, 73–74, 75
Shining, The, 151–152
Siegel, Don, 95–96
signifier, 7, 23, 42, 100, 126, 142, 165, 190
Signs, 117–119
   alienation, 118
   crop circles, 117
   divine intervention, 117
   faith, 117–118
   lack, 119
   love, 119
   narrative, 117
   synchronicity, 117

Silence of the Lambs, The, 14–16
   Sphinx, 15
   subject supposed to know, 15
Single White Female, 168–172
   borderline personality disorder, 170–172
   double, 169–172
   identity, 170–172
   imitation, 170–172
   obsession, 170–171
   phantom pain, 169
   secondary identification, 170
Six, Tom, 56–61
Shyamalan, M. Night, 117–119
Slumber Party Massacre, The, 162–165
   Driller Killer, 163–165
   female sexuality, 164
   Hylas and the Nymphs, 163
   liminal phase, 163
   phallic penetration, 164
   phallus, the, 165
   Twin Peaks, 164
Smith, Graham, 153
Solaris, 113
Sophocles, 10, 101
Spielberg, Steven, 87–90, 93–95
Sproul, R.C., 144
Strangers 1 and 2, The, 179–182
   enantiodromia, 180–181
   individuation, 182
   masks, 180–182
   persona, 180–182
   relationship breakdown, 180
   unfamiliarity, 180–182
strategy of containment, 25–26, 107–108
subject supposed to know, 15–16, 30
subjectivity, 19, 21, 90
sublimation, 88, 91, 189
sublime, the, 81–84, 91
substance abuse, 133–134, 142
Superego, 38, 75, 88–91, 136, 150–151, 154, 173, 198
surveillance, 24–26, 107, 150, 159–162
surveillance capitalism, 17–18, 30
Symbolic Order, 6, 19, 22, 25, 30, 42, 48, 75, 118, 123, 132, 141–142, 146–147, 154, 168, 198
synchronicity, 117–118, 123

taboo, 10–11, 13, 39, 51, 55, 121, 139–140, 149, 164, 147, 177
Tarkovsky, Andrei, 113
Taylor, Drew, 149
Teague, Lewis, 84–86
technology, 17–19, 24–26
Teeth, 49–56
   abstinence, 49–50, 52
   female sexuality, 49–56
   sex education, 51
   vagina dentata, 51–56
Thanatos (death drive), 43, 74, 79, 100, 120–121, 173, 196
They Live, 114–116
   cognitive dissonance, 116
   dictatorship, 115
   ideology, 114–115
   neoliberalism, 116
   political subtext, 114
   projection, 116
   Žižek, Slavoj, 114–115
Thing, The, 108–111
   capitalism, 110
   chest stop scene, 109
   lamella, 109–110
   misanthropy, 109
   paranoia, 110
trauma, 15, 23, 34, 43, 50, 59, 90, 93, 104, 113, 118, 133, 141, 151, 153, 158, 168, 182, 184, 190
Twilight Saga, The, 144–149
   baseball, 147
   desire, 146–148
   heroin, 147
   Mormonism, 146
   Muse, 147
   objet petit a, 146–149
   stalking, 147

uncanny, 6, 37, 60, 79, 81, 86, 92, 99, 123, 169, 198
unconscious, 11, 85, 88, 91, 105, 112–113, 123, 173–179, 198

vampires, 124–154
von Trier, Lars, 7–10
   depression, 8
   female protagonists, 8
   paternity, 7–8

voyeurism, 17, 24–26, 106–108, 123, 159–162

War of the Worlds, 93–95
   9/11 imagery, 93
   camera structure, 93–95
   madness, 95
   parenthood, 94
   sentimentalism, 95
Waterhouse, John William, 163

Weir, Peter, 80–84
What We Do in the Shadows, 152
Wilde, Oscar, 109
Williams, Linda, 68
Williams, Tony, 179
Wise, Robert, 130

Žižek, Slavoj, 79, 94–95, 114–116, 146
Żuławski, Andrzej, 20–23

For Product Safety Concerns and Information please contact our EU representative GPSR@taylorandfrancis.com
Taylor & Francis Verlag GmbH, Kaufingerstraße 24, 80331 München, Germany

www.ingramcontent.com/pod-product-compliance
Lightning Source LLC
Chambersburg PA
CBHW070315240426
43661CB00057B/2655